NIETZSCHE'S VOICES

THE COLLECTED WRITINGS OF JOHN SALLIS
Volume III/7

NIETZSCHE'S VOICES

John Sallis

Edited by Richard Rojcewicz

Indiana University Press

This book is a publication of

Indiana University Press
Office of Scholarly Publishing
Herman B Wells Library 350
1320 East 10th Street
Bloomington, Indiana 47405 USA

iupress.org

© 2022 by John Sallis

Based on a lecture course of 1971–72 at Duquesne University.

All rights reserved
No part of this book may be reproduced or utilized in any form or by any means, electronic or mechanical, including photocopying and recording, or by any information storage and retrieval system, without permission in writing from the publisher. The paper used in this publication meets the minimum requirements of the American National Standard for Information Sciences—Permanence of Paper for Printed Library Materials, ANSI Z39.48-1992.

Manufactured in the United States of America

Collected Writings of John Sallis printing 2022

Library of Congress Cataloging-in-Publication Data
Names: Sallis, John, author. | Rojcewicz, Richard, editor.
Title: Nietzsche's voices / John Sallis ; edited by Richard Rojcewicz.
Description: Bloomington, Indiana, USA : Indiana University Press, 2022. | Series: The collected writings of John Sallis ; volume 111/7 | Includes index.
Identifiers: LCCN 2022020154 (print) | LCCN 2022020155 (ebook) | ISBN 9780253063595 (hardback) | ISBN 9780253063601 (paperback) | ISBN 9780253063618 (ebook)
Subjects: LCSH: Nietzsche, Friedrich Wilhelm, 1844-1900.
Classification: LCC B3317 .S275 2022 (print) | LCC B3317 (ebook) | DDC 193—dc23/eng/20220907
LC record available at https://lccn.loc.gov/2022020154
LC ebook record available at https://lccn.loc.gov/2022020155

In any case what spoke here—which was admitted with as much curiosity as antipathy—was a *strange* voice. . . . What spoke here—as was said with suspicion—was something like a mystical and almost maenadic soul that stammered with difficulty and randomly, as in a strange tongue, almost undecided whether it should communicate or conceal itself. It should have *sung*, this "new soul"—and not spoken!

—Nietzsche, "Attempt at a Self-Criticism," added to
The Birth of Tragedy in 1886

Contents

Key to the citations of Nietzsche's works   *xi*

I. Introduction   *1*

II. Nietzsche's life   *2*
   A. Life in relation to thought.   *2*
   B. Boyhood.   *3*
   C. University student years.   *4*
   D. The Basel period.   *6*
   E. Last years.   *10*
   F. Behold the man.   *13*

III. The Greeks   *22*
   A. The contemporary relevance of the Greeks.   *22*
   B. *The Birth of Tragedy*.   *23*
   C. Culture.   *26*
   D. The wisdom of Silenus.   *27*
   E. Apollo and Dionysus.   *29*
   F. Apollinian culture.   *31*
   G. Lyric poetry.   *32*
   H. Greek tragedy.   *33*
   I. The death of tragedy and the birth of Socratism.   *39*
   J. The contemporary task.   *44*

IV. Truth   *48*
   A. General issues in Nietzsche's essay on truth.   *48*
   B. The value and nature of truth.   *49*
   C. Falsification and forgetfulness.   *50*
   D. A music-practicing Socrates.   *53*

V. History   *55*
   A. Human temporality.   *55*
   B. History and life.   *55*
   C. Kinds of history.   *56*
   D. History as threat to life.   *58*
   E. Nihilism.   *59*

VI. Morality 60
   A. Freedom and morality. 60
   B. The ground of morality. 61
   C. Life as will to power. 62
   D. Morality and life. 63
   E. The slave revolt. 65
   F. Contradictions. 66

VII. The death of God 68
   A. The madman. 68
   B. God as crime against life. 69
   C. Our role in the killing of God. 69
   D. The lantern. 73
   E. This-worldly comfort. 74
   F. Transformation into overman. 74
   G. Beginning of a higher history. 75
   H. The shadows of God. 75
   I. Madness. 76

VIII. *Thus Spoke Zarathustra* 77
   A. The task of becoming overman. 77
   B. The task of homecoming. 81
   C. Image-language. 91
   D. The central idea of *Thus Spoke Zarathustra*. 93
   E. *Thus Spoke Zarathustra* as tragedy. 96
   F. Images in the Prologue. 98
   G. First stage of homecoming: the camel. 100
   H. Second stage of homecoming: the lion. 104
   I. Final stage of homecoming: the child. 111
   J. The child in the First Part of *Thus Spoke Zarathustra*. 117
   K. Marriage and women. 120
   L. The child in the Second Part of *Thus Spoke Zarathustra*. 122
   M. The night song. 126
   N. The dancing song. 131
   O. The tomb song. 133
   P. Metaphysics. 134
   Q. Knowledge and truth. 145
   R. Night. 149
   S. Priority of art over truth. 152
   T. The sublime man. 153

U. Philosophy and art.   *155*
V. The eternal recurrence.   *155*
W. Conclusion. Song.   *170*

Editor's Afterword   *173*
Index   *175*

Key to the Citations of Nietzsche's Works

NIETZSCHE'S WRITINGS WILL be cited according to the following abbreviations. The translations provided in the lectures are at times modifications of the published versions. The standard German text is the ongoing critical edition in two series: complete works (Friedrich Nietzsche, *Werke: Kritische Gesamtausgabe*, 48 volumes) and complete correspondence (Friedrich Nietzsche, *Briefwechsel: Kritische Gesamtausgabe*, 24 volumes) edited by Giorgio Colli and Mazzimo Montinari (Berlin: de Gruyter, 1967–).

A: *The Antichrist: Attempt at a Critique of Christianity*, tr. Walter Kaufmann in *The Portable Nietzsche* (New York: Viking, 1968).

BGE: *Beyond Good and Evil: Prelude to a Philosophy of the Future*, tr. Walter Kaufmann in *Basic Writings of Nietzsche* (New York: Random House, 1968).

BT: *The Birth of Tragedy out of the Spirit of Music*, tr. Walter Kaufmann in *Basic Writings of Nietzsche* (New York: Random House, 1968).

D: *The Dawn of Day: Thoughts on Moral Prejudices*, tr. John McFarland Kennedy (London: Foulis, 1911).

EH: *Ecce Homo: How One Becomes What One Is*, tr. Walter Kaufmann in *Basic Writings of Nietzsche* (New York: Random House, 1968).

GM: *On the Genealogy of Morals: A Polemic*, tr. Walter Kaufmann in *Basic Writings of Nietzsche* (New York: Random House, 1968).

GS: *The Gay Science*, tr. Walter Kaufmann (New York: Random House, 1967). Occasionally the quotations are taken from the translation by Thomas Common (*The Joyful Wisdom*, London: Foulis, 1910).

HATH: *Human, All Too Human: A Book for Free Spirits*, tr. R. J. Hollingdale (Cambridge: Cambridge University Press, 1986).

IB: *The Innocence of Becoming: Selections from Nietzsche's Literary Remains*. No published English translation; references are to the German edition. See *Die Unschuld des Werdens* in the chronology below.

NCW: *Nietzsche Contra Wagner: Out of the Files of a Psychologist*, tr. Walter Kaufmann in *The Portable Nietzsche* (New York: Viking, 1968).

PT: *Philosophy and Truth: Selections from Nietzsche's Notebooks of the Early 1870's*, tr. Daniel Breazeale (Atlantic Highlands, NJ: Humanities Press, 1979). Contains "On truth and lies in a nonmoral sense."

PTAG: *Philosophy in the Tragic Age of the Greeks*, tr. Marianne Cowan (Chicago: Regnery, 1962).

SL: *Selected Letters of Friedrich Nietzsche*, ed. and tr. Christopher Middleton (Chicago: University of Chicago Press, 1969).

TI: *Twilight of the Idols: Or, How One Philosophizes with a Hammer*, tr. Walter Kaufmann in *The Portable Nietzsche* (New York: Viking, 1968).

TSZ: *Thus Spoke Zarathustra: A Book for All and None*, tr. Walter Kaufmann in *The Portable Nietzsche* (New York: Viking, 1968).

UM: *Untimely Meditations*, tr. R. J. Hollingdale (Cambridge: Cambridge University Press, 1983). Translation of the second meditation, "On the uses and disadvantages of history for life," modified according to the version by Adrian Collins, *The Use and Abuse of History* (Indianapolis: Bobbs-Merrill, 1957).

WeP: *We Philologists*, tr. John McFarland Kennedy (London: Foulis, 1911).

WP: *The Will to Power: Attempt at a Revaluation of All Values. Studies and Fragments*, tr. Walter Kaufmann and R. J. Hollingdale (New York: Random House, 1967).

Chronology of the original German, by date of composition, including the volume number of the Colli-Montinari edition of the *Werke*:

1872	*Die Geburt der Tragödie aus dem Geiste der Musik* (BT) Vol. III/1	
1873	*Die Philosophie im tragischen Zeitalter der Griechen* (PTAG) Vol. III/2	
1873	"Über Wahrheit und Lüge im außermoralischen Sinne" (PT) Vol. III/2	
1873–76	*Unzeitgemässe Betrachtungen* (UM) Vols. III/1 and IV/1	
1874	*Wir Philologen* (WeP) Vol. IV/1	
1878–80	*Menschliches, Allzumenschliches: Ein Buch für freie Geister* (HATH) Vol. IV/2–3	
1881	*Die Morgenröte: Gedanken über die moralischen Vorurteile* (D) Vol. V/1	
1882	*Die fröhliche Wissenschaft* (GS) Vol. V/2	
1883–85	*Also sprach Zarathustra: Ein Buch für Alle und Keinen* (TSZ) Vol. VI/1	

1883–88	*Der Wille zur Macht: Versuch einer Umwertung aller Werte. Studien und Fragmente* (WP) Vols. VII–IX but only as literary remains without a title
1883–88	*Die Unschuld des Werdens: Der Nachlaß*, 2 vols., ed. A. Baeumler (Stuttgart: Kröner, 1956) (IB)
1886	*Jenseits von Gut und Böse: Vorspiel einer Philosophie der Zukunft* (BGE) Vol. VI/2
1887	*Zur Genealogie der Moral: Eine Streitschrift* (GM) Vol. VI/2
1888	*Der Antichrist: Versuch einer Kritik des Christentums* (A) Vol. VI/3
1888	*Ecce Homo: Wie man wird, was man ist* (EH) Vol. VI/3
1888	*Götzen-Dämmerung: oder, Wie man mit dem Hammer philosophirt* (TI) Vol. VI/3
1888	*Nietzsche Contra Wagner: Aktenstücke eines Psychologen* (NCW) Vol. VI/3

NIETZSCHE'S VOICES

I. Introduction

"I AM NO MAN, I am dynamite." That is what Nietzsche once said of himself (EH, p. 782), and his words were prophetic, for if we have learned anything from the wretched abuses to which his thought has been subjected, it is this: like dynamite, Nietzsche must be handled with the greatest care.

Nietzsche is easy to read; his is apparently the easiest of all the great philosophies. Yet the easy intelligibility is deceptive. Nietzsche's writings make us believe we have understood when in fact we have not. His philosophy is actually the exact opposite of easy. Most of the opinions about Nietzsche that have been bandied about for decades result from this illusion of immediate intelligibility. So we must be constantly on guard to unlearn what we have heard about him.

The full title Nietzsche gave to one of his last works is *Twilight of the Idols: Or, How One Philosophizes with a Hammer*. It is ironic that, as Nietzsche himself declares, the kind of hammer he will take up is not a sledgehammer but the tiny hammer used to strike a tuning fork. Nietzsche does not propose to smash idols but to touch them delicately in order to see whether they ring true. Yet all too many of Nietzsche's readers have interpreted him by wielding a sledgehammer; they have not applied to Nietzsche the same delicate hammer with which he carefully touches the idols. Let us then try to take seriously what Heidegger says: "This, too, we must still learn, to read a book such as Nietzsche's *Thus Spoke Zarathustra* in the same rigorous manner as one of Aristotle's treatises" (*What Is Called Thinking?* [New York: Harper & Row, 1968], p. 70).

II. Nietzsche's life

A. Life in relation to thought.

We need to talk about Nietzsche's life. Yet, in the case of Nietzsche, talk about a philosopher's life is extremely problematic and can hardly be undertaken without some deliberate reflection on its appropriateness. Why? —Because Nietzsche's philosophy is itself a reflection on the relation of philosophy to life and at the same time is an exemplification of that relation.

What then about the thought of the philosopher Nietzsche and the life of the person Nietzsche? Indeed, Nietzsche says: "I am one thing, my writings are another matter" (EH, p. 715). Thus we are warned against any facile psychologizing. On the other hand, in his writings Nietzsche often speaks of himself and relates what he says about himself to his thought. He even composed a work, *Ecce Homo*, which is a sort of, a very curious sort of, autobiography. Nietzsche stresses the importance of not just stating what theories he puts forth but of saying who he is.

Furthermore, in one of his many discussions of the illnesses he endured and of their relation to his work, Nietzsche says explicitly: "I turned my will to health, to *life*, into a philosophy" (EH, p. 680). That remark is elaborated in *On the Genealogy of Morals*: "Our ideas, our values, our yeas and nays, our ifs and buts, grow out of us with the necessity with which a tree bears fruit—related and each with an affinity to each, evidence of *one* will, *one* health, *one* soil, *one* sun" (GM, p. 452).

Finally, this issue—the relation of philosophy and life—is addressed perhaps most directly in a fragment from an early draft of *Ecce Homo*: "I speak only of what I have lived through, not merely of what I have thought through; the opposition of theory and life is lacking in my case. My 'theory' grows from my 'practice'—oh, from a practice that is not by any means harmless or unproblematic" (EH, p. 796).

In some way, therefore, Nietzsche's life needs to be taken into account. But how? Two possible ways seem obvious. First, we could recount the events of his life as we know them from various sources. But his life was not particularly eventful. Of course, some incidents were clearly of significance, such as his encounters with Wagner. Yet Nietzsche's most productive years were almost entirely uneventful; he lived them in solitude. Nevertheless, Nietzsche himself goes to great lengths to relate many seemingly insignificant details—for example, about his illnesses and recoveries. A second way would not simply look at Nietzsche's life from the outside but would take up what Nietzsche actually says (as in *Ecce Homo*) about the relation of his life to his thought.

Let us begin with the first way and afterward pursue the second. The question remains as to whether either of these actually is an appropriate way to bring the life and thought of a philosopher into relation.

B. Boyhood.

Friedrich Wilhelm Nietzsche was born on October 15, 1844, in the village of Röcken, Germany. He was the son of the village pastor. Nietzsche's grandfathers on both sides had also been Lutheran ministers. In addition to Nietzsche's parents, the household consisted of a grandmother; two mildly neurotic old-maid aunts; Nietzsche's sister, Elisabeth (born in 1846); and a brother who died in infancy.

Nietzsche's first years were spent in an idyllic rural setting. When he was five, however, his father, to whom he was very attached, suddenly became ill and died. Afterward, the family moved to Naumburg, where Nietzsche lived until he was fourteen.

Throughout his boyhood, Nietzsche was not overly studious but was extremely pious. At fourteen, he wrote:

> I have already experienced so much—joy and sorrow, cheerful things and sad things—but in everything God has safely led me as a father leads his weak little child.... I have firmly resolved within me to dedicate myself forever to His service. May the dear Lord give me strength and power to carry out my intention and protect me on my life's way. Like a child, I trust in His grace: He will preserve us all, that no misfortune befall us. But His holy will be done! All He gives I will joyfully accept: happiness and unhappiness, poverty and wealth, and will boldly look even death in the face, which shall one day unite us all in eternal joy and bliss. Yes dear Lord, let Thy face shine upon us forever! Amen. ("Aus meinem Leben," cited in R. J. Hollingdale, *Nietzsche: The Man and His Philosophy*. Baton Rouge: Louisiana State University Press, 1965, p. 21)

These words were written by the same person who three decades later described himself as an "atheist by instinct" and who wrote *The Antichrist*, containing statements such as the following: "The Christian conception of God—God as God of the sick, God as a spider, God as spirit—is one of the most corrupt conceptions of the divine ever attained on earth" (A, p. 585).

At this same time, fourteen years of age, Nietzsche was awarded a scholarship to Pforta, a famous and very rigorous school that specialized in Greek, Latin, and the German classics. At Pforta, Nietzsche rebelled in the beginning but gradually accustomed himself. It was during his time at Pforta that Nietzsche first came into contact with Wagnerian music. Also, Nietzsche's opinions and way of life underwent a drastic change. He often drank heavily, and he criticized religion, declaring it to be "the product of the people's childhood." Nietzsche even composed a poem depicting a drunkard throwing a bottle of beer at a figure of Christ on the cross.

In the lengthy essays Nietzsche wrote at this period of his life, several themes of his mature thought can be glimpsed:

1. In "Ohne Heimat," Nietzsche introduces the idea of home in relation to freedom: "Fleet horses bear me, without fear or dismay, through distant places. And whoever sees me knows me, and whoever knows me calls me: the homeless man. No one dares to ask me where my home is: perhaps I have never been fettered to space and the flying hours and am as free as an eagle" (cited by Hollingdale, p. 27).
2. In an essay on Hölderlin, Nietzsche defends Hölderlin's attack on provincialism, narrow patriotism, and philistinism. Here Nietzsche foreshadows his later antipathy toward the "herd" and "petty politics."
3. According to the essay "On the Childhood of the Peoples," religion is at first a sign of creativity, but its eventual outcome is to rob this world of all value in favor of the next world: "That God became man shows only that man is not to seek his bliss in eternity but to found his heaven on earth; the delusion of a supra-terrestrial world has placed the spirit of man in a false relation to the terrestrial: it was the product of the people's childhood" (cited by Hollingdale, p. 30).
4. "On Moods" presents the idea of strife, opposition, as an essential ingredient of life: "Strife is the perpetual food of the soul, and it knows well enough how to extract the sweetness from it" (cited by Hollingdale, p. 31).

C. University student years.

In 1864, Nietzsche enrolled at the University of Bonn. The year he spent there is significant mainly because during this time he tried to live the life of an ordinary college student. He joined a social fraternity dedicated to drinking and dueling, and Nietzsche was even involved in a kind of duel. Eventually he was repulsed by such a life.

At Bonn, Nietzsche attached himself to the eminent philologist Friedrich Ritschl. When, after Nietzsche's first year, Ritschl left Bonn for the University of Leipzig, Nietzsche followed and remained at Leipzig until 1869, except for a year of military service in the field artillery. Nietzsche devoted his university studies to ancient literature and classical philology.

Two significant events occurred during Nietzsche's stay at Leipzig. First, in 1866 Nietzsche had the opportunity to meet Richard Wagner, the Romantic composer. Nietzsche, himself a talented pianist, had already been captivated by Wagner's music; now he was equally entranced by Wagner's personality. The relationship with Wagner was to be decisive. The other event, equally decisive, was

Nietzsche's discovery of Schopenhauer, whose book (*World as Will and Representation*) he stumbled across in a secondhand bookshop. Nietzsche immediately became an admirer of Schopenhauer, although from the beginning he also had reservations.

Schopenhauer's philosophy of will, with the dualism of noumenal and phenomenal inherited from Kant, was crucial for Nietzsche's development, as is most evident in *The Birth of Tragedy*. Especially important was Schopenhauer's pessimism.

Schopenhauer's thinking takes its departure from two conclusions Kant had demonstrated. First, the world of natural science is the phenomenal world versus the noumenal world of the intellect: a dualism of appearances versus things-in-themselves. It becomes for Schopenhauer the dualism of representation and will. Second, Kant maintained the primacy of practical reason over the theoretical. Schopenhauer identifies practical reason with will and theoretical reason with intellect. So, for Schopenhauer, the dualism is one of will and intellect. For him, there is at first an underlying unity beneath all wills, but conflict is inevitable. Schopenhauer argues along the following lines. According to Kant, space and time are forms of appearances; they apply only to the phenomenal world. The noumenal world, the will, has nothing to do with space and time. But, since it is precisely space and time that constitute the principle of individuation, there is no plurality of wills but only one primordial will underlying what appear to be many individual wills. Through self-intuition, we become aware of this unity. Life itself is the throbbing of the primordial will that underlies all other things. This will is the primary source of life.

In Nietzsche's eyes, the crux of Schopenhauer's philosophy consists in its ethical position, that is, its pessimism: the nature of will is to strive, and when the underlying unity is broken, as is inevitable, a plurality of wills strive in conflict with one another, resulting in unhappiness. Schopenhauer's view that the ultimate is the will leads him in the end to the most pessimistic philosophy in our tradition. Life is incurably miserable. One who has realized this ends by adopting an attitude of denial, using his intellect to lift himself out of the conflict of the world. Thus what we should do is deny the will, renounce all striving, and become ascetics.

Even in his later years, Nietzsche never lost respect for Schopenhauer as a man. Nietzsche admired him as one who was a master of style and who had the courage to stop at nothing in his search for truth, that is, for an honest atheism. Nevertheless, Nietzsche did come to regard Schopenhauer's philosophy as decadent. Nietzsche rejected Schopenhauer's pessimism about life in general. But this does not mean Nietzsche adopted some naive optimism or some theological or teleological optimism. Instead, Nietzsche's position dialectically surpasses the simple distinction between optimism and pessimism, between Yes-saying to life and No-saying: "I contradict as has never been contradicted before and am nevertheless the opposite of a No-saying spirit" (EH, p. 783). "The psychological problem in the type of Zarathustra is how he who says No and *does* No to an unprecedented degree, regarding everything to which one has so far said Yes, can nevertheless be the opposite of a No-saying spirit; how the spirit that bears the heaviest fate, the fatality of a task, can nevertheless be the lightest and most transcendent—Zarathustra is a dancer" (EH, p. 762).

Nietzsche also rejected Schopenhauer's dualism of intellect and will. The problem, as Nietzsche sees it, is that the intellect cannot overcome the will unless the intellect itself partakes of the will or is itself a kind of will. What Schopenhauer requires (asceticism through an overcoming of the will by the intellect) is possible only if the intellect itself is a will, that is, only if there exists no dichotomy between them. Will can be overcome only by will or, in other words, by itself. But that is *self-overcoming*, a fundamental idea of Nietzsche's philosophy; he moves from Schopenhauer's dualism to a self-overcoming. Thus the seeds of Nietzsche's theory of the will to power lie in his interpretation of Schopenhauer's dualism.

D. The Basel period.

Nietzsche remained at Leipzig until 1869. Then the chair of classical philology at the University of Basel, Switzerland, became vacant. At Ritschl's insistence, Nietzsche was awarded a doctorate at Leipzig without an examination and was appointed to this chair. Nietzsche became professor at the unheard-of age of twenty-four.

Nietzsche was far from certain this appointment was best for him. He was already growing weary of philology; nevertheless, he accepted the position. His inaugural lecture was "Homer and classical philology" and presented philology as a handmaid of art. There followed a series of lectures, all of which were preparatory studies for *The Birth of Tragedy*: "The Greek Music-Drama," "Socrates and Tragedy," and "The Dionysian Principle."

As soon as Nietzsche came to Basel, he found he had a talent for teaching, although he was never content with academic life. His friend Erwin Rohde (with whom he shared an enthusiasm for the Greeks, for Schopenhauer, and for Wagner) tells that during this period Nietzsche often discussed the idea of setting up a kind of secular monastery in the spirit of Wagner. Despite the fact that Nietzsche gradually grew antipathetic to classical philology—scholarly busyness—his preoccupation with the ancients was crucial for all his later thought.

Nietzsche's little book on the pre-Socratics (*Philosophy in the Tragic Age of the Greeks*), not published until after his death, was perhaps more responsible than anything else for the twentieth-century renewal of philosophical interest in the pre-Socratics. Furthermore, in his own thinking Nietzsche always retained his kinship to the early Greek philosophers—especially Heraclitus. In 1888, his last productive year, Nietzsche wrote of "Heraclitus, in whose proximity I feel altogether warmer and better than anywhere else. The affirmation of passing away *and destroying*, which is the decisive feature of a Dionysian philosophy; saying Yes to opposition and war; *becoming*, along with a radical repudiation of the very concept of *being*—all this is clearly more closely related to me than anything else thought to date" (EH, p. 729).

Shortly after Nietzsche came to Basel, he visited Wagner at the latter's home in Tribschen, in the neighboring Swiss canton, and soon was a regular visitor. During this time, Wagner was at the height of his powers, composing *Die Meistersinger*, *Siegfried*, and *Götterdämmerung*. Nietzsche's association with Wagner was an awakening: Wagner was proof that genuine creativity was still possible. Nietzsche was overwhelmed by Wagner and came to address him as *Meister* ("master"). Even after his painful break with Wagner, Nietzsche said: "I call Wagner the great benefactor of my life."

Nietzsche admired not only Wagner's creative genius but also the revolutionary character of Wagner's art and of his conception of art. Nietzsche and Wagner also shared an enthusiasm for Schopenhauer.

As regards art, Wagner maintained (in *Art and Revolution*) that art is essentially non-Christian; it is a theme Nietzsche takes up in his own work. Wagner also held that the individual arts were once component parts of a single artwork: Greek tragedy. Thus Wagner influenced Nietzsche's attention to drama. Wagner took as his task the restoration of the "total artwork" in which all the individual arts are synthesized and reach their highest form.

* * *

A year after Nietzsche arrived in Basel, the Franco-Prussian War broke out (1870). Nietzsche volunteered and served a short time as a nursing orderly. In less than a month, he collapsed with dysentery and diphtheria after having tended casualties for three days and nights continuously. Nietzsche returned to Basel, but soon his poor health forced him to ask for a leave of absence. Rather than resting, however, he worked furiously on *The Birth of Tragedy*. After a year he did appear to have regained his health, but he was never really well again.

The Birth of Tragedy, Nietzsche's first major work, was published in 1872. Here Nietzsche attempts to account for the origin of Greek tragedy in terms of dual principles, Apollinian-Dionysian. The work served the Wagner cause: Wagnerian music-drama is presented as a rebirth of Greek tragedy.

The Birth of Tragedy aroused great controversy. It was bitterly attacked by most philologists and denounced as extremely unscholarly (it lacked even a single footnote). Nietzsche immediately lost all his students, and his career as a philologist was virtually finished. Only many years later did philologists finally come to appreciate the depth of Nietzsche's insight into Greek culture.

During the years at Basel, Nietzsche made four friends (besides Wagner) who were especially important in his life:

1. Jacob Burckhardt. The great historian shared Nietzsche's enthusiasm for the Greeks. Nietzsche attended Burckhardt's lectures, and these had a significant influence on *The Birth of Tragedy*.
2. Franz Overbeck. He was chair of "critical theology" at Basel. The friendship with Overbeck was perhaps Nietzsche's only one on a personal basis; their opinions never agreed. This friendship was also unique inasmuch as Nietzsche and Overbeck never seriously quarreled.
3. Paul Rée. This atheist tried to understand religion through a psychological investigation of human nature. Nietzsche was especially attracted to Rée's view that morality is a matter of custom or convention.
4. Peter Gast. He was a composer who moved to Basel in 1875. Gast almost idolized Nietzsche and served him faithfully. Nietzsche, in turn, managed to secure performances of several of Gast's works. When Nietzsche's eyesight eventually deteriorated almost to blindness, Gast prepared his manuscripts for him.

* * *

During 1873–74, Nietzsche became more and more torn between his personal loyalty to Wagner and his growing dissatisfaction with what Wagner represented. In August 1874, he paid his last private visit to Wagner (in Bayreuth, Germany). At the time, Wagner was engaged in building his festival house and in completing *Götterdämmerung*. Nietzsche's arrival was unexpected, and he was not made welcome. Nietzsche carried a score by Brahms, played a little from it, and then purposely left it on the piano in Wagner's music room. When Wagner entered, there was the detested name of Brahms staring him in the face. The result, as described by Nietzsche's sister, was an unpleasant scene, with Wagner red-faced, angry, and shouting, Nietzsche icy and silent.

Nietzsche did not see Wagner again for two years. In 1876, the inaugural Bayreuth Festival was held, and Nietzsche attended the first "Ring" cycle but only as just another festival-goer and not as an intimate of Wagner. Nietzsche gave away his ticket to the second cycle. He could no longer ignore the ideological side of Wagner: the German nationalist and anti-Semite. In *Ecce Homo*, Nietzsche recounts his experience of the festival and speaks of how he felt when

> one day I woke up in Bayreuth. As if I were dreaming! Wherever was I? There was nothing I recognized; I scarcely recognized Wagner. In vain did I leaf through my memories. Tribschen—a distant isle of the blessed: not a trace of

any similarity. The incomparable days when the foundation stone was laid, the small group of people that had belonged, had celebrated, and did not need first to acquire fingers for delicate matters—not a trace of any similarity. What had happened? —Wagner had been translated into German! The Wagnerian had become master over Wagner.—*German* art. The *German* master. *German* beer.

I think I know the Wagnerians.... In truth, a hair-raising company!... Not a single abortion is missing among them, not even the anti-Semite.—Poor Wagner! Where had he landed!—If he had even entered into swine! But to descend among Germans! (EH, p. 740–41)

Nietzsche was arriving at his mature philosophical evaluation of the real meaning of Wagner's work: Wagner's operas represented—in the highest artistic way—sensual abandon. At the same time, there was a constant association of sensual abandon with death. The yearning for death, the search for redemption in annihilation, comes to be the dominant theme. Wagner's characters suffer from life as from a burden, and they will their own destruction. The next step is the death of desire itself, which is the exact point Wagner reached in his last opera, *Parsifal*. But this is just Schopenhauer's pessimism again. So, for Nietzsche, Wagner is a decadent; he says "No" to life.

* * *

On two occasions during the late 1870s and early 1880s, Nietzsche considered marriage. He met the two women (Mathilde Trampedach, Lou Salomé) through friends (Hugo von Senger, Rée) who were already enamored of the women they introduced to Nietzsche. In both cases, Nietzsche proposed marriage through the friend and in both cases was turned down.

* * *

From 1873 to 1876, Nietzsche published the four parts of his second work, *Untimely Meditations*:

1. "David Strauss, Confessor and Writer." Nietzsche attacks Strauss for eliminating God while still clinging to Christian morality.
2. "On the Uses and Disadvantages of History for Life." Nietzsche attacks the much-praised "historical consciousness" (of post-Hegelian thought) as having become burdensome and destructive.
3. "Schopenhauer as Educator." Nietzsche pays homage to the intellectual independence and courage of Schopenhauer. Nietzsche later said this text is not about Schopenhauer but about Nietzsche himself; it is his self-reflection carried out by thinking back on one whose teaching affected him most profoundly.
4. "Richard Wagner in Bayreuth." Praise of Wagner.

E. Last years.

In 1875, Nietzsche suffered his first general collapse. He recovered briefly, but thereafter his health deteriorated. Nietzsche settled into a rhythmic cycle of sickness and recovery that was to persist for the rest of his life. In 1879, he suffered a more serious collapse and resigned permanently from the university. Nietzsche said later that he merely used his illness as a pretext to resign.

Now Nietzsche began the European wandering that continued for the rest of his days. The only place he felt somewhat at home was the Alpine village of Sils-Maria. Nietzsche expressed his sense of lacking a home in this poem from the literary remains, dated fall 1884 (*Werke: Kritische Gesamtausgabe*, vol. VII/3, p. 37):

Der Freigeist.
Abschied

"Die Krähen schrei'n
Und ziehen schwirren Flugs zur Stadt:
Bald wird es schnei'n—
Wohl dem, der jetzt noch—Heimat hat!

Nun stehst du starr,
Schaust rückwärts ach! wie lange schon!
Was bist du Narr
Vor Winters in die Welt—entflohn?

Die Welt—ein Thor
Zu tausend Wüsten stumm und kalt!
Wer Das verlor,
Was du verlorst, macht nirgends Halt.

Nun stehst du bleich,
Zur Winter-Wanderschaft verflucht,
Dem Rauche gleich,
Der stets nach kältern Himmeln sucht.

Flieg', Vogel, schnarr'
Dein Lied im Wüsten-Vogel-Ton!—
Versteck', du Narr,
Dein blutend Herz in Eis und Hohn!

Die Krähen schrei'n
Und ziehen schwirren Flugs zur Stadt:
Bald wird es schnei'n—
Weh dem, der keine Heimat hat!"

The Free Spirit.
Farewell

"The crows caw
And fly townwards with whirring wings:
Soon it will snow—
Happy is he who now still—has a home!

Now you stand rigid,
You look back, oh! how long!
You fool, why fled you
Into the world before winter?

The world—a gate
To a thousand deserts mute and cold!
Whoever has lost that,
Which you have lost, will never come to a halt.

Now you stand pale,
To winter-wanderings condemned,
Like the smoke
That always seeks colder skies.

Fly, bird, grate out
Your song in the tone of a desert-bird!—
You fool, conceal
Your bleeding heart in ice and scorn!

The crows caw
And fly townwards with whirring wings:
Soon it will snow,
Woeful is he who has no home!"

During 1878–80, Nietzsche published *Human, All Too Human*. Later he said about this book: "The title means 'where *you* see ideal things, I see what is human, alas, all-too-human.' . . . On closer inspection you discover [in this book] a merciless spirit that knows all the hideouts where the ideal is at home—where it has its secret dungeons and, as it were, its ultimate safety. With a torch whose light never wavers, an incisive light is thrown into this *underworld* of the ideal. One error after another is coolly packed in ice" (EH, pp. 739–40).

* * *

Although Nietzsche's books aroused virtually no interest outside his immediate circle, Nietzsche continued to write:

The Dawn (1881). Nietzsche later said of it: "With this book, my campaign against morality begins" (EH, 746). "With *The Dawn* I first took up the fight against the morality that would un-self man" (EH, 748).

The Gay Science (1882). This work carries even further the attack already begun against morality. Nietzsche later described the poem with which this work concludes as "an exuberant dancing song in which, if I may say so, one dances right over morality" (EH, p. 750). At the same time, *The Gay Science* is preparatory for *Thus Spoke Zarathustra*; several distinctive themes (the death of God, the eternal recurrence) first appear here.

During 1883–85, Nietzsche wrote what is rightfully regarded as his greatest work, *Thus Spoke Zarathustra*. More and more he now withdrew into solitude and lived only to write. He developed *Thus Spoke Zarathustra* in three other books: *Beyond Good and Evil* (1886), *On the Genealogy of Morals* (1887), and *Twilight of the Idols* (1888). At the same time, he began to make notes for a major philosophical work that would go beyond *Thus Spoke Zarathustra*, but Nietzsche never completed it. After his death, Gast and Nietzsche's sister published an extensive collection of these notes as *The Will to Power*.

The year 1888 was the last active one of Nietzsche's life and was also one of his most productive, in which he wrote five books: *The Case of Wagner*, *Twilight of the Idols*, *The Antichrist*, *Ecce Homo*, and *Nietzsche contra Wagner*.

* * *

The final collapse came in Turin, Italy, on January 3, 1889. Upon leaving his lodgings that morning, Nietzsche saw a cabman beating a horse in the Piazza Carlo Alberto. And then:

> With a cry, Nietzsche flung himself across the square and threw his arms around the animal's neck. Then he lost consciousness and slid to the ground, still clasping the tormented horse. A crowd gathered, and Nietzsche's landlord, attracted to the scene, recognized his lodger and had him carried back to his room. For a long time Nietzsche lay unconscious. When he came to he was no longer himself. At first he sang and shouted and thumped the piano, so that the landlord, who had already called a doctor, threatened to call a policeman. Then Nietzsche quieted down and began writing the famous series of letters to the courts of Europe and to his friends announcing his arrival as Dionysus and the Crucified. How many letters he wrote is not certain. Those directed to public figures announced that he, "the Crucified," would be going to Rome "on Tuesday" (the 8th of January), where the princes of Europe, together with the Pope, were to assemble; a notice to this effect was addressed to the secretary of state of the Vatican. (Hollingdale, p. 282)

Among the letters just mentioned were the following (Hollingdale, p. 283).

To Georg Brandes: "After you had discovered me, it was not difficult to find me: the difficulty now is to lose me. The Crucified."

To Burckhardt: "In the last resort, I would much rather have been a professor at Basel than God."

To Gast: "To my maestro Pietro. Sing me a new song: the world is transfigured and all the heavens rejoice. The Crucified."

To Overbeck: "Although you have hitherto showed a poor opinion of my ability to pay, I hope still to prove that I am one who pays his debts—for example to you.... I have just had all anti-Semites shot. Dionysus."

As soon as Overbeck received the letter, he set out for Turin. He arrived on January 8 and found Nietzsche's lodgings in a state of chaos. When Nietzsche saw Overbeck he embraced him fervently and burst into tears.

Nietzsche never regained his sanity. He was occasionally violent, sometimes almost lucid. After a short stay in clinics in Basel and Jena, he was taken by his mother back to his childhood home in Naumburg. She looked after him with devotion, and he gradually became calm and docile, sinking finally into complete apathy.

In the years following his collapse, Nietzsche's work began to attract attention. By the time he died on August 25, 1900, at the age of fifty-six, he was world-famous.

F. Behold the man.

Having outlined Nietzsche's life history from an exterior point of view, let us now take up the other way of looking at the relation of the philosopher's philosophy to the philosopher's life, namely, by considering what Nietzsche himself says about his own life.

The task seems simple enough. Nietzsche wrote *Ecce Homo*, and there he speaks extensively about himself, as the title "Behold the Man" would lead us to expect. Here we presumably have Nietzsche's autobiography—at least, the book has been understood as such. Yet is it Nietzsche's autobiography in any usual sense? Is Nietzsche simply recounting the events of his life and the circumstances surrounding his writings? If so, he has certainly chosen a curious, untactful, and even repulsive way of telling his life story, namely, by telling us why he is so wise, so clever, and why he writes such good books.

If read as autobiography, *Ecce Homo* is the most pompous document of its sort ever produced. Listen to these typical passages: "It is my fate that I have to be the first decent human being" (EH, p. 782). "I am a bringer of glad tidings like no one before me; I know tasks of such elevation that any notion of them has been lacking so far. Only beginning with me are there hopes again.... With me, truth enters into a fight with the lies of millennia" (EH, p. 783).

Thus *Ecce Homo* has been taken as a product of Nietzsche's approaching insanity, as an interesting autobiographical document but one marred by the author's loss of inhibition and full of the ravings of a near-madman.

But is this work an autobiography at all in any usual sense? Nietzsche said that we ought to be most distrustful of people when they speak or write about themselves and that in such cases we must read between the lines. Do we not also need to do likewise in the case of Nietzsche's own supposed autobiography?

Nietzsche rarely writes in the straightforward manner characteristic of a philosophical treatise. Instead, he writes books of aphorisms (such as *Human, All Too Human*), poetry, diatribes, attacks (such as "David Strauss"), in a way for which we have no name (*Thus Spoke Zarathustra*), in a way that only appears to be autobiographical, and in a way that resembles a philosophical treatise (*On the Genealogy of Morals*) but where the resemblance is merely external. Nietzsche said the beginning of each of the essays in *On the Genealogy of Morals* was calculated so as to mislead, and then he goes on to talk of the importance of the tempo of the book and speaks of the way truths are made to sound there, namely, by "grumbling in the distance" (EH, p. 768).

Why does Nietzsche write in these curious ways? Why does he not simply present his philosophical theories straightforwardly, in direct treatises? Perhaps the reason is that to do so would take for granted something eminently questionable, something that *must* be questioned. Let me suggest, specifically, that a principal reason Nietzsche does not adopt a straightforward style is his sensitivity to the questionable relation of philosophical writers to what they write about.

The philosopher claims in his writing to speak the truth, specifically the truth that is fundamental (grounding all other truths) and universal (binding on everyone). Now, in order for what the philosopher writes to express the universal truth, the philosopher himself must in no way enter into the writing—otherwise, there would be expressed not only the universal truth but also the individuality of the philosopher, which means it would not be universal truth that was expressed. What is written must bear no essential reference to the writer and must instead be an image of truth itself. The writing must be a linguistic articulation mirroring the articulation of truth itself; the writing must therefore be a philosophical treatise.

The philosopher must claim to be only a mouthpiece for the truth; he must disappear as an individual and become a transparent medium through which the truth speaks. Thus the philosopher is involved simultaneously in the greatest hubris (claiming to speak ultimate truth) and the greatest humility (suppressing his individuality in order to serve as mouthpiece for truth). Plato was aware of this duality, and to him it indicated a profound affinity of philosophy with both tragedy and comedy.

This idea of philosophy takes it for granted that man is able more or less to become a mouthpiece for the truth. But Nietzsche insists on calling this into question—to wonder whether philosophy has been and is able to be such a mouthpiece. For Nietzsche, this relation—of human beings to the truth they profess to speak—has to be made questionable. But how is it to be questioned? After all, any questioning of it is itself an attempt to speak the truth; in other words, the questioning (as search for truth) already involves what is being questioned.

The questioning can therefore not proceed straightforwardly. It is insufficient just to write a treatise on the relation of man to truth, for already the choice of writing a treatise (that is, the style appropriate to one who serves as a mouthpiece for truth) assumes an answer to the question of man's relation to truth. So this relation can remain genuinely questionable only if one avoids dogmatically assuming that a definite style is self-evidently appropriate. Any choice of style already involves a certain kind of relation of man to truth.

The style of philosophical writing needs to remain questionable. More positively, the relation of man to truth can be explored by taking up various styles (various ways of relating oneself to what is spoken about) and working these out. To work them out means to let what is written about and the writing itself recoil on each other dialectically. Therefore, the way Nietzsche writes, his style, is not independent of what is at issue in the writing. We have to try to understand Nietzsche not only in *what* he writes but also in *how* he writes.

In this connection, we should note Nietzsche's statement: "Everything profound loves masks" (BGE, p. 240). There are many masks in Nietzsche. Eugen Fink even speaks of Nietzsche's entire philosophy as a "philosophy behind masks" (*Nietzsches Philosophie* [Stuttgart: Kohlhammer, 1960], p. 7). But it should be remembered that the masks are not something extrinsic but instead are bound up with the very questioning in which Nietzsche is engaged.

* * *

So we now turn to *Ecce Homo*. As with every one of Nietzsche's writings, we must try to understand the character of the work itself. We must ask how it ought to be read. Nietzsche tells us a number of things about how to read his books, about what is required on our part in order to be able to read them.

In *The Dawn*, Nietzsche describes himself as "a teacher of slow reading." He continues:

> At present it is not only my habit, but even my taste—perhaps a perverted taste—to write nothing but what will drive to despair everyone who is "in a hurry." For philology is that venerable art which exacts from its followers one thing above all: to step to one side, to leave themselves spare moments, to grow

silent, to become slow. Philology is the leisurely art of the goldsmith applied to language, teaching us how to read well, that is, slowly, profoundly, attentively, prudently, with inner thoughts, with the mental door ajar, with delicate fingers and eyes.... My patient friends, this book appeals only to perfect readers and philologists: *learn* to read me well! (D, preface, §5)

So Nietzsche's works are not to be read "head-on." We need to "step to one side," have "inner thoughts," leave the "mental door ajar." Nietzsche's writings must be read slowly, for it is as important to hear what Nietzsche does *not* say as it is to hear what he does say. Nietzsche tells us that one of his instincts is silence: "Silence is as much of an instinct with me as is garrulity with our dear philosophers. I am brief; my readers themselves must become long and comprehensive in order to bring up and together all that I have thought and thought deep down" (from a discarded draft for section 3 of "Why I Write such Good Books," EH, p. 796).

Nietzsche continues in the same fragment: "My writings are difficult; I hope this is not considered an objection. To understand the most abbreviated language ever spoken by a philosopher—and also the language poorest in formulaic phrases, most alive, most artistic—one must follow the opposite procedure of that generally required by philosophical literature. Usually, one must condense or run the risk of upsetting one's digestion; I have to be diluted, liquefied, mixed with water, for the sake of good digestion" (EH, p. 796).

Or again, Nietzsche says in the *Twilight of the Idols*: "It is my ambition to say in ten sentences what everyone else says in a book—what everyone else does *not* say in a book" (TI, p. 556).

Reading Nietzsche's works not only requires a certain skill and care. In addition, as he claims again and again, his writings make a certain demand on the reader, a certain "existential demand." At the beginning of *Ecce Homo*: "Those who can breathe the air of my writings know it is an air of the heights, a strong air. One must be made for it. Otherwise there is no small danger that one may catch cold in it. The ice is near, the solitude tremendous.... Philosophy, as I have so far understood and lived it, means living voluntarily amid ice and high mountains" (EH, p. 674). In reference to *Thus Spoke Zarathustra*: "Such things reach only the most select. It is a privilege without equal to be a listener here. No one is free to have ears for Zarathustra. Is he not ... a *seducer*?" (EH, 675–76). Again: "Ultimately, no one can get more out of things, including books, than he already knows. For what one lacks access to from experience, one will have no ear" (EH, p. 717).

Just as something is demanded of us in order to read Nietzsche's works, so also our reading—if genuine—must affect us, must affect what and how we are. Thus, negatively, Nietzsche speaks of men who are honey-gatherers of the spirit, interested only in storing away items of knowledge without ever really assimilating them: "*Our* treasure is where the beehives of our knowledge are. We are constantly making for them, being by nature winged creatures and honey-gatherers of the spirit; there is one thing alone we really care about from the heart: 'bringing something home'" (GM, p. 451). Or again, with respect to *Thus Spoke Zarathustra*: "having understood six sentences from it—that is, having really experienced them—would raise a person to a higher level of existence than 'modern' men could attain" (EH, 715). Finally, Nietzsche says: "Of what is great, one must either be silent or speak with greatness. With greatness—that means cynically and with innocence" (WP, preface, §1). How is such speaking possible?

* * *

Ecce Homo is subtitled: How one becomes what one is. That is the decisive clue for understanding the work—with regard to both what is said there and how it is said. Let us consider the way the Platonic tradition—which is something quite different from Plato—understood the task of becoming what one is. It is to become *in fact* what one already *essentially* is. In other words, it is to realize, to fulfill, an ideal—that ideal which defines what man is. Furthermore, this ideal (what man essentially is) is something we always already know, though for the most part confusedly. However far a person may be from the ideal, he is never devoid of knowledge of it; he has only *forgotten* the ideal. It can always be recollected. So the important element in becoming what one is is the recollection in which one comes explicitly to know the ideal and thus to actualize it in oneself.

From Nietzsche's perspective, nothing is changed if we talk about Christianity rather than Platonism. Christianity is merely "Platonism for the people" (BGE, p. 193), the mere substitution of faith for knowledge. This substitution makes no matter, for the crucial point remains—namely, to become what one is means to actualize an ideal given in advance, an ideal having its source beyond oneself.

In contrast, Nietzsche writes: "To become what one is, one must not have the faintest notion *what* one is" (EH, p. 710). Otherwise put, to become what one is does not mean to actualize some pregiven ideal. Accordingly, if *Ecce Homo* addresses itself to this question of becoming what one is, then its task does not amount to presenting new ideals, erecting new idols: "The last thing I should promise would be to 'improve' mankind. No new idols are erected by me" (EH, p. 673). "I want no 'believers'" (EH, p. 782).

What then is the task of *Ecce Homo* if neither to present a new ideal nor, of course, to revive some old ideal? And how does this task make it necessary for Nietzsche to say who he is? Nietzsche states at the very beginning: "Since I must before long confront humanity with the most difficult demand ever made of it, what seems indispensable is for me to say *who I am*" (EH, p. 673). This statement raises three questions: (1) What is the demand? (2) Why is it the most difficult one? (3) How does the posing of this demand require that Nietzsche say who he is?

1. The demand.
It is a call for a revaluation of all values: "Revaluation of all values: that is my formula for an act of supreme self-examination on the part of humanity" (EH,

p. 782). The demand is for supreme self-examination, for a discovery of one's self in order that one might *be* oneself. It is the demand that man become what he is.

2. The difficulty.

Let us ask: How is it possible to demand of someone that he become what he is? The easiest way would be to tell him what he is, give him a new ideal. But Nietzsche refuses to do any such thing, for to impose an ideal on someone is precisely the best way of ensuring that he will not become what he is.

One can also confront men with this demand by destroying the ideals in terms of which men have previously tried to understand themselves. That is, one can smash the idols that have kept men from becoming themselves. One can destroy the ideals so that men are freed to become themselves rather than imitating ideals imposed on them. Certainly *Ecce Homo*—and Nietzsche's work as a whole—has this destructive intention, to destroy all ideals, to usher in a "twilight of the idols":

> No new ideals are erected by me; let the old ideals learn what it means to have feet of clay. Overthrowing idols (my word for "ideals"): that comes closer to being part of my craft. One has deprived reality of its value, its meaning, its truthfulness, to precisely the extent to which one has mendaciously invented an ideal world. . . . The lie of the ideal has so far been a curse on reality; due to this lie, mankind itself has become mendacious and false down to its most fundamental instincts—to the point of worshipping the opposite values of those which alone would guarantee its health, its future, and the lofty right to its future. (EH, pp. 673–74)

We can see, then, not only why this demand is difficult to pose but also why it is the most difficult demand for those on whom it is placed. It demands that they become what they are, but it refuses to tell them what they are. Furthermore, it destroys all the ideals in terms of which they think they understand what they are. So, first, Nietzsche's work wants to place a demand on men by destroying the ideals, by freeing men from every idol that has kept them from becoming themselves. But listen to Zarathustra:

> Alas, there are so many great thoughts which do no more than a bellows: they puff up and make emptier.
>
> You call yourself free? Your dominant thought I want to hear, and not that you have escaped from a yoke. Are you one of those who had the right to escape from a yoke? There are some who threw away their last value when they cast off their servitude.
>
> Free *from* what? As if that mattered to Zarathustra! But your eyes should tell me brightly: free *for* what?
>
> Can you give yourself your own evil and your own good and hang your own will over yourself as a law? (TSZ, p. 175)

Thus something else is required besides the destruction. It is for the sake of this "something else" that Nietzsche has to say who he is.

3. The demand and who Nietzsche is.

The destruction of idols must be accompanied by an indication of what it means to become what one is. It does not mean to actualize some ideal nor simply to destroy all ideals. Instead:

> To become what one is, one must not have the faintest notion *what* one is. From this point of view, even the blunders of life have their own meaning and value. . . . The whole surface of consciousness—consciousness *is* a surface—must be kept clear of all great imperatives. Beware even of every great word, every great pose! Such words and poses are so many dangers that the instinct comes too soon to "understand itself." Meanwhile the organizing "idea" that is destined to rule keeps growing deep down—it begins to command; slowly it leads us back from side roads and wrong ways. (EH, p. 710)

This says: *become* what you are—*let* yourself become what you are instead of binding yourself to ideals. To become what you are is *not* to strive to realize an ideal: "I cannot remember that I ever tried hard—no trace of struggle can be demonstrated in my life. Mine is the opposite of a heroic nature. 'Willing' something, 'striving' for something, envisaging a 'purpose,' a 'wish'—I know none of this from experience" (EH, p. 711). But that still puts it negatively. What is involved positively?

The decisive indication is the following: "Zarathustra once defines, quite strictly, his task—it is mine, too—and there is no mistaking his meaning: he says Yes to the point of justifying, redeeming, even all the past" (EH, p. 764). This says that to become what one is means *to affirm what one has become*—to affirm all the side roads, errors, suffering, everything that has made one what he is.

In other terms, to become what one is means *amor fati*, love of one's fate: "My formula for greatness in a human being is *amor fati*: wanting nothing to be different, not forward, not backward, not in all eternity. Do not merely bear what is necessary, still less conceal it—all idealism is mendacity in the face of what is necessary—but instead *love* it" (EH, p. 714). Or again: "What is necessary does not hurt me; *amor fati* is my inmost nature" (EH, p. 780).

Now we can see why Nietzsche tells us who he is: in that way, he shows us what it means to become what one is, to love one's fate. Thus Nietzsche says: "How could I fail to be grateful to my whole life? —and so I tell my life to myself" (EH, p. 677).

Ecce Homo is Nietzsche's own Yes-saying, affirming, loving, of his life—of *everything* in his life, and that is why he needs to speak not only of the great things but also of the most insignificant and unpleasant events of his life. He talks about everything: family, friends, lodgings, climate, diet, illness, relation to

Wagner, and on and on. In telling who he is, Nietzsche speaks not of his ideals and goals but of chance happenings and the chaos of instincts. He speaks of his attacking instinct, his instinct for cleanliness, his instinctual atheism. He speaks not of striving and seeking but of play: "I do not know any other way of associating with great tasks than play: as a sign of greatness, that is an essential presupposition" (EH, p. 714).

Yet there is great danger involved in *Ecce Homo*, the danger that Nietzsche's own becoming who he is will be turned into a new ideal to be imitated. Much of what is especially strange about the book derives from Nietzsche's intention to ward off that danger:

> I want no "believers"; I think I am too malicious to believe in myself; I never speak to the masses. I have a terrible fear that one day I will be pronounced holy; you will guess why I publish this book beforehand; it shall prevent people from doing me mischief.
>
> I do not want to be a holy man; sooner even a buffoon.—Perhaps I am a buffoon. (EH, p. 782)

Yet Nietzsche is well aware that it is not sufficient merely to *say* this—he must *be* it. In much of *Ecce Homo*, Nietzsche is playing the buffoon. Perhaps we should ask regarding Nietzsche what he himself asks regarding Shakespeare: "What must a man have suffered to have such a need of being a buffoon!" (EH, p. 702).

Nietzsche wants to show us the path of becoming what one is—but then he immediately wants to send us away from himself, to repulse us. The preface to *Ecce Homo* concludes with a passage taken from *Thus Spoke Zarathustra*:

> Now I go alone, my disciples; you, too, go now, alone. Thus I want it.
>
> Go away from me and resist Zarathustra! And even better: be ashamed of him! Perhaps he deceived you.
>
> The man of knowledge must not only love his enemies; he must also be able to hate his friends.
>
> One repays a teacher ill if one remains nothing but a pupil. And why do you not want to pluck at my wreath?
>
> You revere me; but what if your reverence tumbles one day? Beware lest a statue slay you.
>
> You say you believe in Zarathustra? But what matters Zarathustra? You are my believers—but what matter all believers?
>
> You had not yet sought yourselves; and you found me. Thus do all believers; therefore all faith amounts to so little.
>
> Now I bid you lose me and find yourselves; and only when you have all denied me will I return to you. (EH, p. 676; TSZ, p. 190)

To affirm what one is, to love one's fate, to say "Yes" to life, even in what is strangest and most questionable about it, is what Nietzsche calls the Dionysian.

The last words of *Ecce Homo* are: "Have I been understood? —*Dionysus versus the Crucified*" (EH, p. 791). In this connection, Nietzsche speaks of himself as "the first tragic philosopher," as bringing about a "transposition of the Dionysian into a philosophical pathos" (EH, p. 729). Nietzsche says he promises a tragic age, a rebirth of the highest art in saying "Yes" to life, a rebirth of tragedy. All of this refers us to Nietzsche's reflections on tragedy and the Dionysian, that is, to *The Birth of Tragedy*.

* * *

Nietzsche said of *Thus Spoke Zarathustra*: "This work stands altogether apart" (EH, p. 760). Our goal in this course is to read and interpret *Thus Spoke Zarathustra*. Yet access to this work is immensely difficult, as Nietzsche himself warns us. Therefore, a great deal of preparation is needed before we can even approach it. All of Nietzsche's works preceding *Thus Spoke Zarathustra* (especially *The Birth of Tragedy* and *The Gay Science*) prepare the way for it, and all subsequent works (especially *Beyond Good and Evil, On the Genealogy of Morals, Twilight of the Idols,* and *The Antichrist*) are designed to explain and expand it. So these works surrounding *Thus Spoke Zarathustra* can serve us as a means of access. Accordingly, our procedure will be to prepare for reading *Thus Spoke Zarathustra* by, first, considering the context and major concerns of *The Birth of Tragedy*; second, by closely examining two other early works, "On Truth and Lies in a Nonmoral Sense" and "On the Uses and Disadvantages of History for Life"; and third, by drawing from many of the later writings insofar as they cast light on *Thus Spoke Zarathustra*.

III. The Greeks

A. The contemporary relevance of the Greeks.

If we consider not only Nietzsche's associating of himself with the Dionysian but also his statement that what was thought by Heraclitus is more closely related to him than anything else ever thought, we get a further indication of how much Nietzsche's philosophy depends on his encounter with the Greeks—with Greek thinking and especially with Greek tragedy. Nietzsche's encounter with the Greeks is the *beginning* of his philosophy—not only the temporal beginning but also the beginning in the sense of the source that sustains all his thinking.

Nietzsche signals in many places the fundamental role the Greeks play for him. In *The Birth of Tragedy*, he calls the Greeks "the highest of all teachers" and says that to be capable of learning from them is "a high honor and rare distinction" (BT, p. 121). The essay "We Philologists" argues that "it is only as a creator that one is able to take anything from the Greeks" (WeP, §171). In *Philosophy in the Tragic Age of the Greeks*, Nietzsche speaks of the Greek philosophers (that is, the pre-Socratics) as they who "once and for all *justified* philosophy simply by having engaged in it and having done so more fully than any other people" (PTAG, p. 28). He goes on to say that the Greeks invented "the archetypes of philosophical thought" and that "nothing essential has been added" since the Greeks (PTAG, p. 31).

It is as a *creator* that Nietzsche wants to learn from the Greeks. His task is a creative one, namely, the overcoming of nihilism, the revaluation of all values, the transformation of man into overman, or—in the form most clearly demonstrative of his link to the Greeks—the rebirth of tragedy. Yet Nietzsche's task is a contemporary one. It is bound to the situation of contemporary man and hence is no mere repetition of the birth of tragedy as occurred among the Greeks. Instead, Nietzsche's task requires that the condition of contemporary humanity be made transparent. Nevertheless, even here—in understanding the contemporary situation—the Greeks are decisive for Nietzsche.

In the second essay of the *Untimely Meditations*, Nietzsche considers the contemporary situation by drawing out the significance of a characteristic feature of his age, its historical consciousness. Yet he insists that he is able to penetrate what is most *timely* only because he occupies an *untimely* position from which to interrogate the age. It is "only to the extent that I am a pupil of earlier times, especially the Hellenic, that although a child of the present time I was able to acquire such untimely experiences" (UM, p. 60).

In other words, the Greeks provide a standpoint from which to understand the basic phenomena of the contemporary age: "We are experiencing phenomena so strange that they would hang in the air as incomprehensible if we could not look back over a tremendous expanse of time and connect them with their Greek counterparts" (UM, p. 208).

Greek culture serves Nietzsche not only as a means to expose the contemporary age but also as a means of self-interrogation. In *Ecce Homo*, Nietzsche says that through his insight into the foundations of Greek culture, he "discovered the only parable and parallel in history" for his "own inmost experience" (EH, p. 727). Furthermore, such parallels are not just accessory; they do not simply illustrate something that in their absence would still be available through reflection. On the contrary, Nietzsche says: "Immediate self-observation is not nearly sufficient for learning to know ourselves. We need history, since the past continues to flow within us in a hundred waves" (HATH, vol. II, pt. 1, §223). Self-knowledge requires history—it is by gaining access to the past that we bring before ourselves an image of that which imperceptibly flows within us and forms us.

B. *The Birth of Tragedy*.

The work that is most crucial for understanding Nietzsche's encounter with the Greeks—hence for understanding the beginning of his thought—is *The Birth of Tragedy*. It was Nietzsche's first book, published in 1872. There has been a tendency to depreciate it, because in the late 1880s Nietzsche came to speak critically of what he wrote there. This tendency is grossly mistaken. If we look carefully at Nietzsche's criticism, we see that it does not pertain to the core of the work. We might even say that because *The Birth of Tragedy* so decisively set Nietzsche on his way, it became necessary for him again and again to retrieve this genuine core.

The Birth of Tragedy is a complex work. Nietzsche himself later spoke of it as "disagreeable," "a strange and almost inaccessible book," lacking in "the will to logical cleanliness" (BT, pp. 17–19). A principal source of its complexity and inaccessibility lies in the fact that it moves simultaneously on several different levels. At least five distinct levels can be delineated:

1. *The Birth of Tragedy* is a treatise on Greek tragedy—its birth, its nature, its death.

It was on this level that *The Birth of Tragedy* was viciously attacked by the philologists of Nietzsche's day, especially by Wilamowitz in a piece called *Zukunftsphilologie!* ("Philology of the future!"). What Nietzsche said about Greek tragedy appeared outrageous, an arbitrary construction oblivious to the canons of sound scholarship. *The Birth of Tragedy* was even more suspect because the entire discussion of tragedy could be seen merely as propaganda for Wagner's cause.

There are two fundamental reasons for the hostility. First, Nietzsche's view of Greek tragedy is not based simply on a careful analysis of tragedies and the ancient reports about them. Instead, his view is rooted in the deeper levels of the book, that is, in Nietzsche's insights into the relation of art and life and into the character of art in general. The philologists hardly noticed these levels. Second, Nietzsche is proposing a new and indeed revolutionary comprehensive view of the Greeks. The traditional view, handed down from Winckelmann, Goethe, and Schiller, considered the Greeks the embodiment of beauty, perfection, serenity, and harmony (the attributes of Greek sculpture). The Greeks were regarded as "fortunate children," ones spared an overpowering awareness of the horror and absurdity of life and the concomitant pessimism. A common epithet was "Greek cheerfulness." By contrast, Nietzsche views the Greeks not as oblivious to misery, suffering, and absurdity but rather in terms of the greatness with which they *overcame* their propensity to suffering and pessimism: "How much did this people have to suffer to be able to become so beautiful!" (BT, p. 144). Furthermore, according to Nietzsche it was precisely when Greek culture lost its connection with the substratum of suffering and pessimism that its decline set in, the decline embodied in Socrates. Socrates and Plato are not for Nietzsche the pinnacle of Greek culture but instead are the beginning of its decline. The greatest Greek philosophers are not Socrates, Plato, and Aristotle but Anaximander, Heraclitus, and Empedocles.

2. *The Birth of Tragedy* is an aesthetics, a treatise about art as such.

Here two general issues can be delineated. First, the aesthetic problem can be seen in terms of the apparent contradiction between a pair of necessary components of art: aesthetic distance and aesthetic involvement. The requirement of distance is evident in the fact that we place paintings in a frame and enact dramas on a stage. The artwork has to be held at a distance from the spectator, who must take it as art, not as reality. On the other hand, if art is to be of significance, it must not merely be something played out at a distance, leaving our lives untouched; it must involve us profoundly. This duality is a very general form of the one Nietzsche tries to account for in terms of the contrast between the Apollinian and the Dionysian. In Greek tragedy, Nietzsche sees these two forms welded together so that each reaches its consummation.

The second general issue about the aesthetics of *The Birth of Tragedy* has to do with music. With a few exceptions, music has never been accorded much significance by philosophers. Viewed from the perspective that places the highest value on cognition, music appears inferior to most other arts (especially poetry) since it is furthest removed from the representation and articulation of conceptual language. Yet is this an appropriate perspective? Is music merely imperfect representation? Is there not rather a fundamental gulf between cognition and music? The latter is Nietzsche's position, and his problem is to understand this gulf, one he thematizes as the conflict between Dionysus and Socrates.

3. *The Birth of Tragedy* is a treatise about art and life.
Nietzsche's concern is not primarily to describe the nature of artworks or even the character of artistic creation. Instead, he wants to regard art as a human activity and to ask about the meaning of art within life as a whole. How is it that man creates works of art? What in life—what need, what end—drives man to create artworks? Nietzsche, as he later puts it, is concerned to examine art in the perspective of life—to understand how "art represents the highest task and the truly metaphysical activity of this life" (BT, p. 31–32).

4. *The Birth of Tragedy* is a metaphysics of art.
Nietzsche himself uses this expression and relates it to his statement that "it is only as an aesthetic phenomenon that existence and the world are eternally justified" (BT, p. 52). The question is: Why should this be called metaphysics? Metaphysics is presumably concerned with knowledge of existence and of the world, whereas Nietzsche speaks not of knowing but of justifying. Or are knowing and justifying perhaps the same? Perhaps knowing is not a matter of pure seeing but of justifying—in the sense of covering the world and existence with a veil of illusion that allows life to continue, that holds us back from suicide. According to Nietzsche, "Truth is the kind of error without which a certain species of living being could not live" (WP, §493).

5. *The Birth of Tragedy* is a metaphysics of life.
If aesthetic justification (art) is simply a means used by life to secure its own continuation, then the most fundamental problem is not art but life as such. *The Birth of Tragedy* is, most fundamentally, a metaphysics of life. But that is the case with Nietzsche's thought as a whole, and thus *The Birth of Tragedy* can serve as a way for us to approach that thought.

We have spoken of *The Birth of Tragedy* as a treatise (about Greek tragedy, about art, about art and life) and as a metaphysics; presumably, it is then a metaphysical treatise. As we already noted, however, the very character and appropriateness of a "philosophical treatise" need to be called into question, granted the radicality of Nietzsche's questioning. In fact, a tension between Nietzsche's thought and the traditional philosophical way of writing is already evident in *The Birth of Tragedy*. That work is an attack on theoretical man but is carried out precisely through what looks like a scholarly theoretical inquiry. That is, in attacking the theoretical attitude (Socratism), Nietzsche seems to be attacking precisely the kind of endeavor he himself is carrying out.

Nietzsche refers to this tension in a paradoxical way at one point in *The Birth of Tragedy*: "Thus all our knowledge of art is basically quite illusory, because as knowledgeable beings we are not one and identical with that being which, as the sole author and spectator of this comedy of art, prepares a perpetual entertainment for itself. Only insofar as the genius in the act of artistic creation coalesces with this primordial artist of the world, does he know anything of the eternal essence of art" (BT, p. 52). (The primordial artist is the will itself.) Accordingly, Nietzsche takes distance from what he is saying in the book. In his later self-criticism, he claims that what spoke in *The Birth of Tragedy* was "a *strange voice*"—someone "who concealed himself for the time being under the scholar's hood.... It should have *sung*, this 'new soul'—and not spoken! What I had to say then—too bad I did not dare say it as a poet" (BT, p. 20).

C. Culture.

Having outlined these levels, let us now look more closely at the last one, the deepest level, the metaphysics of life or, in different terms, the view of the nature of culture.

What is culture? It is that by which man is stimulated to life despite the suffering, horror, and absurdity inherent in the nature of things and in life itself. Culture

> is an eternal phenomenon; the insatiable will does always find a way to detain its creatures in life and compel them to live on, by means of an illusion spread over things. One person is chained by the Socratic love of knowledge and by the delusion of being able thereby to heal the eternal wound of existence; another is ensnared by art's seductive veil of beauty fluttering before his eyes; still another by the metaphysical comfort that beneath the whirl of phenomena eternal life flows on indestructibly—to say nothing of the more vulgar and almost more powerful illusions which the will always has at hand.... Everything we call culture is made up of these stimulants. (BT, pp. 109–10)

So there are these three profound stimulants by which man is impelled to live; corresponding to them are Socratic, artistic, and tragic culture. All three stimulants are related to myth: artistic and tragic culture directly, Socratic negatively (destruction of myth). The theme of myth allows us to connect *The Birth of Tragedy* with Nietzsche's demand to become what we are. That such a demand is posed to modern man presupposes modern man is *not* what he is, remains estranged from what he is. It is the same as Nietzsche's demand for *homecoming* and presupposes modern man is homeless, uprooted. This uprootedness of modern man is precisely what Nietzsche tries to understand through myth in *The Birth of Tragedy*.

What is the function of myth? Nietzsche says: "Without myth, every culture loses the healthy natural power of its creativity: only a horizon defined by myths completes and unifies a whole cultural movement. Myth alone saves all the powers of imagination and of the Apollinian dream from aimless wanderings. The images of the myth have to be the unnoticed omnipresent demonic guardians, under whose care the young soul grows to maturity and whose signs help a man interpret his life and his struggles" (BT, p. 135).

Modern man, under the impact of the Socratic destruction of myth, has become mythless—that is why he is rootless: "There we have the present age, the result of that Socratism which is bent on the destruction of myth. And now the mythless man stands eternally hungry, surrounded by all past ages, and digs and grubs for roots, even if he has to dig for them among the remotest antiquities. The tremendous historical need of our unsatisfied modern culture, the assembling around one of countless other cultures, the consuming desire for knowledge— what does all this point to, if not to the loss of myth, the loss of the mythical home, the mythical maternal womb?" (BT, p. 136).

How is myth the instrument of rootedness? Myth defines the horizon by which we can "interpret" our lives and our struggles. But this horizon is not one of intelligibility; it does not allow us to *understand* life, for understanding (that is, the Socratic tendency) always pushes on beyond every defined horizon. Instead, myth is a horizon of *justification*. Myth roots us in life by aesthetically justifying life, by convincing us, as Nietzsche says, that "even the ugly and disharmonic are part of an artistic game which the will in the eternal amplitude of its pleasure plays with itself" (BT, p. 141). Myth roots us in life by making life lovable, by making possible an *amor fati*.

Myth, Nietzsche says, "reveals to us the playful construction and destruction of the individual world as the overflow of a primordial delight. Thus the dark Heraclitus compares the world-building force to a playing child who places stones here and there and builds sand hills only to knock them down again" (BT, p. 142). In myth, not only man's self-becoming but also the pulsations of the world as a whole appear free of all ideals, goals, and striving—that is, free of all morality. These are rather a matter of *play*. And in the world seen in this manner, man discovers the image of his own genuine, playful self-becoming, an image providing him a horizon within which to become what he is.

D. The wisdom of Silenus.

On its first level, as we noted, *The Birth of Tragedy* is a treatise on Greek tragedy. In the book, Nietzsche relates an ancient story according to which King Midas once captured the wise Silenus, companion of Dionysus, and put to him the question: What is the best and most desirable of all things for man? Nietzsche presents Silenus' response as follows: "Fixed and immovable, the demigod said not a word, until at last, urged by the king, he gave a shrill laugh and broke out into these words: 'O, wretched ephemeral race, children of chance and misery, why do you compel me to tell you what it would be most expedient for you not to hear? What is best of all is utterly beyond your reach: not to be born, not to *be*, to be *nothing*. But the second best for you is—to die soon'" (BT, p. 42).

For Nietzsche, this wisdom of Silenus, this profound pessimism, stands at the root of Greek culture. Greek culture consists in a series of *overcomings* of the wisdom of Silenus. The greatest such overcoming takes place in the event of Greek tragedy, and Nietzsche's view of Greek tragedy is rooted in his aesthetics.

What is involved in the project of formulating a general view of the nature of art? Presumably it means to form a system of concepts adequately describing what is essential to art. But such a project encounters two difficulties at the very outset. First, from what source are we to derive these concepts? Are we to obtain them merely by abstraction from all particular works of art? If we abstract from all differences, we would supposedly obtain what all artworks have in common. But is there any such common feature? What do a Bach fugue and a poem by Hölderlin have in common? Besides, what guarantee do we have that such an abstraction would yield the *essence* of art? Even more, in order to gather together the particular artworks from which to abstract, would we not need to have decided already what is and is not art, just in order to know what to gather up and what to omit? Therefore, if we want to describe the general features of art, we need something to guide us toward what is essential. Nietzsche's guide is the relation of art to life. In other words, the essence of art could be discovered in the way art is related to life.

The second difficulty is the following. In proposing to develop an aesthetics, it seems we presume it is possible to "capture" art in a net of concepts. But is this so? A short while ago, we considered Nietzsche's remark that "all knowledge of art is basically quite illusory." Presumably, then, it is not a matter of conceptual comprehension *in contrast* to the kind of activity the artist is engaged in. For only in artistic creation do we know anything of the essence of art. By its own dicta, *The Birth of Tragedy* is more nearly art than science, and indeed Nietzsche later wrote that he should have dared to speak there as a poet.

What does all this entail concretely regarding the character of *The Birth of Tragedy*? Nietzsche says: "For a genuine poet, metaphor is not a rhetorical figure but a vicarious image that he actually beholds in place of a concept" (BT, p. 63). Thus what Nietzsche attempts—regardless of whether he succeeds—is not a conceptual representation of art (or even specifically of Greek tragedy) in terms of *concepts* of the Apollinian and the Dionysian. Instead, these are "vicarious images"—images presented in the figures of the two gods. Here we have already a form of what Nietzsche later refers to (commenting on *Thus Spoke Zarathustra*) as "the return of language to the nature of imagery" (EH, p. 761).

E. Apollo and Dionysus.

Let us begin with the gods themselves in whom the images are presented. Apollo is the god of light; so much so that there is no darkness at all in him. Apollo is the shining god par excellence; his epithet "Phoebus" means "brilliant" or "shining." Apollo is entirely beneficent; he is the purifier and healer and teaches men the art of healing. Apollo is a soothsayer, the god of prophesy, the source of divine wisdom. He shows men how to make peace with the other gods and in this way is a god of harmony. Apollo's oracle at Delphi was the most famous one in the ancient world. The character of Apollo is expressed very well in the famous injunctions of the oracle: "Know thyself" and "Nothing in excess."

Dionysus scorns those injunctions and instead stands for self-oblivion and immoderation. Dionysus is the only god whose parents (Zeus and the mortal Semele) were not both divine. Dionysus is a god, not a demigod, but through his mother he retains a special relation to the earth. Dionysus is the god of wine and accordingly the god of ecstasy and inspiration. In stories of his capture by pirates and later by Pentheus, the king of Thebes, Dionysus is presented as unable to be bound—he breaks all bonds, all constraints, all limits. As the god of the grapevine, Dionysus dies each year with the coming of winter. He suffers a terrible death, torn to pieces by Titans, but he is always brought back to life in the spring. Ancient tradition says it was his resurrection that was celebrated through the presentation of tragedies. The companions of Dionysus were the satyrs, wild goat-men who played the flute, the instrument that enchanted humans and drove them mad. In Greek tragedy, the members of the chorus are regarded as satyrs. The most famous worshippers of Dionysus were the Maenads. These were women who, frenzied with wine and swept up in ecstasy, roamed in bands through the wilderness, uttering sharp cries and waving wands tipped with pine cones. When the Maenads caught sight of a wild animal, they would descend on it, tear it to pieces, and eat its flesh raw.

What is imaged in these two contrasting deities? —According to Nietzsche, nothing less than the preconditions of art, the two fundamental art-impulses. Apollo and Dionysus represent "artistic energies which burst from nature herself, without the mediation of the human artist, energies in which nature's art-impulses are satisfied in the most immediate and direct way. . . . With reference to these immediate art-states of nature, every artist is an 'imitator'" (BT, p. 38). So these artistic energies were constituted before the advent of the human artist. We will see that in the development of art, the artistic energies are transformed: the Apollinian and the Dionysian, as they finally enter into the domain of tragedy, are not simply identical with those pre-artistic forms in which they arise from nature.

In his description of the Apollinian and Dionysian, Nietzsche takes as his point of departure the weaker form in which, as he says (WP, §798), these art-impulses are rehearsed in ordinary life: dreams and intoxication. The Apollinian is linked to "the beautiful illusion of the dream world" in which we take joy in the apprehension of form. Thus the Apollinian is the spirit of the plastic arts. It is especially important that in the dream vision we are distanced from the illusion. Indeed in a sense we live through, even suffer through, what appears, but there always radiates from the apprehended form the sensation that it is mere appearance, mere semblance. In shining and shimmering, the form betrays that it is illusion. Furthermore, the shining is such that the Apollinian involves a perfecting, namely, of the incompletely intelligible everyday world, a healing of its imperfection. The Apollinian is an urge to everything that simplifies and distinguishes, that makes clear, unambiguous, and typical (WP, §1050). The Apollinian embodies distinctness, measured restraint, clear delineation of boundaries, hence individuation and freedom from the wilder emotions in which we lose ourselves in something external, unite with others. Apollo is "the glorious divine image of the *principium individuationis*, and through his gestures and glances all the joy and wisdom of 'illusion,' together with its beauty, speak to us" (BT, p. 36).

The Dionysian, on the other hand, is the embodiment of that intoxication and ecstasy, of those profound emotions that overstep and dissolve all limits and all determinateness. The Dionysian is linked to the collapse of intelligibility and of the principle of individuation. Dionysus, the god of intoxicating wine, is a god who dissolves bounds. In Dionysian ecstasy, everything individual and subjective vanishes into total self-oblivion. It dissolves into the dark primordial unity at the ground of all things. Man is reunited with man and with nature: "He feels himself a god, and he himself wanders about now just as enchanted and exalted as the gods he saw in his dreams. Man is no longer an artist; he has become a work of art" (BT, p. 37). This reunion with the "mysterious primordial unity" corresponds to the reuniting of the dismembered Dionysus and his return to life. The mysterious primordial unity is the primal will that, according to Schopenhauer, is the thing-in-itself underlying all phenomena. Nietzsche says: "By the mystical triumphant cry of Dionysus, the spell of individuation is broken, and the way lies open to the mothers of being, to the innermost core of things" (BT, pp. 99–100).

The Apollinian-Dionysian duality forms the basis of Nietzsche's view of the epochs of Greek culture. The old Greek culture of Homer's time was Apollinian. Its Apollinian character insulated and protected the Greeks from the savagery of the Dionysian festivals that spread throughout the ancient world. Eventually, however, Dionysian impulses began to appear among the Greeks. The greatest achievement of Greek culture was its synthesis of the Dionysian and the Apollinian—first, in lyric poetry and finally (in a more perfect form) in Greek tragedy. Specifically, the development of Greek culture falls into five epochs:

1. the age of the Titans (background of the old Apollinian culture);
2. the Homeric world (Apollinian);
3. influx of the Dionysian;
4. Apollinian reaction: Doric culture, rigid Apollinian culture of Sparta; and
5. lyric poetry and Greek tragedy.

We need to consider: first, the old Apollinian culture and its background; second, the initial synthesis of the Apollinian and Dionysian in lyric poetry; third, the consummation of this synthesis in Greek tragedy; fourth, the death of tragedy and the birth of Socratism; and, fifth, the contemporary task.

F. Apollinian culture.

The harmony and measure of the old Greek culture have been regarded as manifestations of a natural paradise, a natural state of blessedness with which the Greeks were endowed. But one of Nietzsche's main ideas is that the roots of every culture are savage and barbaric: any degree of culture is achieved only by the most strenuous act of overcoming the primitive substratum. Such overcoming requires casting an illusion over the world and existence, "justifying" them and providing a stimulus to life. Nietzsche says of the old Apollinian culture: "It is by no means a simple condition that comes into being naturally and as if inevitably. . . . It must first overthrow an empire of Titans and slay monsters and . . . must have triumphed over an abysmal and terrifying view of the world and the keenest susceptibility to suffering through recourse to the most forceful and pleasurable illusions" (BT, p. 43).

What was the illusion that made Apollinian culture possible? —The Olympian Gods. All these gods are Apollinian; they all embody the same impulse as does Apollo himself. How did these gods provide an illusion so as to act as a stimulus to life? —By deifying, sanctifying, life as such, by giving the Greeks a transfiguring mirror in which they saw their own lives glorified. "Thus do the gods justify the life of man: they themselves live it—the only satisfactory theodicy!" (BT, p. 43). The fact that the Greeks had to create such a glorification of life—such a "fantastic excess of life" (BT, p. 41)—points back to the sensitivity with which they felt the *need* to glorify life. The greater the experience of the need, the greater the act of overcoming in which this need is fulfilled. Thus, it was not because the Greeks were oblivious to the abyss of horror and suffering but because they experienced this abyss most painfully that they veiled it as they did.

Accordingly, Nietzsche asks: "What terrific need was it that could produce such an illustrious company of Olympian beings?" (BT, p. 41). The need resides in the experience of terror, of suffering, and of the absurdity of existence. It is the experience behind the wisdom of Silenus: best of all is never to have been born. Such profound pessimism growing out of the experience of the horrors of life is what the Greeks veiled from sight and overcame by means of their gods: "It was in order to be able to live that the Greeks had to create these gods—from a most profound need" (BT, p. 42).

* * *

With respect to the Dionysian, Nietzsche is drawing on the metaphysics of Schopenhauer, specifically on the latter's notion of a primal will. Let us relate this notion to the Apollinian-Dionysian duality. Through the Apollinian art-world of the Olympian gods, the Greeks are stimulated to life. That is to say, the Apollinian art-world *redeems* ordinary existence. An analogous kind of redemption is also in play at the level of the primal will. The primal will (thing-in-itself) involves eternal suffering inasmuch as it is divided against itself through a plurality of conflicting wills. Thus arises the need for a "redemption in appearances," a need for appearances that veil the eternal strife and suffering. These appearances are those of ordinary empirical existence, where the strife of will is veiled by the forms that constitute the phenomenal world. It is because the eternal suffering and strife are normally veiled in our everyday phenomenal existence that a glimpse beneath to the primal will is so terrifying and pessimistic. The greatness of Apollinian art is that it veils the strife of the primal will more opaquely than does everyday phenomenal existence.

In Nietzsche's account, what transpires in the course of Greek history is that the Apollinian veil—which cuts man off from the primal will—proves ineffective. The Dionysian union with the primal will reasserts itself and challenges the Apollinian culture. The outcome is a transformation of Apollinian culture through a synthesis of the Apollinian and the Dionysian in lyric poetry and finally in Greek tragedy.

G. Lyric poetry.

Nietzsche finds two clues for understanding Greek lyric poetry. The first is Schiller's observation that before he created anything he did not have in mind any images but rather felt a musical mood. The second is the circumstance that the Greeks always took for granted the union, even the identity, of the lyric poet with the musician. Nietzsche takes these as clues that lyric poetry is dependent on, rooted in, born out of, the spirit of music.

In music, Schopenhauer said, there is produced an immediate copy of the primal will itself. Music is an image of the pulsing, the rising and falling, of the will. For Nietzsche, the poem is the projection of music into a world of pictures and symbols, a projection of Dionysian ecstasy into an Apollinian image-world. As a musician, the poet is Dionysian; as a lyrist, the poet is Apollinian. "As a Dionysian artist, the lyric poet has identified himself with the primal unity, with its pain and contradiction.... He produces a copy of this primal unity as music. Now, however, under the Apollinian dream inspiration, this music reveals itself to him again as a symbolic dream-image. The inchoate, intangible reflection of the primordial pain in music, with its redemption in mere appearances, now produces a second mirroring as a specific symbol or example" (BT, p. 49). So in the case of the lyric poet—in marked contrast to the purely Apollinian artist—the image-world of the poem grows out of the poet's Dionysian identification with the will and thus is an image of the poet's own self in its oneness with this ground. The projection of the image-world is no longer merely a counterpart to the process in which the will seeks redemption in appearances; instead, the projection is itself caught up precisely in that redemptive process.

Thus the poet, as an individual, is *not* the true artist. On the contrary, he is the medium through which the primal will is projected into appearances, the medium through which the primal will (with which the poet must first be reunited) achieves its redemption in appearances. So art is not some activity carried on by phenomenally existing individual human beings; instead, the individual is only a medium for the play of the will itself: "To our humiliation *and* exaltation, one thing above all must be clear to us. The entire comedy of art is neither performed for our betterment or education nor are we the true authors of this art-world. On the contrary, we may assume that we are merely images and artistic projections for the true author and that we have our highest dignity in our significance as works of art—for it is only as an aesthetic phenomenon that existence and the world are eternally justified" (BT, p. 52; see also BT, pp. 22 and 141).

H. Greek tragedy.

Shortly after composing *The Birth of Tragedy*, Nietzsche abandoned the metaphysical distinction between the thing-in-itself (primal will) and the world of appearances (empirical world). In his later writings, Nietzsche most severely attacks the concept of the thing-in-itself. Yet already in *The Birth of Tragedy*, especially in the discussion of Greek tragedy, this distinction is undermined. *The Birth of Tragedy* overcomes its own external framework. We now need to see how it does so.

What Nietzsche says about Greek tragedy seems relatively straightforward, merely an elaboration of the same basic structure involved in lyric poetry. But this is one of those cases in which Nietzsche is deceptively clear. I will first sketch the apparently straightforward outline of Nietzsche's account of tragedy. Then I will pose some questions and through them try to see the fundamental issues in the background.

Nietzsche begins with the problem of the role of the chorus. According to ancient tradition, tragedy arose from the tragic chorus and was originally only chorus. Yet the chorus cannot be considered (in the usual way) an ideal spectator commenting on what is transpiring in the scene, for the chorus lacks ideality. That is to say, the chorus lacks aesthetic distance and regards what is transpiring in the scene as real (BT, p. 57). So Nietzsche takes up a hint offered by Schiller: the chorus is a living wall with which the tragedy closes itself off from the everyday world (BT, p. 58). Yet in what way is it closed off? And for what purpose?

In Nietzsche's view, the chorus is a separated domain in a very special sense: the separation from the everyday world that it provides is of the same order as Dionysian ecstasy. The chorus is "the mirror image in which Dionysian man contemplates himself" (BT, p. 63). Thus the chorus is the artistic counterpart of the Dionysian throng. In its presence, the separations among human beings give way to an overwhelming feeling of unity with the primal will. The individual, the everyday world, is overcome, and man is led back to the very core of all things. This holds both for members of the chorus and for the spectators in the audience, who indeed in the Greek view are not entirely cut off from the chorus. This Dionysian enchantment, the overwhelming feeling of unity, is a precondition for tragedy. Under the spell of the enchantment, the Dionysian reveler sees himself as a satyr. But then in turn he sees a new vision outside himself in his god, Dionysus. This new vision—the scene of the tragedy—is just the Apollinian consummation, the transfiguring of the spectator's own state.

Originally the scene and the action were regarded merely as a *vision* generated by the chorus and spoken of by the chorus in the symbolism of dance, song, and word. In this vision the satyric chorus sees its master, Dionysus. The only stage hero was for a long time Dionysus, and even when the celebrated figures (such as Prometheus and Oedipus) of Greek tragedy appear on stage, they are only masks for Dionysus—hence the typicality of these figures. So tragedy involves the same basic structure as does lyric poetry, namely, Dionysian ecstasy projected into an Apollinian image-world:

> We must understand Greek tragedy as the Dionysian chorus which ever anew discharges itself in an Apollinian world of images. Thus the choral parts with which tragedy is interlaced are, so to speak, the womb that gave birth to the whole of the so-called dialogue, that is, the entire world of the stage, the real drama. In several successive discharges this primal ground of tragedy radiates this vision of the drama which is by all means a dream apparition and to that extent epic in nature; but, on the other hand, being the objectification of a Dionysian state, it represents not Apollinian redemption through mere appearances but, instead, the shattering of the individual through his fusion with primal being. (BT, pp. 64–65)

With this outline in mind, we need to pose some questions. In his "Attempt at a self-criticism," Nietzsche says that *The Birth of Tragedy* viewed art in relation to life. So what is the relation of tragedy to life? In other words, how is it that tragedy was able to exercise such immense power over the Greeks?

Nietzsche speaks of "the highest and indeed the truly serious task of art" (BT, p. 118). What is this task? It is "to save the eye from gazing into the horrors of night and to deliver the subject by the healing balm of illusion from the spasms and agitations of the will" (BT, p. 118).

In reference to the Greeks, Nietzsche speaks of the man who "sees everywhere only the horror and absurdity of existence." Nietzsche goes on: "Here, when the danger to his will is greatest, art approaches as a saving sorceress, expert at healing. She alone knows how to turn these nauseating thoughts about the horror and absurdity of existence into notions with which one can live. . . . The satyr chorus . . . is the saving deed of Greek art" (BT, p. 60).

Nietzsche also says in the same vein: tragedy "forces us to look into the terrors of individual existence—yet we are not to become rigid with fear. A metaphysical comfort tears us momentarily from the bustle of the changing figures" (BT, p. 104).

So how is tragedy related to life? It saves life from the will-negating pessimism that results from an awareness of the horror and absurdity of life. It saves us from the wisdom of Silenus. Tragedy saves, however, not by projecting a world of Apollinian gods opposed to the Dionysian—tragedy does not cut us off from the Dionysian. Instead, tragedy saves in the very midst of the Dionysian. The Dionysian is not the opposite of tragedy but its precondition. Tragedy saves by turning the nauseating thoughts into notions with which one can live—that is, by transforming the Dionysian in such a way that what results is not pessimism but "metaphysical comfort."

Now we can formulate the central question: *How* does tragedy provide metaphysical comfort? How is it that the projection of Dionysian ecstasy (the chorus) into the Apollinian image-world (the scene) provides metaphysical comfort? The simplest answer would be that the chorus *discharges* itself through its vision, through the projection of the Apollinian image-world. In other words, through this projection, man purges himself, throws off the terror and nausea brought on by the Dionysian awareness. But Nietzsche insists that such an Aristotelian answer is wrong: "Not in order to get rid of terror and pity, not in order to purge oneself of a dangerous affect by its vehement discharge—Aristotle misunderstood it that way—but in order to be oneself the eternal joy of becoming beyond all terror and pity—that joy which includes even joy in destroying" (EH, p. 729).

Therefore, to be metaphysically comforted means to be the eternal joy of becoming. Tragedy draws one out of pessimism into the sphere of the eternal joy of becoming. But what does this mean, and how is it related to the Apollinian projection?

The clue to answering these problems lies in this statement: "Just as tragedy, with its metaphysical comfort, points to the eternal life of this core of existence which abides through the perpetual destruction of appearances, the symbolism of the satyr chorus proclaims this primordial relationship between the thing-in-itself and appearance" (BT, pp. 61–62).

This passage refers to the eternal life of the core of existence. That is simply the primal will. So to be the eternal joy of becoming (to be metaphysically comforted) means to be identified with the primal will. Nietzsche says: "We are really for a brief moment primordial being itself" (BT, p. 104). In tragedy, there is an identification with the primal will. Yet the identification with the primal will is precisely what gives rise to the pessimism that tragedy is supposed to overcome. So if in tragedy there is identification with the primal will, it must be a different sort of identification than the one of mere Dionysian ecstasy. And the difference must be what is provided by the Apollinian projection.

The passage tells us what is accomplished by the Apollinian projection. The symbolism of the satyr chorus (its Apollinian projection) proclaims the relationship between the thing-in-itself and appearances, that is, between the primal will and the empirical world. So the transformation from the wisdom of Silenus to metaphysical comfort is accomplished by this proclamation.

How does the Apollinian projection accomplish this proclamation and yield metaphysical comfort? How does it so transform the Dionysian that what results is metaphysical comfort rather than pessimism?

To answer, we need to return to the problem of the primal will. Specifically, we need to see how Nietzsche relates the primal will to the Apollinian-Dionysian duality and how he thereby goes beyond the Schopenhauerian framework.

Thus far we have spoken of the Apollinian and Dionysian primarily in reference to the artist. We associated the Apollinian with dreams, the Dionysian with intoxication. The Apollinian involves man's projecting of an image-world, and the Dionysian is man's reunion with his primal ground. But we have also seen that when the artist (lyric poet) projects an image-world, he is only a medium for a more primordial projecting by the will itself. That means the Apollinian-Dionysian duality is not simply a distinction between two human capacities. Instead, the Apollinian and Dionysian express the fundamental character of the primal will itself. The interplay of the Apollinian and Dionysian in the artist is a mirroring, an imitation, of that process which constitutes the will itself.

Recall Nietzsche's statement that the Apollinian and Dionysian are "artistic energies which burst forth from nature herself." Then what is the character of the primal will if its basic features are expressed in the Apollinian-Dionysian duality? We know what the Apollinian and Dionysian mean with respect to man. But what are they as dimensions of the will?

The Apollinian embodies boundaries, individuation, perfecting. Let us then say that the Apollinian is a *constructive* force. The Dionysian is the disintegration of boundaries, the breakdown of individuation, the collapse of everything into mysterious unity. Let us then say that the Dionysian is a *destructive* force. Consequently, the duality *as duality of the primal will* is the duality of constructing and destroying, of building up and tearing down.

Recall what we quoted earlier in the context of a discussion of myth. For Nietzsche, the playful construction and destruction of the individual world is the overflow of a primordial delight: "Thus the dark Heraclitus compares the world-building force to a playing child who places stones here and there and builds sand hills only to knock them down again." Also, in the "Attempt at a Self-Criticism," Nietzsche identifies this creating-destroying play as the only meaning that *The Birth of Tragedy* recognizes behind events: "In fact, the whole book knows only an artistic meaning and crypto-meaning behind all events—a 'god,' if you will, but certainly only an entirely reckless and amoral artist-god, who, in building as in destroying, in the good as in the bad, wants to experience his own joy and glory—who, creating worlds, frees himself from the distress of fullness and overfulness, from the suffering of the contradictions compressed in him. The world: at every moment the attained salvation of God, as the eternally changing, eternally new vision of the most deeply afflicted, discordant, and contradictory being" (BT, p. 22). So it is in terms of its creating-destroying play that the primal will is to be understood.

What is most significant here is the way this understanding shifts the focal point away from the will regarded as thing-in-itself over against the world of appearance (Schopenhauer) and concentrates instead on the play of constructing and destroying, that is, on the game in which appearances are built up and torn down. In other words, what is essential is not so much the will as primal ground but rather the process, the play, the building and destroying. Here very little would be required to abandon the empty subject behind the creating-destroying play, to dissolve the distinction between the thing-in-itself and appearance, and thus to transform utterly the metaphysical framework taken over from Schopenhauer. But this step is still not expressly taken. Nietzsche will take it shortly after *The Birth of Tragedy*, and the eventual outcome will be the theory of the will to power.

* * *

Let us now return to the issue of tragedy. We saw that tragedy involves a peculiar kind of identification with the primal will—different from sheer Dionysian ecstasy, distinguished from it by the Apollinian projection. What is the character of the identification? —It is a mirroring. That is to say, in tragedy the basic structure (Apollinian-Dionysian) of the will is imitated, mirrored. That means in tragedy, man mirrors in himself the building-destroying play of the will. How so?

We know tragedy involves Dionysian ecstasy; that is a precondition for tragedy. So there is no difficulty in seeing how in tragedy man imitates the *destructive* dimension of the will, namely, through his own Dionysian ecstasy, through the destruction or obliteration of himself as an individual. But as long as there is only Dionysian ecstasy and not tragedy, the result is pessimism. The reason is that the will is then imitated only in its destructiveness.

So in tragedy everything depends on a further imitation—of the *constructive* dimension of the will. That imitation is what the Apollinian projection accomplishes, since this projecting is nothing else than a mirroring of precisely that process—namely, projection—in which the primal will builds up appearances. In Apollinian projection, man imitates the constructive dimension of the play of the will and does so most decisively when that Apollinian projection is born, as in tragedy, out of a condition of Dionysian identification with the primal will.

Thus tragedy brings man metaphysical comfort, delivers him from pessimism, by involving him in an imitation of the primordial creating-destroying play of the will itself. The metaphysical comfort derives from the fact that such imitation of the creativity of the will produces within man the *joy of creating*. Nietzsche says, as I partially quoted earlier:

> We are to recognize how all that comes into being must be ready for a sorrowful end; tragedy forces us to look into the terrors of individual existence—yet we are not to become rigid with fear. A metaphysical comfort tears us momentarily from the bustle of the changing figures. We are really for a brief moment primordial being itself and feel its raging desire for existence and joy in existence; the struggle, the pain, and the destruction of appearances now appear necessary to us, in view of the excess of countless forms of existence which force and push one another into life, in view of the exuberant fertility of the universal will. (BT, p. 104)

The metaphysical comfort by which tragedy delivers man from the abyss of pessimism is the "metaphysical comfort of realizing that beneath the whirl of appearances eternal life flows on indestructibly" (BT, p. 109–10). Yet even if we grant that tragedy, by imitating the constructive dimension of the will, produces in man the joy of creating, nevertheless tragedy also exposes man to the destructiveness. Does tragedy then simply comfort man and along with that bring pessimism? Is the result a mere juxtaposition of comfort and pessimism?

Nietzsche answers "No." Metaphysical comfort is not simply added alongside pessimism so as to mitigate it and render it endurable. Instead, the metaphysical comfort of tragedy is a radical transformation, a decisive overcoming, of the wisdom of Silenus. According to Nietzsche, "The joy aroused by the tragic myth has the same origin as the joyous sensation of dissonance in music" (BT,

p. 141). He adds that this analogy with dissonance is the only way to make this tragic joy concretely intelligible.

What characterizes dissonance is that the experience of pleasure cannot at all be separated from the simultaneous feeling of pain. Here one does not merely *tolerate* the painful. For Nietzsche, this is the apex of the tragic. It not only mirrors the constructive and destructive dimensions of the play of the will but also embodies the absolute inseparability of joy and suffering, of creation and destruction. In other words, tragedy is the affirmation of the *necessary unity* of creation and destruction.

The will to hold onto, to retain permanently, to affirm, the joy of one's life is also the will to all the pain and suffering with which that joy is intertwined. It is the will to hold onto one's life as a whole. It is to love one's fate. It is to will the eternal recurrence of the same. Thus in *The Birth of Tragedy* Nietzsche is already what he later, in *Ecce Homo*, tells us he is: the tragic philosopher and the philosopher of the eternal recurrence.

I. The death of tragedy and the birth of Socratism.

We have been considering the birth of tragedy out of the spirit of music, that is, out of the Dionysian. In taking up the death of tragedy we will obtain our first view of Nietzsche's own philosophical task, and we will see how *The Birth of Tragedy* is the beginning of Nietzsche's thought.

According to Nietzsche, Greek tragedy met a violent end—by suicide, at the hands of one of its own practitioners, Euripides. Euripides withdrew tragedy from its Dionysian element and sought to reconstruct it on a basis incapable of supporting it. Euripides abandoned Dionysus and thereby abandoned tragedy itself. Yet Euripides was little more than a mask for someone much more profound and problematic, for "the most problematic phenomenon of antiquity" (BT, p. 88), namely, Socrates.

In the death throes of tragedy a new opposition arose: Dionysus versus Socrates. The death of tragedy was the birth of Socratism, and this birth represents the "turning point" (BT, p. 96) of the whole of human history. It is this opposition which even today characterizes the situation of Western man and hence determines the task of contemporary philosophy.

What is significant about the death of tragedy is not so much the particular changes, transformations, and processes of decay but rather the fundamental opposition that emerged between the tragic and the Socratic. To grasp this opposition we first need to understand Nietzsche's interpretation of Socrates.

1. Nietzsche and Socrates.

Nietzsche's statements about Socrates display a certain ambivalence. The relation to Socrates is certainly not one of sheer opposition. In many passages, Nietzsche expresses genuine respect. For example, Nietzsche speaks of "the courage and wisdom of Socrates" and says Socrates was one who knew when and how to remain silent—he was "great in his silence" (GS, §340). Nietzsche also refers to "the heroism of this free spirit" (HATH, vol. I, §433) and praises Socrates' subtle "compromise between piety and freedom of spirit," something Socrates achieved by taking his religious task to be that of "putting Apollo to the test" to see whether the oracle had spoken the truth regarding who is wisest (HATH, vol. II, pt. 2, §72). In an early manuscript, Nietzsche says: "Socrates . . . stands so near to me that I am almost always fighting a battle with him" (PT, p. 127).

Yet such passages are far outweighed by those in which Nietzsche is highly critical of Socrates. In *Twilight of the Idols*, Nietzsche regards Socrates as a symptom of decadence, as one whose instincts had turned against themselves and who therefore, in self-defense, resorted to dialectic as the alternative to being "absurdly rational" (TI, p. 478). An early manuscript says that in the person of Socrates "the self-destruction of the Greeks fulfilled itself" (PT, p. 136). Nietzsche explains that with Socrates the plebeian resentment gained its victory over the noble taste of the Greek aristocracy (TI, p. 475). It was with Socrates that the development of Greek philosophy came to a halt: "The real philosophers of Greece are those prior to Socrates" (WP, §437). Thus Socrates ushers in the end of both tragedy and philosophy among the Greeks: "Socrates represents a moment of the profoundest perversity in the history of values" (WP, §430).

What is the source of the ambivalence in Nietzsche's relation to Socrates? To answer, we must realize that Nietzsche regards Socrates as initiating a fundamentally new kind of culture, one radically opposed to that represented by tragedy. With Socrates, in Nietzsche's view, there arises a new form of illusion capable of serving as a stimulus to life, capable of holding man back from the suicidal wisdom of Silenus. This new form of illusion and culture Nietzsche calls Socratism. It is only because Socratism is able to assume the redemptive role previously played by tragedy that it is able to banish tragedy. So we obtain a first glimpse of the ground of Nietzsche's ambivalence: Socratism redeems and yet is opposed to tragedy.

2. Socratism and tragedy.

What is Socratism? In the simplest terms, it is a demand for intelligibility, a demand for rationality at any price. Its law is that whatever is good or beautiful must be intelligible. It is this demand that Socrates places on Greek culture. When he discovered a lack of transparent intelligibility in traditional institutions, he could see only negativities—the lack of insight and the power of ignorance. This was the case most of all with the tragedies of Aeschylus and Sophocles, tragedies built on an enigmatic background, an unintelligible Dionysian substratum.

In tragedy, man imitates the primordial building-destroying play of the will itself. This play is the substratum that supports tragedy. But this play, as we saw, is that of "an entirely reckless and amoral artist-god." It is a play devoid of aim and purpose, an "overflow of primordial delight" (BT, p. 142), a play involving discord, apparent impossibilities (for example, Aeschylus has a character identify a snippet of hair and an ordinary footprint as those of her long-lost brother, whereas she does not recognize him when they meet face-to-face), and contradiction. In short, the play is something radically unintelligible. That is what Euripides as thinker and spectator experienced, the fact that he did not *understand* the tragedies of his predecessors. So he radically transformed tragedy. His fundamental mistake was to suppose that one *ought* to understand tragedy, that it ought to be plausible and intelligible. With this supposition, Euripides was merely the victim of Socratism: he misunderstood his own misunderstanding.

The result was that the chorus and the whole musical-Dionysian substratum of tragedy appeared objectionable and eventually was eliminated. Thereby, tragedy was destroyed: "Optimist logic drives music out of tragedy using the scourge of syllogisms; that is, logic destroys the essence of tragedy, which can be interpreted only as the manifestation and projection into images of Dionysian states, as the visual symbolizing of music, as the dream-world of a Dionysian intoxication" (BT, p. 92).

Thus, under the power of the Socratic demand, one becomes blind to the Dionysian. Fink says: "Socratism, the origination of the domination of the logical, of rational intelligibility, no longer has eyes for the life flowing behind all forms, building and destroying them.... With Socrates... man loses, as it were, his openness to the dark night-side of life" (*Nietzsches Philosophie*, p. 28).

Furthermore, with the exclusion of the Dionysian, the Apollinian also virtually collapses. It is placed in the service of philosophical thought—of the demand for transparency and intelligibility—and becomes mere logical schematizing: "Here philosophic thought overgrows art and compels it to cling close to the trunk of dialectic. The Apollinian tendency has withdrawn into the cocoon of logical schematism" (BT, p. 91).

3. The power of Socratism.

The characterization of Socratism as the demand for intelligibility makes evident how Socratism could challenge and condemn tragedy. But in order for Socratism to succeed, it needed not only to *make* this demand. The demand had to be taken up; it had to become binding on man. Thus it had to have the *power* to bind, to compel man into its service. What is the source of this power, the power to compel man to heed the demand for intelligibility and thus to abandon tragedy? In other words, how is it that Socratism serves as such a great stimulus to life that it is able to force man to abandon the stimulus provided by tragedy? We can answer by pointing to three features of Socratism.

First, Socratism is an unlimited uncovering. It is a demand for intelligibility, but this intelligibility is soon found to reside not on the surface but hidden within. So the demand for intelligibility leads to another demand: the demand that intelligibility be discovered, uncovered. In the case of existing institutions, with their lack of transparency, the relevant intelligibility is to be uncovered independently of what exists and is to be established through a radical reform of the institutions.

So Socratism takes the shape of an uncovering that goes to any lengths in its search for intelligibility; Socratism issues in an unlimited uncovering. Socratic man is the theoretical man, the man who "finds the highest object of his pleasure in the process of an ever happy uncovering that succeeds through his own effort" (BT, p. 94).

Second, Socratism involves a profound illusion, one that keeps company with an instinct. What is required in order that man might be bound to the project of an unlimited uncovering, might find there the highest object of pleasure? What is required, what sustains the project, is a profound illusion. Socratism receives its binding power not from something uncovered (known) but from something that lies beneath the uncovering, accompanying it as an instinct.

The illusion is the promise of a total uncovering, a promise that the uncovering will never reach an abyss of unintelligibility. It is the illusion that man can by means of logical tools penetrate to the core of things. But it is also an illusion that through knowledge man can *correct* what is amiss in things and do so with a view to his own well-being. Nietzsche speaks of "a profound illusion that first saw the light of day in the person of Socrates: the unshakable faith that thought, using the thread of logic, can penetrate the deepest abysses of being and that thought is capable not only of knowing being but even of correcting it. This sublime metaphysical illusion accompanies science as an instinct" (BT, p. 95).

Note how Nietzsche, with almost Socratic irony, links Socratism to instinct. The irony is that Socratism, with its demand for intelligibility, is a reversal of the usual relation between conscious knowledge and instinct, a reversal in favor of conscious knowledge. This reversal is displayed in the daimon of Socrates: in contrast to the usual relation between knowledge and instinct, Socrates' instinctual wisdom (in the guise of the daimon) plays no creative-affirmative role but appears only as a critic of conscious knowledge, as a restraining force. Instinct is virtually banished and is merely a seldom used dissuading power. The irony is that this banishing of instinct in favor of knowledge results not from knowledge but precisely from the instinct that underlies Socratism; the Socratic reversal in which conscious knowledge usurps the role of instinct is itself founded on instinct.

Third, Socratism is an optimism. The optimistic mission of Socratism is symbolized in the figure of the dying Socrates, whose insight has freed him even from the fear of death. The mission is to make existence (all of it, including death) appear intelligible and hence justified, to blind man by the light of intelligibility to whatever remains fearful and enigmatic, to cast over everything a cloak of rationality. So this is the promise Socratism holds out to man: knowledge is salvation and knowledge is achievable. Man is thereby lured to seek the continuation of life rather than yield to the wisdom of Silenus. "Socrates is the prototype of the theoretical optimist who, with his faith that the nature of things can be fathomed, ascribes to knowledge and insight the power of a panacea" (BT, p. 97).

So the power of Socratism resides in (a) its capacity to harness man to a search for knowledge, whereby he is distracted from the abyss into which Dionysian man gazes, (b) its capacity to conceal that abyss beneath the radiance of rationality, to blind man to it, and (c) its assurance that through knowledge man can transform existence and the world so as to compel them to conform to the conditions of his own well-being.

This latter assurance is the promise of technology: "Socratism believes it can correct the world by knowledge, guide life by science, and actually confine the individual within a limited sphere of solvable problems, from which he can cheerfully say to life: 'I desire you; you are worth knowing'" (BT, p. 109).

Socratism promises not simply to cover over the abyssal unintelligibility encountered by Dionysian man but to dissolve that abyss through human knowledge and knowledge-directed action. Accordingly, Socratism holds out the promise that man can gain a decisive victory over suffering. Socratism promises to deliver man from suffering, in contrast to the comportment toward suffering that tragedy achieves by proclaiming the inseparability of joy and suffering. Socratism promises the *abolition* of suffering, whereas tragedy achieves a *transformed relation* of man to suffering. This expresses the sense of the opposition between Socrates and Dionysus that is most decisive for Nietzsche's thought.

4. Socrates and Socratism.

What is the relation between Socrates and Socratism? Certainly Socrates is the spokesman for Socratism. But what is especially important for Nietzsche is that Socrates was not totally overcome by Socratism—that is, in the end Socrates came to some awareness of the limitation of Socratism. Nietzsche sees this awareness betrayed in two remarks made by Socrates at the end of his life. First, Socrates relates that in dreams he was commanded to practice music (*Phaedo*, 60E). Here Socrates is betraying his experience of a gap, a void left by the banishing of Dionysus. Second, in his very final words about owing a sacrifice to Asclepios (*Phaedo*, 118A), Socrates is expressing a profound distrust of that optimism which gives Socratism its power. In Nietzsche's eyes, Socrates is here revealing that he has suffered from life and has felt the impotence of the optimistic promise of a banishment of suffering. So Socrates, the foremost advocate of Socratism, came in the end to some awareness of its limits, a recognition of a need it leaves unsatisfied, a need it itself generates. Here in this tension between

Socrates and Socratism we see the genuine source of the ambivalence we found in Nietzsche's statements about Socrates.

Nietzsche writes: "A profound experience in Socrates' own life impels us to ask whether there is necessarily only an antipodal relation between Socratism and art, and whether the birth of an 'artistic Socrates' is altogether a contradiction in terms" (BT, p. 92). That is to say, in Socrates' misgivings, in his sense of a void underlying Socratism, Nietzsche detects a dynamic interrelation between Socratism and art, a relation such that Socratism might even "prompt a regeneration of art," and that Socratism's "own infinity might also guarantee the infinity of art" (BT, p. 93).

Socrates' own misgivings pose for Nietzsche the question of a rebirth of tragedy out of Socratism, the question of a music-practicing Socrates. That for Nietzsche is the contemporary task and his own task: the birth of a music-practicing Socrates.

J. The contemporary task.

Throughout his discussion of Socratism, Nietzsche insists that there is no more powerful stimulus than that provided by Socratic uncovering. Nevertheless, *The Birth of Tragedy* concludes with an announcement of the destruction of Socratism: "The age of Socratic man is over" (BT, p. 124). What is the character of this destruction? We can see it from the historical cast of the announcement: it is a destruction brought about not by some external force but by the historical unfolding of Socratism itself. This unfolding is not a mere dissipation of the power of Socratism, not a gradual decay. Instead, it is an unfolding in which the power of Socratism is so enhanced that eventually it comes to supply the means for its own destruction. Thus Nietzsche is able to announce the destruction of Socratism because his own age is the one in which Socratism has unfolded to the point of *self*-destruction. Socratism is destroyed not by some superior power but by itself.

Nietzsche provides three somewhat distinct accounts of this self-destructive unfolding. The first account portrays the point of self-destruction as the moment Socratism (science) is transformed into art. In reference to the propelling illusion of Socratism, Nietzsche writes: "This sublime metaphysical illusion accompanies science as an instinct and leads science again and again to its limits, at which point it must turn into art—which is really the aim of this mechanism" (BT, pp. 95–96). What Nietzsche is saying finds beautiful expression in Camus:

> Here yet are trees, and I sense their roughness; here yet is water, and I taste its flavor. These fragrances rising up to me from the lawn, under the stars, in the dark, on certain evenings when the heart relaxes—how could I deny this world whose power and forces I experience? All the science on earth, however, will not yield anything that could assure me this world is mine. You describe it to

me and teach me to classify it. You enumerate its laws, and in my thirst to know I grant they are true. You dismantle its mechanism, and my hope increases. Ultimately you teach me that this majestic and variegated universe is reducible to the atom and the atom itself reducible to the electron. All this is good, and I wait for you to continue. But then you speak to me of an invisible planetary system where electrons gravitate around a nucleus. You explain the world to me with an image. I realize then that you have converted to poetry.... So this science which was supposed to teach me everything ends up in a hypothesis, this lucidity founders in metaphor, and this uncertainty resolves into a work of art. (Albert Camus, *Le mythe de Sisyphe* [Paris: Gallimard, 1942], p. 35)

The second account elaborates this transformation by introducing *myth* as the mediating link by which Socratism—in function of its own propelling illusion—is led over into art. Nietzsche claims it is the mission of Socratism "to make existence appear intelligible and thus justified" (BT, p. 96). Then he says in reference to the dying Socrates: "And if reasons do not suffice, myth has to come to their aid in the end—myth which I have just called the necessary consequence, indeed the purpose, of science" (BT, p. 96).

Thus Socratism founders inasmuch as it proves incapable of making good the promise of an uncovering that would eventually exhibit the intelligibility at the ground of existence and the world. In place of the promised intelligibility, Socratism is forced to inscribe myth—that is, forced to pass over from uncovering to creating, from science to art.

Third, Nietzsche speaks specifically of the way the diversion from science to art takes place:

Science, propelled by its powerful illusion, speeds irresistibly toward its limits where its optimism, concealed in the essence of logic, suffers shipwreck. The periphery of the circle of science has an infinite number of points, and while there is no telling how this circle could ever be surveyed completely, noble and gifted men nevertheless reach, even at mid-life and inevitably, such boundary points on the periphery from which they gaze into what defies illumination. When they see to their horror how logic coils up at these boundaries and finally bites its own tail, suddenly a new form of insight breaks through, tragic insight which, merely to be endured, needs art as a protection and remedy. (BT, p. 97–98)

Socratism by its own propulsion comes eventually to a point of self-destruction, a point where its logic "bites its own tail" and its optimism suffers shipwreck. Yet Socratism is able to do this only because there is a peculiar negativity inherent in it from the beginning—only because it involves, contrary to its very principle, a certain concealment, one necessary in order for it to sustain itself.

What does it conceal? —The Dionysian, the abyss of unintelligibility. It conceals this while promising to banish all opacity and render everything intelligible. In different terms, Socratism projects in advance a transparency, an order of reasons, at the root of life. Yet the fact that Socratic man is driven to such a projection and experiences it as binding him indicates that even he is not totally oblivious to the Dionysian abyss. Any covering over requires at least an oblique awareness of what is being covered over.

Socratism projects intelligibility in advance and places man under the demand for an uncovering of the intelligibility projected. Socratism demands an unlimited uncovering, demands that the uncovering activity be directed at everything, *even at itself.* Thus the demand requires that Socratic man attempt finally to uncover (exhibit in its intelligibility) what lies at the root of the demand and of the uncovering activity itself. That is to say, logic coils up and comes to be directed back at itself and its own roots. To the extent that these roots prove impenetrable, Socratism founders: its logic bites its own tail.

It is not simply that something encountered resists the effort by Socratic man to exhibit it in its intelligibility; instead, the very drive to intelligibility proves incapable of subjecting itself to the demanded uncovering. The very progress of Socratic uncovering serves to uncover an opacity in its own foundations: the desire to make intelligible is itself uncovered as something unintelligible.

* * *

The outcome of the self-destruction of Socratism is the recovery of the Dionysian. In other words, the outcome is the renewal of the need for tragedy, for the metaphysical comfort with which man might be able to endure the gaze into the abyss, a gaze that accompanies the collapse of Socratic optimism. What is called for is a rebirth of tragedy out of the spirit of music. What is called for is "a form of culture for which we should have to use the symbol of a music-practicing Socrates" (BT, p. 106).

The task called for has two sides, destructive and constructive. First, Socratism must be brought to the point at which it destroys itself; that is, the self-destruction must be carried out. Then, arising from this situation, there must be a renewal of tragedy and not a mere repetition of what happened among the Greeks. Instead, the rebirth of tragedy must be mediated by the destruction of Socratism.

In *The Birth of Tragedy*, this twofold task is announced—not so much as a future goal but as something already virtually accomplished. As for the destruction, Nietzsche believes that Socratism has already been brought to its point of self-destruction through the work of Kant and Schopenhauer. Specifically, these two thinkers, through the radical limitation they placed on knowledge by restricting it to appearances, undermined Socratism by its own means.

Nietzsche says that Kant and Schopenhauer managed "to make use of the paraphernalia of science itself to point out the limits and the relativity of knowledge generally and thus to deny decisively the claim of science to universal validity and universal aims" (BT, p. 112). Thereby Kant and Schopenhauer prepared the way for a rebirth of tragedy "out of the Dionysian root of the German spirit" (BT, p. 119).

Accordingly, regarding the constructive side of the task, the rebirth of tragedy takes place in German music and reaches its culmination in the music-dramas of Wagner. So the great task has been accomplished. All that remains is to reform culture in conformity with the spirit of Wagnerian drama. Presumably, then, the task of the philosopher is to promote this reformation—that is, to become a philosopher of culture and to champion the extension of the new tragic spirit into all areas of contemporary life.

Nietzsche says: "There is but one hope and guarantee for the future of man, and it is that Wagner's sense for the tragic may not die out" (UM, p. 213). The philosopher is not so much to bring about the rebirth of tragedy but rather to make this rebirth effective. That is what Nietzsche attempted in his *Untimely Meditations*, especially in his attack on contemporary culture in the first meditation and in his praise of the Wagnerian cause in the fourth.

Nietzsche's later view of the contemporary task remained essentially the same as in *The Birth of Tragedy*. He continued to regard it as the task of a rebirth of tragedy out of the ashes left by the self-destruction of the culture that had guided man since Socrates. What changes, however, is Nietzsche's conviction that this task has already been accomplished by Kant, Schopenhauer, and Wagner. In the "Attempt at a Self-Criticism" of 1886, fourteen years after *The Birth of Tragedy*, Nietzsche says that his view is "a hundred times more demanding" (BT, p. 19) than it was in that book. Nietzsche came to realize how much more is demanded for accomplishing the contemporary task, how much more radical this task is. Thus he criticizes *The Birth of Tragedy* for adhering to Kantian and Schopenhauerian formulas and even more for praising German music. As Nietzsche comes to grasp the contemporary task in its full depth, he realizes it is a task that has not even been seen, much less already carried out by Kant, Schopenhauer, and Wagner. Indeed their work belongs to that which must be overcome.

Most generally, Nietzsche comes to see that what he called the self-destruction of Socratism is in fact the destruction of everything by which Western man has previously taken his bearings—that it is the fulfillment of nihilism. Thus the task of a rebirth of tragedy coincides with the task of overcoming nihilism.

IV. Truth

A. General issues in Nietzsche's essay on truth.

In the "Attempt at a Self-Criticism," Nietzsche says the problem he really confronted in *The Birth of Tragedy* was "*the problem of science itself,* science considered for the first time as problematic, as questionable" (BT, p. 18). Nietzsche formulates the issue as follows: "What is the significance of all science, viewed as a symptom of life?" (BT, p. 18). In *The Birth of Tragedy,* this problem is most evident in Nietzsche's criticism of Socrates and Socratic culture. Nietzsche undertakes to show that by turning away from tragedy and from everything belonging to it, Socratism was set on a course of unlimited uncovering. This course was ultimately self-destructive and in the present age is coming to its end. Yet, as we noted, Nietzsche soon realized how far short of such destruction the present age actually is. Something more radical is required than the critiques of knowledge in Kant and Schopenhauer. Thus it became Nietzsche's task to promote a more radical self-destruction of Socratism. Important for this undertaking is Nietzsche's essay written the year after *The Birth of Tragedy,* though published only posthumously: "On Truth and Lies in a Nonmoral Sense."

This essay is transitional. In many ways it is still tied to *The Birth of Tragedy* but in other respects goes decisively beyond. So we can begin to see here how certain problems of *The Birth of Tragedy* will be taken up into the framework of Nietzsche's later thought.

Two issues from the book are central to "On Truth and Lies." First, according to *The Birth of Tragedy* it is with Kant that science reaches the decisive point at which it strikes up against its own limits, that is, the point of self-destruction. In a sense, Nietzsche's essay—as an attempt to drive science to its limits—remains bound to Kant. The Kantian spirit (the "Copernican Revolution") is evident in this statement from the essay: "If someone hides a thing behind a bush, seeks it again, and finds it in the same place, then there is not much to praise regarding this seeking and finding. Yet that is how matters stand with the seeking and finding of 'truth' in the realm of reason" (PT, p. 85). In Kantian language: if by reason I can discover something about nature, it is only because reason has placed this something in nature in advance. Kant's famous statement is: "We can know apriori of things only what we ourselves place into them" (*Critique of Pure Reason,* B xviii).

Yet Nietzsche is concerned not only with what man places in things and not only with the placing activity. Instead, he is concerned with the ground of the necessity of this placing. That is, he wants to ask: What is the underlying ground that determines what Kant held to be the a priori? In other words: What is the need driving man to impose an order on the world?

Second, the essay is akin to *The Birth of Tragedy* by interrogating science (knowledge, truth) from the perspective of life. It considers knowledge in relation to the basic conditions and impulses inherent in life. Right from the beginning of the essay, knowledge is presented as in service to life: "There is for the intellect no further mission that would transcend human life" (PT, p. 79). But here again Nietzsche goes beyond *The Birth of Tragedy*. Now he considers not merely how truth became the highest value (as in Socratism) but how the sense of truth arose in the first place. That is, he wants to trace the sense of truth back to its rootedness in life itself. So his question becomes: What is the role of the intellect in life? In other words, what are those conditions (needs) inherent in life which are fulfilled by intellect? That is to say, what is the *origin* of truth?

B. The value and nature of truth.

Nietzsche's most general answer is that the intellect is "a means for the preservation of the individual" (PT, p. 80). How does intellect serve as such a means? Originally, it does so as a capacity for dissimulation, a power of deception, fraud, pretentiousness, disguise. In other words, originally the human intellect served as a vehicle not of truth but of lies—of lies in service to life, of lies necessary for the preservation of life. Furthermore, the very distinction between truth and lie (which is tied to the origination of language) is governed by preservation-needs. Specifically, the demand that one speak the truth arises as the demand that one properly use the linguistic conventions of one's society. And this demand serves to protect the individual and the society from those persons who would abuse the conventions for their own gain and others' injury.

Therefore, the sense of truth arose from preservation-needs, as a way of fulfilling certain conditions required by life. Nietzsche's unbelievably brief account is provocative. We are provoked to challenge what Nietzsche says, but it is perhaps more important to question what is behind it all, such as by asking: What are these beginnings, these origins, which Nietzsche is claiming to retrieve? More specifically, are they simply historical in the emptiest, most straightforward sense—that is, origins which "civilized man" has left behind? Or are they origins that are in some way retained? Furthermore, how are we to understand Nietzsche's manner of gaining access to these origins? How does he come to have knowledge of them? Most importantly, what are we to make of his claim to speak the truth about the origin of truth? Does not an inquiry calling truth into question call itself into question thereby? In other words, if truth is nothing but sanctified lie, what are we to make of this statement itself? Is it not simply another sanctified lie? Here we can only be astonished at Nietzsche's utter silence regarding these matters.

In any case, let us focus on Nietzsche's central point: the desire for truth does not stem from some commitment (some ideal) independent of the conditions and needs of life; on the contrary, it is decisively linked to life and its preservation. According to Nietzsche, "It is only in a similarly limited sense that man desires truth: he covets the agreeable, life-preserving consequences of truth. Man is indifferent toward pure, ineffective knowledge; he is even hostile toward truths which possibly might prove harmful and destructive" (PT, p. 81).

Thus Nietzsche proposes to trace both the value of truth and the nature of truth back to preservations-needs. Truth is a value because of its "life-preserving consequences." And the nature of truth is to be understood in terms of the social and linguistic sanctification of those lies preservative of society and the individual. As Nietzsche later says and I already cited: "Truth is the kind of error without which a certain species of living being could not live."

In the case of both the value of truth and the nature of truth, Nietzsche stands in marked contrast to the usual, traditional views. Usually man takes his commitment to truth not as necessitated by the preservation-needs of life but rather as dictated by an unconditional ideal. So we assume it is not necessary to ask why we should be truthful and should seek the truth; we do not ask why truth, why not rather untruth. And the nature of truth is taken to consist in the correspondence between language (concepts) and reality, so that truth is once and for all distinguished from lie.

Nietzsche wants to see how these usual views arise. He wants to show how man's *moral sense* of truth arises, how, despite the fact that the desire for truth is rooted in life, man can come to take his commitment to truth as a commitment to an unconditional ideal independent of life. And he wants to show how the transition occurs from truth as sanctified lie to a view of truth as correspondence with reality. So Nietzsche's question is: How does truth as moral value and as correspondence arise from originary truth as life-preserving lie?

C. Falsification and forgetfulness.

In the most general terms, for Nietzsche the transition from originary truth to the usual views about the nature and value of truth is a matter of forgetting. Man forgets the origin of those concepts and words in which he professes to speak the truth. And only therefore is man able to presume that the nature of truth consists in correspondence and that the search for truth is something unconditional.

In order to develop this thesis, Nietzsche proceeds to describe the falsification (the lie) involved in our words and concepts. The falsification is built into them by the very way they originate, and it is this falsification that must be forgotten in order for our traditional view of truth to arise.

Nietzsche begins by rejecting outright the view of truth as correspondence. His statement is: "In general it seems to me that the 'right perception'—which would mean the adequate expression of an object in the subject—is an absurdity full of contradictions: for between two utterly different spheres, as between subject and object, there is no causality, no correctness, no expression, but at the utmost an *aesthetic* relation" (PT, p. 86). Much of "On Truth and Lies" is concerned with pointing to this aesthetic relation at play in the origin of words, concepts, and laws. Nietzsche wants to show that each—far from involving some correspondence with reality—is rather the outcome of an aesthetic, creative activity in which there is no trace of correspondence.

1. Words.

For Nietzsche, the creative activity at play in language is the unjustifiable translation of experience into metaphor and the subsequent forgetting that such translation is unjustified.

> What is a word? It is the copy in sounds of a nerve-stimulus. But to infer a cause outside us from the nerve-stimulus is already the result of a false and unjustifiable application of the principle of sufficient reason. If truth alone had been the deciding factor in the genesis of language, and if the standpoint of certainty had been decisive for designations, then how could we still dare to say: the stone is hard. As if "hard" were known to us otherwise and not merely as an entirely subjective stimulus! We divide things according to grammatical genders. . . . What arbitrary metaphors! How far flown beyond the canon of certainty! (PT, pp. 81–82)

Thus language does not originate as an imitation of things as they really are—words are not copies of things-in-themselves: "The 'thing-in-itself' (it is just this which would be the pure ineffective truth) is also quite incomprehensible to the creator of language and not worth making any great endeavor to obtain. This creator designates only the relations of things to man and for their expression calls to his aid the most daring metaphors. A nerve-stimulus first transformed into an image! First metaphor! The image again copied into a sound! Second metaphor!" (PT, p. 82).

So what is to be made of that truth which we claim to speak in our words? Nietzsche says: "Truths are illusions of which one has forgotten that they are illusions and worn-out metaphors" (PT, p. 84). Thus we claim that our language is true in the sense of corresponding with reality only because we are oblivious to, forgetful of, the falsification built into our language from its very beginning. That is, in order to presume that one's speech can be truthful in the sense of corresponding to reality, one must forget oneself as creative, artistic subject.

2. Concepts.

A similar kind of falsification (and subsequent forgetfulness of it) is at work in our concepts. Nietzsche asks: What is involved in the formation of concepts? He answers: a concept is something general, something applicable to many more or less similar—but nevertheless dissimilar, unequal—cases. So concepts arise by the equating of unequals, by deliberate falsification: "Let us especially think about the formation of concepts. Every word becomes at once a concept . . . by having simultaneously to fit innumerable, more or less similar (which really means never equal, therefore altogether unequal) cases. Every concept originates through equating the unequal. Just as certainly as no one leaf is exactly similar to any other, so certain is it that the concept 'leaf' has been formed through the arbitrary omission of these individual differences, through a forgetting of the differentiating qualities" (PT, p. 83).

Furthermore, in this constructing of concepts, we tend to separate the concept from the individual things: "This concept now awakens the notion that in nature there is, besides the leaves, a something called *the* 'leaf,' the original model according to which all leaves were woven, drawn, accurately measured, colored, crinkled, and painted, but by unskilled hands, so that no copy had turned out correct and trustworthy as a true copy of the original model" (PT, p. 83).

Nietzsche's point is that this antithesis (concept versus thing) is not something we discover but something we invent—that is, a falsification. So at the root of our concepts, there is a dual falsification: the equating of unequal things and the erecting of a realm of concepts in distinction from individual things.

3. Laws.

Nietzsche's account of the laws of nature follows the same lines as his account of concepts: scientific laws concern only spatiotemporal, mathematical relations among things. And, following Kant, Nietzsche insists that these relations are merely the determinations we have added to things. So the lawfulness and regularity we think we find in nature are only expressions of a lawfulness we have put there: "All conformity to laws which impresses us so forcibly in the orbits of stars and in chemical processes coincides at bottom with those qualities we ourselves attach to those things, so that it is we who thereby make the impression on ourselves" (PT, p. 88). As Nietzsche said, there is nothing to praise in finding something we ourselves have previously hidden. I would add: unless we have *forgotten* that we hid it.

Nietzsche wants to regard intellect (knowing) from the perspective of life. So the question is: How does the origination of language and especially of concepts and laws serve life? We have seen in general that intellect serves preservation-needs. Now we can understand more clearly how: it institutes order in the midst of chaos.

> Everything that makes man stand out in bold relief against animals depends on his faculty of volatizing the concrete metaphor into a schema and thus resolving a perception into a concept. For, within the range of those schemata, something becomes possible that never could succeed under the first perceptual impressions: to build up a pyramidal order with castes and grades, to create a new world of laws, privileges, sub-orders, delimitations, a world which now stands opposite the other perceptual world of first impressions and assumes the appearance of being the more fixed, general, known, and human of the two and therefore is the regulating and imperative world. (PT, p. 84)

So intellect establishes something fixed, stable, relatively permanent—establishes order, structure. Nietzsche adds: "Only by all this does man live with some repose, safety, and consistency" (PT, p. 86). Nietzsche's aim in this essay regarding truth and lies is not to condemn knowledge and the search for truth on the ground that they involve falsity and forgetfulness. Instead, Nietzsche wants to point to these origins in order to show how knowledge is related to life, namely, as a requirement of life itself, a requirement for preservation. Therefore, the title speaks of truth regarded not as some sort of moral imperative imposed externally on life but rather as truth in a nonmoral sense, that is, as arising out of life to fulfill a condition imposed by life itself.

D. A music-practicing Socrates.

According to *The Birth of Tragedy*, there is an inner dynamism in science bringing it to a limit at which it destroys itself and is transformed into art. The essay on truth and lies illuminates that issue. It seeks out the origin of the very means used by Socratic man: language, ideas, laws. What it finds there, however, is precisely the *creative* subject—not the discoverer but the inventor, not the Socratic man but the artist. In other terms, Nietzsche finds that the very possibility of the notion of truth definitive of Socratism depends on a forgetfulness of oneself as "artistically creative subject." Thus the artist stands not only at the end of Socratism but also at its beginning. It is then appropriate that Nietzsche concludes his essay by drawing out the contrast between Socratic ("rational") man and the artistic ("intuitive") man. Specifically, Nietzsche contrasts the rational man as one engaged in constructing a framework of concepts that grant to life stability, permanence, and order versus the artist as one who hurls metaphors into confusion, shifts the boundary stones of the framework of concepts, and throws that framework out of joint: "There are ages when the rational and intuitive man stand side by side, the one full of fear of intuition, the other full of scorn for abstractions.... Both desire to rule over life: the one by knowing how to meet the most important needs with foresight, prudence, and regularity; the other as an 'over-joyous' hero by ignoring those needs and taking as real only that life which simulates appearance and beauty" (PT, p. 90).

Rational man attends to the order necessary for the preservation of life. The artist uses this order only as a scaffolding for a movement beyond. The one fulfills the need for preservation; the other the need for enhancement. That contrast forms the basic structure of the will to power.

The question we are left with is the same as the one *The Birth of Tragedy* leaves: On which side does Nietzsche himself belong? Is the recalling of the artist beneath Socratism the work of Socratic man or of the artist? Or is it perhaps the work of both? Thus the work of a music-practicing Socrates!

V. History

A. Human temporality.

In 1873-76, Nietzsche published the four parts of his *Untimely Meditations*. The first two parts, on David Strauss and on history, are "untimely" in a very definite sense—they attack something highly prized by Nietzsche's age. They attack as decadent and destructive certain aspects of modern culture that Nietzsche's contemporaries took as signs of greatness. Specifically, the essay on history, "On the Uses and Disadvantages of History for Life," attacks the "sense of history," the "historical consciousness," that was the legacy of Hegelian philosophy to the nineteenth century.

In a sense, *Untimely Meditations* belongs to the same stage of Nietzsche's work as does *The Birth of Tragedy*: Nietzsche as champion of culture, of a new spirit born of German music. Nietzsche is at this stage bent on destroying the decadent scientific culture, the culture claiming, for example, to make history an objective science.

The essay on history deals with an issue that will eventually stand at the center of Nietzsche's thought: man's relation to history, to the past, or, more generally, to time. Nietzsche considers different ways man can comport himself to time: the unhistorical way is obliviousness to time, the historical way is the dissipation and destruction of the self by time, and the superhistorical way is a turning from time to the eternal. These considerations are important because in *Thus Spoke Zarathustra* the central idea, that of the eternal recurrence, concerns the same issue: man's comportment to time, that is, human temporality.

B. History and life.

"On the Uses and Disadvantages of History for Life" begins with a contrast between the unhistorical (sheer animality) and the historical. Nietzsche says that man can genuinely become man only by suppressing the unhistorical—only by becoming historical. It is a painful and difficult transition to become historical, to come to have a memory, to be able to be bound by the past, and to bind oneself to the future and thus be able to make promises.

On the Genealogy of Morals discusses this transition and the means by which it is accomplished. Nietzsche asks at the outset of that book: "To breed an animal with the right to make promises—is not this the paradoxical task nature has set for itself in the case of man? Is it not the real problem regarding man?" (GM, p. 493). The point on which "Uses and Disadvantages" focuses is that, however essential it may be for man to become historical, nevertheless the unhistorical must be retained, the historical must be limited. In other words, an excess of history, an unlimited historical sense (a Socratic relation to the past, an unlimited drive to an uncovering of the past) is destructive. The basic sense of the destructiveness can be understood in terms on Nietzsche's statement: "This is a universal law: a living thing can be healthy, strong, and productive only within a certain horizon" (UM, p. 63).

An excess of history is destructive because it makes man unable to draw a horizon around himself. Unlimited uncovering of everything past and foreign destroys every horizon, uproots man, leaves him homeless. So Nietzsche's task is to fix the limits of the historical in function of the needs of life itself—to view history in the perspective of life. So he must examine the use, the need, that life has for history and the limits of this need, the limits beyond which history poses a threat to life. Thus the title: "On the Uses and Disadvantages of History *for Life*."

C. Kinds of history.

According to Nietzsche, history serves life in three ways. These correspond to the three kinds of history he distinguishes: monumental, antiquarian, critical.

1. Monumental history.

This kind of history presents the great, the rare, the classic. It is necessary especially to the man of action, who needs "examples, teachers, and comforters" (UM, p. 67). It is needed by the man who, radically out of step with his times, can find no teacher or example among his contemporaries. Nietzsche suggests the greatest use of this kind of history for modern man is simply to provide "the knowledge that great things once existed and were therefore possible and so may be possible again" (UM, p. 69).

Along with the *use* of monumental history, Nietzsche points to its inherent *disadvantage*, the danger bound up with such history. In order to learn from the past, it must be comparable to the present. But what about such comparison? It is always vague and elusive. If we are to gain strength from the past, then "many of the differences must be neglected" (UM, p. 69). Therefore: "As long as the past is principally used as a model for imitation, it is always in danger of being a little altered and touched up and brought nearer to fiction" (UM, p. 70). Thus monumental history "lives by false analogy" and thereby can mislead as well as instruct.

An even greater danger, however, arises if those who are weak and inactive, the inartistic, come to make use of monumental history. In their hands it can become a weapon against the creative man, a means of depreciating what is accomplished in the present—depreciating it by means of the great examples from history: "For the weak do not want greatness to arise; their method is to say, 'See, the great thing is already here!' Their motto is: 'Let the dead bury the living'" (UM, p. 72).

2. Antiquarian history.

This is the use of history by which man is connected with his origins and identifies himself with the spirit of his family, city, nation. This identification is a way man can draw a horizon around himself. According to Nietzsche: "How could history serve life better than by anchoring the less gifted races and peoples to the homes and customs of their ancestors and keeping them from ranging far afield in search of something better, to find only struggle and competition" (UM, p. 73). This is history in service to man's conservative side, indeed a necessary service. At the same time, however, since it serves only one side of human nature, it is a threat to the other side: "It understands only how to preserve life, not how to create it; and thus it always undervalues present growth" (UM, p. 75).

3. Critical history.

The dangers inherent in the first two kinds of history, namely, that they pose a threat to genuine creation in the present, point to the need for a third sort of history: critical history. This history subjects the past to judgment, interrogates it, and in the end condemns it by bringing to light the weakness and injustice lying in the background. It destroys our piety regarding the past, the piety that always threatens to overpower the present.

There is a sense in which Nietzsche himself practices all three kinds of history. We see his practice of monumental history expressed when he says regarding Greek tragedy, as already cited: "I had discovered the only parable and parallel in history for my own inmost experience." Also, insofar as he is attempting to overcome the homelessness, the destruction of horizons, introduced by Socratism, Nietzsche's intention is similar to that of antiquarian history. But it is critical history that he is most obviously carrying out, especially in his later writings. We need to make three observations regarding critical history and Nietzsche's own work.

First, the judgment and condemnation of history are not the work of pure knowledge in which a sense of justice would be uppermost. That is to say, this kind of history necessarily does violence to the past: "It is not justice that sits in judgment here, nor mercy that proclaims the verdict, but only life.... Its sentence is always unmerciful, always unjust, as it never flows from a pure fountain of knowledge" (UM, p. 76).

Second, this condemnation of the past is curiously dialectical. Such is evident if we note that, as already quoted from *Human, All Too Human*, there is for Nietzsche a genuine sense in which we *are* our past: "Immediate self-observation is not nearly sufficient for learning to know ourselves; we need history, since the past continues to flow within us in a hundred waves." But if we *are* our past, then the condemnation of it is a condemnation of ourselves. Yet such a condemnation can spur us to overcome ourselves, to create, to make a new beginning: "It comes down to a conflict between our innate, inherited nature and our knowledge, between a stern new discipline and an ancient tradition; and we plant a new way of life, a new instinct, a second nature, that withers the first. It is an attempt to gain a past aposteriori from which we might spring, as against that from which we do spring" (UM, p. 76).

Third, this is "a dangerous attempt, as it is difficult to find a limit to the denial of the past!!" (UM, p. 76). This is a danger Nietzsche himself later experienced most profoundly. And it is the danger which proves the most difficult to overcome. Nietzsche later saw that the denial of the past—more existentially expressed, resentment against the past—is ultimately overcome only in affirmation of the eternal recurrence.

D. History as threat to life.

We have seen the ways history can serve life. What is important is that history "always has a reference to the ends of life and is under their absolute rule and direction" (UM, p. 77). But history is equally capable of becoming a danger, a threat to life. That is what happens when it loses its reference to life—when pursuit of history is not limited (restrained) by the needs of life and by the power of life to appropriate it. The loss of limits is what Nietzsche regards as having occurred in the nineteenth century.

Much of the "Uses and Disadvantages" is devoted to discussing various ways history threatens life. In general, as we saw, the effect of an excess of history is to erase the horizon life must draw around itself. Instead, man becomes a spectator of world history, equally close to what is near and familiar and to what is remote and strange. Man becomes incapable of feelings of strangeness and remoteness. Then, immersed in this chaos of history, man can no longer distinguish what properly belongs to himself—that is, he becomes homeless. His personality is so weakened that he becomes a passive instrument for recording indifferently what parades before him: indifferent to the spectacle in the sense of not responding to it. This homelessness, loss of horizon, is simultaneously the loss of a basis for action, or, in Nietzsche's terms, it is the destruction of our instincts. Every belief, every conviction, and every project must be subjected to the court of world history and either remain simply undecided or else appear foolish. The point is that nothing issues in action: "The banishment of instinct by history has turned men into shades and abstractions" (UM, p. 84). The result is a contrast between the inner and the outer—that is, a cultivation of the inner man which comes to no outer expression and which may exist in the midst of outward barbarism.

That is what Nietzsche saw in Germany in the 1870s. In opposition, he proclaimed his own conception of culture: "Culture is, before all things, the unity of artistic style in every expression of the life of a people" (UM, pp. 5, 79).

E. Nihilism.

There is something curious about the essay on history. Nietzsche's criticism of historical consciousness is itself a work of historical criticism. That is, it makes historical consciousness and its effects visible by historical means, especially by bringing out a contrast with the Greeks. This is a version of the same problem we already encountered in Nietzsche's use of science in order to criticize science and undermine it. Here he uses history against itself. Nietzsche acknowledges this reflexivity: "The origin of historical culture and of its absolutely radical antagonism to the spirit of a new time and to a 'modern consciousness' must itself be known by a historical process. History must solve the problem of history, science must turn its sting against itself. This threefold 'must' is the imperative of the 'new spirit,' if it is really to contain something new, powerful, vital, and original" (UM, pp. 102–3).

We saw in *The Birth of Tragedy* that such a point is the most crucial of all, the point at which logic coils up and bites its own tail, the point at which science overcomes itself. Its importance lies in the fact that precisely here a new insight becomes possible—that which, in *The Birth of Tragedy*, Nietzsche called "tragic insight" and which he saw as re-creating a need for art.

A fundamental structure in Nietzsche's thought consists in a new beginning arising precisely at the point at which the old destroys itself, overcomes itself. Hence a new beginning in values, a revaluation of all values, sets in precisely at the point of the old system of values destroying itself. This point is what Nietzsche calls nihilism.

VI. Morality

A. Freedom and morality.

Between 1878 and 1882, Nietzsche published three books: *Human, All Too Human*, *The Dawn*, and *The Gay Science*. These works are very different from earlier ones. The most striking difference is in form: they are aphoristic. But they also are different with respect to their basic issue. This basic issue is also the one of the later works, *Beyond Good and Evil* (1886) and *On the Genealogy of Morals* (1887). In other words, it is the basic issue of all the writings surrounding *Thus Spoke Zarathustra*.

In *Human, All Too Human*, Nietzsche says: "Writing should always signal a victory, indeed an overcoming of oneself which must be communicated to others for their use" (HATH, vol. II, pt. 1, §152). The issue, then, is one of victory, overcoming, self-overcoming, self-liberation. The same is indicated by the subtitle of *Human*: A Book for Free Spirits. Nietzsche later explains this subtitle: "It means a spirit that has *become free*, that has again taken possession of itself" (EH, p. 739). So the issue is one of freedom or liberation.

Yet in a sense there is also another issue, visible in Nietzsche's explanation of the title *Human, All Too Human*: "The title means: 'Where *you* see ideal things, *I* see what is human, alas, all-too-human!' I know man better.... On closer inspection, you discover a merciless spirit that knows all the hideouts where the ideal is at home—where it has its secret dungeons and, as it were, its ultimate safety. With a torch whose light never wavers, an incisive light is thrown into this *underworld* of the idea" (EH, p. 739). This other issue is indicated even more directly when Nietzsche refers to *The Dawn* as waging a campaign against morality (EH, p. 746). So the second issue is the ideal, morality. These books constitute an attack on morality.

Yet these issues (freedom and morality) are not, in fact, two different ones, for the liberation of man is identical with his liberation from morality. Nietzsche writes in reference to *The Dawn*: "Where does its author seek that new morning, that as yet undiscovered tender redness that marks the beginning of another day—ah, of a whole series, a whole world of new days? —In a revaluation of all values, in a liberation from all moral values, in saying Yes to and having confidence in all that has hitherto been forbidden, despised, and damned" (EH, p. 746). So the issue is man's liberation from morality, and Nietzsche refers to this as a revaluation of all values.

What is the character of this liberation? At first, one might suppose that to free man from morality, from moral values, means to make him simply oblivious of values, to bring him to a condition in which he would cease to regard himself, others, and the world in terms of values. This would be a condition in which man would cease to evaluate, perhaps instead would simply be objective, would simply regard things as they are without attributing any values to them. But that is not at all what Nietzsche means. Even to regard things objectively is to evaluate, since objectivity is itself a value. It belongs to the very nature of life to evaluate, to regard everything in terms of values. So the liberation is not a matter of eliminating man's relation to values but rather of *transforming* that relation. Specifically, what Nietzsche intends is a radical reversal of man's relation to values: "The free spirit asks himself why he now renounces what he once revered and hears in reply something like an answer: You shall become master over yourself, master also over your virtues. Formerly they were your masters, but they must be only your instruments beside other instruments. You shall gain control over your For and Against and learn how to display first the one then the other in accordance with your higher goal" (HATH, preface to vol. I, §6).

B. The ground of morality.

We can liberate ourselves from moral values (transform our relation to values) only if we discover how we are in the first instance bound by them. Nietzsche's basic insight here is that the bond tying us to morality is not itself a matter of morality. He says in *The Dawn*: "One becomes moral—but not because one is moral!" (D, §97). In other words, submitting oneself to morality is not itself a moral act but is due to some other motive. Thus Nietzsche states categorically: "There are no absolute morals" (D, §139). This does not mean simply that there are in fact many different systems of morals, no one of which is absolutely superior to all others. More fundamentally, it means: no morality is absolute in the sense of providing its own sufficient ground, the ground on which men subject themselves to morality. There is always something else presupposed, some other ground on which men bind themselves to a moral system. There are unconscious virtues beneath our conscious moral virtues (GS, §8).

What is this ground? What is it that leads man to bind himself to a moral system? It is, most generally, life itself. Morality—like art, science, and history—must be viewed from the perspective of life. An interrogation of morality from such a perspective is what Nietzsche later calls a reflection "on the genealogy of morals." In the book of that name, Nietzsche expresses the problem of morality as follows: "Under what conditions did man devise the value judgments called good and evil? And what value do they themselves possess?" (GM, p. 453). So Nietzsche proposes to determine the value of our values. But is this not just begging the question, a vicious circle? No. What Nietzsche proposes is that our values be evaluated not in terms of themselves but rather by reference back to life itself. That is, they are to be evaluated in terms of whether they enhance or impoverish life. Like the study of history, they are to be evaluated in terms of their service to life.

In order to evaluate our values in this way, it is necessary to discover how, in general, they are related to life. And that requires a knowledge of the conditions and circumstances in which moral values grow. So the first task is to discover the bond between morality and life, to understand the nonmoral ground on the basis of which man becomes moral.

C. Life as will to power.

To see how Nietzsche relates morality to life, we need to work through the conception of life that began to emerge in earlier works. In *The Birth of Tragedy*, Nietzsche views art and science from the perspective of life. This turns out to mean that he views them in terms of the will, in terms of the way they veil or imitate the primordial will at the core of all things. He views all forms of culture as the means by which man escapes the pessimistic wisdom of Silenus, the life-negating wisdom—that is, as ways by which life secures its continuation, ways in which the fundamental needs of life are fulfilled so that life can be sustained and enhanced.

The Birth of Tragedy, however, still understands the will to some extent within the framework of Schopenhauer's metaphysics, thus as thing-in-itself. But we have seen that Nietzsche came to reject such Schopenhauerian notions. And, after he does so, he speaks not of will but of will to power. So life is will to power. And various cultural forms—hence morality—are means by which the needs inherent in life as will to power are fulfilled.

We can gain an initial understanding of what Nietzsche means by will to power if we recall some of the issues in the essays on truth and history. In the essay on history, Nietzsche says that a living thing can be healthy and productive only within a certain horizon. That is, a basic need of life is the need for a living thing to draw a horizon around itself. The essay on truth indicates one basic way in which this is done, namely, by means of language and ideas, whereby man establishes structure, order, permanence, stability—that is, creates order out of chaos, imposes order on chaos. By imposing this order, man becomes capable of controlling the chaos, gaining mastery over it, gaining *power* over it.

So life (will) has need for order. It needs this order so as to be what it is, namely, a gaining of mastery, a gaining of power. So life or will is a gaining of power over something; power expresses the very nature of will. It is thus that

Nietzsche speaks of will to power. But it is especially important to realize that for Nietzsche power is not something extrinsic, a goal, for which the will strives. It is not as though "will to power" indicates only one kind of willing alongside others such as will to fame or will to pleasure. Instead, power expresses the very nature of the will, so that in the willing of power, the will wills itself. As Heidegger says, will to power is "will to will" (*Nietzsche*, vol. IV [New York: Harper & Row, 1982], p. 31).

D. Morality and life.

It is in terms of this conception of life as will to power that we need to understand how Nietzsche deals with the question of morality. What he tries to show is the way moral values are rooted in the will to power. They are simply ways the will to power fulfills its needs. They are basically ways of gaining power over something or someone. In other words, man binds himself to moral values because they provide a certain way he is able to be what he is: will to power. Of course, it is quite another question whether this way serves in the end to enhance life or impoverish it, whether these values are valuable when viewed from the perspective of life. The point is simply that moral values represent *one* way that life seeks to sustain itself.

In the works we are now dealing with, there are numerous instances in which Nietzsche tries to show how particular values and particular prescribed ways of acting are grounded in life as will to power. We need to consider a few examples.

1. Justice.

What is the origin of justice? How does it come to be an ideal? In *Human, All Too Human*, Nietzsche explains as follows: Justice arises among powers that are fairly equal, where conflict would be useless and would injure both sides. Hence there occurs the idea of coming to an understanding. Justice is thus simply a means of preserving one's power. In this form, justice can exist only among equals. But eventually justice gets generalized into the concept of "rights." Thereby the power relations among unequals are also included. Nietzsche later argued that this is done to contain and control the rancor and resentment of the weak. He summarizes in *The Dawn*: "In this way, rights arise: recognized and guaranteed degrees of power" (D, §112).

2. Distinction.

In *The Dawn*, Nietzsche also considers what he calls "desire for distinction," especially moral distinction, moral excellence: "The desire for distinction is the desire to subject one's neighbor, even if merely in an indirect fashion, perhaps only felt or even only dreamed of. There is a long series of stages in this secretly desired will to subdue, and a very complete record of them would perhaps be an excellent history of culture" (D, §113). Furthermore, Nietzsche observes that even if the social context is eliminated, the desire for distinction (even within the compass of an individual) is still a desire to subdue, to overcome, to overpower—specifically, to overcome oneself, to surpass what one formerly was.

3. Asceticism.

This too is a way of gaining power over: "For certain human beings have such a great need to exercise their force and their lust to rule that, lacking other objects, or because they have always failed elsewhere, they finally have recourse to tyrannizing certain parts of their own nature. . . . In every ascetic morality, man adores part of himself as a God and to that end needs to diabolicize the rest" (HATH, vol. I, §137). Nietzsche adds that the feeling of power "has perhaps never reached a higher pitch of perfection on earth than in the souls of superstitious ascetics" (D, §113).

4. Altruism.

Nietzsche especially interrogates those kinds of acts that appear altruistic, completely unselfish, benevolent, the acts traditional (Christian) morality values so highly. Here again, he wants to show that what is fundamentally involved is an attempt to gain power over. In treating others benevolently, doing good to them (such as in giving them something), we assert and feel our power over them. They need something we have; they are dependent on us, and our benevolence makes them indebted to us—thus even more dependent.

In asserting our power over ones who are dependent, a still more subtle motive is at work: we also strengthen ourselves, thereby guaranteeing our power against other opponents who are not dependent on us. So Nietzsche says that "in doing good and being kind to those who are in any way already dependent on us, . . . we want to increase their power because we thus increase our own; or we want to show them the advantage there is in being in our power—they thus become more contented with their position and more hostile to the enemies of our own power and readier to contend with those enemies" (GS, §13).

This struggle for power is operative not only in the case of the man who is in a superior position and able to assert his power over others in the usual ways. As Nietzsche says in *Thus Spoke Zarathustra*, "even in the will of those who serve, I found the will to be master" (TSZ, p. 226). Such is especially apparent in pity.

5. Pity.

One who pities another asserts thereby his own superiority. But the one who desires to be pitied is basically also motivated by a desire for power. According to Nietzsche, in wanting to be pitied one wants to prove that, in spite of all one's weakness, one still possesses a power, namely, the power of giving pain, of presenting a distasteful, painful spectacle to others (HATH, vol. I, §50).

6. Guilt and punishment.

Nietzsche considers not only "moral acts" but also acts that would be condemned as immoral. The important point is that the ground of moral acts and of immoral acts is the same. Fundamentally, there is no distinction between moral and immoral. For example, according to Nietzsche one does not attack another merely to hurt him but rather primarily in order to become conscious of one's own strength and so to heighten one's feeling of power (HATH, vol. I, §317).

The point is developed in connection with the question of the origin of guilt and punishment. These concepts arose originally in the relation between creditor and debtor. The debtor always pays his debt—not necessarily with money but by granting his creditor the opportunity and pleasure of punishing him, exercising power over him: "An equivalent is provided by the creditor's receiving, in place of material compensation such as money, land, or other possessions, a kind of pleasure. The pleasure is induced by his being able to exercise his power freely upon one who is powerless" (GM, pp. 500–501).

E. The slave revolt.

The most comprehensive discussion of the way the struggle for power is at the root of moral ideals occurs in the context of "the slave revolt in morals" (GM, p. 472). This revolt is central to Nietzsche's interpretation of Christianity. In essence, it is simply the means the impotent used in order to gain a position of power. Specifically, the slave, unable to gain or exercise power directly, brought about a value inversion that condemned his master as evil and provided an elaborate structure (system of moral values) for giving himself, the slave, a feeling of superiority, strength, power.

In effect, the slaves reversed the "morality of good and bad" (according to which the aristocratic, high-born, powerful, active man was good and the plebeian slave bad) so that it became the "morality of good and evil" (which condemns the master as evil, hence making the slave good).

One of Nietzsche's most brilliant presentations of this slave revolt is found in the section of *On the Genealogy of Morals* inviting us to peer into the "workshop" for the manufacture of ideals:

> Would anyone like to take a look at the secret of how ideals are made on earth? Who has the courage? —Very well! Here is a point we can see through into this dark workshop. But wait a moment or two, Mr. Rash-and-curious. Your eyes must first get used to this false iridescent light. All right! Now speak! What is going on in there? Say what you see, man of the most perilous kind of inquisitiveness—now I am the one who is listening.
>
> "I see nothing, but I hear the more. There is a soft, wary, malignant muttering and whispering coming from all the corners and nooks. It seems to me

someone is telling a lie; a sugary sweetness clings to every sound. Weakness is being lied into something meritorious, no doubt of it—so it is just as you said—"

Go on!

"—and impotence which does not requite is lied into 'goodness of heart'; anxious lowliness into 'humility'; subjection to those one hates into 'obedience' (that is, obedience to one of whom they say he commands this subjection—they call him God). The inoffensiveness of the weak man, even the cowardice of which he has so much, his lingering at the door, his being ineluctably compelled to wait, here acquire flattering names, such as 'patience,' and are even called virtue itself. His inability for revenge is called unwillingness to revenge, perhaps even forgiveness ('for *they* know not what they do—we alone know what *they* do!'). They also speak of 'loving one's enemies'—and sweat as they do so."

Go on!

"They are miserable, no doubt of it, all these mutterers and nook counterfeiters, although they crouch warmly together—but they tell me their misery is a sign of being chosen by God. One beats the dogs one likes best. Perhaps this misery is also a preparation, a testing, a schooling, perhaps it is even more—something that will one day be made good and recompensed with interest, with huge payments of gold, no! of happiness. This they call 'bliss.'"

Go on!

"Now they give me to understand that they are not merely better than the mighty, the lords of the earth whose spittle they have to lick (not from fear, not at all from fear! but because God has commanded them to obey the authorities)—that they are not merely better but are also 'better off,' or at least will be better off someday. But enough! Enough! I can't take any more. Bad air! Bad air! This workshop where ideals are manufactured—it seems to me it stinks of so many lies." (GM, pp. 482–83)

So it is the gaining of power, will as will to power, that provides the ground of morality. Man binds himself to morality because morality is a way of gaining power—a way the will to power can be what it is. According to Nietzsche, "The feeling of power in man has been developed in so subtle a manner that, in this respect, he can compare favorably with the most delicately adjusted balance. This feeling has become his strongest propensity: and the various means he discovered for creating it form almost the entire history of culture" (D, §23).

F. Contradictions.

By way of conclusion, I want to point out two fundamental contradictions regarding the issue of morality: a contradiction in morality itself and a contradiction in Nietzsche's own project vis-à-vis morality.

The ground of morality is the struggle, desire, for power. Yet this ground is not only nonmoral, in the sense of being the prior basis for man's first subjecting himself to morality, but furthermore, as something radically egotistic, as the very opposite of selflessness and altruism, it is in fact something *immoral*. In other words, the ground on which man becomes moral is itself something morality condemns. The ground of morality is immoral.

Here we see the basic contradiction inherent in morality. Its ground, its motivation, stands in contradiction to what arises on that ground: man becomes moral for immoral reasons. According to Nietzsche, "The fundamental contradiction in the morality which at present stands in high honor is here signaled: the motives to such a morality are in antithesis to its principle! That with which this morality wishes to prove does itself refute it out of its criterion of what is moral!" (GS, §21).

In this tracing of values back to life, in Nietzsche's attempt to prepare the way for a liberation of man from bondage to moral values, there is a fundamental contradiction, one that is basic to Nietzsche's thought and even determines the structure of that thought. But it is not a contradiction Nietzsche discovers only later, as though it were some kind of mistake he was at first oblivious to. Instead, it is a contradiction in which he is consciously involved from the beginning, a contradiction inherent in the character of what he is doing.

We have seen several forms of this inherent contradiction already, such as the condemnation of science through science or the condemnation of history by means of history. It is equally at play in the critique of morality. Why should man be liberated from morality? —Because that is what the *truth* about man and morality prescribes ought to be done. Now what about this belief in truth, in the value of truth? What about this moral belief, the belief that man's welfare is furthered by the promotion of truth, that man profits from knowing the truth, that he ought to act as the truth prescribes?

Is there a necessary relation between man's welfare and his possession of the truth? Nietzsche suggests not: "A fundamental insight—there is no preestablished harmony between the promotion of truth and the welfare of mankind" (HATH, vol. I, §517). The point is that this is not a preestablished fact; it is simply a moral belief. So if Nietzsche attacks morality in the name of truth, for the sake of truth, then the attack is itself a matter of morality—and thus is dependent on what it attacks! Nietzsche says of *The Dawn* that the book "represents a contradiction and one which it does not fear; in the book, confidence in morals is retracted—but why? Out of morality. . . . There is no doubt that to us likewise there speaks a 'thou shalt.' We likewise obey a strict law that is set above us—and this is the last cry of morals which is still audible to us, which we too must live . . ." (D, preface, §4).

What we have here is, so to speak, morality recoiling on itself and biting its own tail!

VII. The death of God

A. The madman.

Nietzsche first announces the death of God in section 125 of *The Gay Science*, under the heading of "The madman." I will first cite the entire section and then, drawing out eight themes, will provide the extended commentary it deserves.

> *The madman.* Have you not heard of that madman who lit a lantern in the bright morning hours, ran to the market place, and cried incessantly: "I seek God! I seek God!" As many of those who did not believe in God were standing around just then, he provoked much laughter. One asked: Has he got lost? Another asked: Did he lose his way like a child? Or is he hiding? Is he afraid of us? Has he gone on a voyage? Emigrated? Thus they yelled and laughed.
>
> The madman jumped into their midst and pierced them with his eyes. "Whither is God?" he cried; "I will tell you. *We have killed him*—you and I. All of us are his murderers. But how did we do this? How could we drink up the sea? Who gave us the sponge to wipe away the entire horizon? What were we doing when we unchained this earth from its sun? Whither is it moving now? Whither are we moving? Away from all suns? Are we not plunging continually? Backward, sideward, forward, in all directions? Is there still any up or down? Are we not straying as through an infinite nothing? Do we not feel the breath of empty space? Has it not become colder? Is not night continually closing in on us? Do we not need to light lanterns in the morning? Do we hear nothing as yet of the noise of the gravediggers who are burying God? Do we smell nothing as yet of the divine decomposition? Gods, too decompose. God is dead. God remains dead. And we have killed him.
>
> "How shall we comfort ourselves, the murderers of all murderers? What was holiest and mightiest of all that the world has yet owned has bled to death under our knives. Who will wipe this blood off us? What water is there for us to clean ourselves? What festivals of atonement, what sacred games shall we need to invent? Is not the greatness of this deed too great for us? Must we ourselves not become gods simply to appear worthy of it? There has never been a greater deed; and whoever is born after us—for the sake of this deed he will belong to a higher history than all history hitherto."
>
> Here the madman fell silent and looked again at his listeners; and they, too, were silent and stared at him in astonishment. At last he threw his lantern on the ground, and it broke into pieces and went out. "I have come too early," he said then; "my time is not yet. This tremendous event is still on its way, still wandering. It has not yet reached the ears of men. Lightning and thunder require time; the light of the stars requires time. Deeds, though done, still

require time to be seen and heard. This deed is still more distant from men than the most distant stars—*and yet they have done it themselves.*"

It has been related further that, on the same day, the madman forced his way into several churches and there struck up his *Requiem aeternam Deo*. Led out and called to account, he is said always to have replied nothing but: "What after all are these churches now if they are not the tombs and sepulchers of God?"

B. God as crime against life.

Those who were milling about in the marketplace obviously did not understand the madman. They yelled, laughed, and made jokes. After he spoke to them, they responded with silence and stared at him in astonishment. Yet it was not because they were believers that they failed to understand. The passage tells us they were men who did not believe in God—that is even the reason they laughed and joked. Thus Nietzsche's declaration of the death of God is far removed from any usual atheism, mere unbelief. Nietzsche's declaration is not merely a statement of the fact that God does not exist. On the contrary, this declaration involves a profound experience of what this God was, of why he had to die, and of the overwhelming consequences his death has for man—the immense burden it places on man.

Nietzsche himself says in *The Antichrist* that his declaration is not simply a theoretical denial of God's existence: "That we find no God—either in history or in nature or behind nature—is not what differentiates us, but that we experience what has been revered as God, not as 'godlike' but as miserable, absurd, harmful, not merely an error but a *crime against life*. We deny God as God. If this God of the Christians were proved to exist, we should be even less able to believe in him. In a formula: God, as Paul created him, is the negation of God" (A, p. 627). Thus, integral to Nietzsche's declaration of the death of God is the experience of God as a crime against life, God as the negation of God, God as self-negating.

C. Our role in the killing of God.

The madman says *we* have killed God. We are the murderers of God. How is this so? And why have we killed God? In the first instance, it is because we have experienced God as a lie—because we can no longer maintain the lie involved in belief in God. That is to say, we have killed God because of our sense of truthfulness. This leads directly into that contradiction we already considered: What about this sense of truthfulness, this belief in the value of truth, this inability to maintain the lie? What is its source, its ground? Its source is precisely the Christian faith: it is Christianity that has instilled in us a sense of truth. Nietzsche says: "Even we men of knowledge, we men of today, we godless men and antimetaphysicians, even we light our torches from the flame kindled by a millennial faith, the Christian faith, which was also the faith of Plato, that God is truth, that truth is divine. But what if this becomes more and more unbelievable, if nothing proves to be divine any longer unless it be error, blindness, lies? What if God himself proves to be our longest lie?" (GS, §344; GM, p. 588).

What then is the situation of the atheist—who denies God out of loyalty to the truth? The ground of his denial (his belief in the value of truth, his demand for truth at any price) is provided precisely by what he is denying. Even the atheist remains bound to the Christian moral idea: "Unconditional honest atheism (and its air is the only one we breathe, we more spiritual men of this age!) is therefore not the antithesis of that ideal, as it appears to be; it is rather only one of the latest phases of its evolution, one of its terminal forms and inner consequences. The awe-inspiring catastrophe of two thousand years of training in truthfulness is what finally forbids itself the lie involved in belief in God" (GM, p. 596).

Therefore, the basis for the negation of the Christian moral ideal is not something external to that ideal but is rather contained in it. The ideal contains the seeds of its own destruction. It is an inherently self-destructive, self-negating ideal. But how can something that negates itself persist for two thousand years? — Only if its negative character is such that it does not immediately negate itself, only if its basic negativity is at first concealed and becomes explicit only through a development, through the unfolding of its "logic of decadence" (WP, §43).

How then did we come to kill God? It is not simply because we are more truthful, more courageous, more honest than the men of the past. Nietzsche even insists that modern man is vastly inferior to the ancients and the men of the Renaissance. We are the murderers of God because our age is the one in which the divine ideal reaches the point of total *self*-negation, the point at which its self-destructive character has unfolded into explicit self-destruction. In answer to the madman's question, we were able to kill God because our age provides us with the presupposition, namely, that the ideal come to the point at which its self-negation is explicit. Nietzsche says, "Only we, we spirits who have become free, have the presuppositions for understanding something that nineteen centuries have misunderstood" (A, §36). Nietzsche even says that men of the past are not to be blamed for not proclaiming the death of God, whereas today (that is, because we are men of today) we know better: "I am careful not to hold mankind responsible for its mental disorders [namely, Christianity]. But my feeling changes, breaks out, as soon as I enter modern times, our time. Our time knows better. What was formerly just sick is today indecent—it is indecent to be a Christian today. And here begins my nausea" (A, §38). Thus it is not so much that *we* have killed God; instead, God, as embodiment of the Christian moral ideal, has killed himself. Our negation of the Christian ideal is subordinate to the self-negation of the ideal itself.

Accordingly, to understand what is at issue in the death of God requires that we understand what is involved in this self-negating character of the Christian moral ideal. That is to say, we must try to understand the basic character of that negativity which was inherent in this ideal from the beginning and which has reached it consummation in our age.

As we have seen, Nietzsche's view is that morality has its roots in life, in the will to power. In Nietzsche's terms, the Christian moral ideal (as a system of values) is projected by man as will to power—projected as a means of preserving and enhancing power, a means of self-affirmation. It is one of the ways life draws a horizon around itself. We know, however, that in the moral ideal there is a basic contradiction: those values that are set up contradict the very grounds in life on the basis of which they are set up. Moral values, although grounded in life, constitute a negation of that very ground, a negation of life. Those values that are established as a means of preserving and enhancing life end up being a negation of life; they reflect back on life in such a way as to negate it.

So Christianity affirms life but only in such a way as, in the end, to negate it. It is this negation of life that constitutes the inherent negativity of the moral ideal, and it is the conflict between affirmation and negation that gives rise to the development (the unfolding of the logic of decadence) which is consummated in our time. And it is this negativity which Nietzsche condemns and which lies at the basis of his entire polemic against Christianity.

Let us look more carefully at the moral ideal and the negativity belonging to it. How is it possible for an ideal to arise while harboring such a contradiction, the contradiction of affirming and denying, affirming by denying? Nietzsche answers: "In the Christian world of ideas, there is nothing that has the least contact with reality—and it is in the instinctive hatred of reality that we have recognized the only motivating force at the root of Christianity" (A, §39).

That is central: the negativity inherent in the moral ideal has its roots in the hatred of reality. But what leads man to hate reality? Nietzsche's answer: suffering. "But this explains everything. Who alone has good reason to lie his way out of reality? —He who suffers from it" (A, §15). So the Christian moral ideal originated through those who suffered from life, especially those who suffered at the hands of the strong. It originated out of the resentment of the sufferers, the weak—a resentment against reality and life and in particular against the higher examples of life, persons who are strong, noble, masterly. The moral ideal is simply the means by which this resentment is exercised.

The moral ideal is a means by which life—and hence the suffering inherent in the lives of the weak—is devalued and by which war is waged, in the only way possible, on those at whose hands the weak suffer. Recall the glimpse into the workshop for the manufacture of ideals: there weakness is made meritorious, subjection made into obedience to God. "Christianity . . . has waged deadly war against this higher type of man. . . . Christianity has sided with all that is weak and base, with all failures; it has made an ideal of whatever contradicts the instinct of the strong life to preserve itself" (A, §95).

Christianity has its root in the slave revolt in morals, and in turn the root of this revolt is resentment. The Christian moral ideal arose from the resentment fostered by weakness and suffering. It arose as the negation of conditions promoting life itself, enhancing it and strengthening it. The young Hegel had already said the same: "Christianity made an honor of disgrace; it sanctified and immortalized every incapacity by turning into a sin any possible belief in human strength" (*Die Positivität der christlichen Religion*, in *Werke*, vol. 1: *Frühe Schriften* [Frankfurt: Suhrkamp, 1971], p. 209. Original text dated 1795–96).

How precisely is God involved in all this? The answer would be that God is simply the ultimate embodiment and guarantee of the anti-natural system of values, of the moral ideal erected on the ground of resentment. God is the authority who makes these values unquestionable: "The concept of 'God' was invented as a counterconcept to life—everything harmful, poisonous, slanderous, the whole hostility unto death against life synthesized in this concept in a gruesome unity! The concept of the 'beyond,' the 'true world' invented in order to devaluate the only world there is" (EH, p. 790). In *The Antichrist*, God is described as follows: "This hybrid product of decay, this mixture of zero, concept, and contradiction, in which all the instincts of decadence, all cowardices and wearinesses of the soul, find their sanction!" (A, §19).

The genuine "high point" in this projection of God out of resentment against life is reached in the Christian idea of the crucifixion: "God on the cross—are the horrible secret thoughts behind this symbol not understood yet? All that suffers, all that is nailed to the cross, is divine. All of us are nailed to the cross, consequently we are divine. We alone are divine. Christianity was a victory, although the vanquished was a nobler outlook—Christianity has been the greatest misfortune of mankind so far" (A, §51).

Thus the Christian God is God of the sick, a god erected as support and vindication of resentment:

> The Christian conception of God—God as god of the sick, God as a spider, God as spirit—is one of the most corrupt conceptions of the divine ever attained on earth. It may even represent the low-water mark in the descending development of divine types. God degenerated into the contradiction of life, instead of its transfiguration and eternal Yes! God as the declaration of war against life, against nature, against the will to live! God—the formula for every slander against "this world," for every lie about the "beyond"! God— the deification of nothingness, the will to nothingness pronounced holy! (A, §18)

Note, however, that this passage suggests another possibility: the projection of God as affirmation, transfiguration, Yes-saying to life—in radical contrast to the Christian God. What Nietzsche intends are the Greek gods. According to

The Birth of Tragedy, as already cited, "the gods justify human life by living that life—the only satisfactory theodicy."

Let us return to the madman. He says we ourselves are the ones who have killed God. Of course, as discussed above, we of today are able to kill God only because God has killed himself, that is, because the moral ideal has come to the point of radical self-negation. But, in a deeper sense, it is still we, we human beings, who have killed God. We killed him from the very beginning; we deprived him of life by making him the counterconcept to life, the denial of life, rather than the highest exemplification of life.

D. The lantern.

The madman lit a lantern in the bright morning hours. Why? He would do so only if the light of the sun no longer allowed him to see, only if he had recognized it as a false light. The sun, since Plato, has stood for the highest, perfect, all-illuminating reality, the metaphysical, supersensible reality, the divine reality, the God of philosophy. So the madman's actions already betray his awareness of the death of God—the only light the madman has for his search is a lantern he himself lights.

So we need to ask what the death of God means philosophically. A clue is found in Nietzsche's discussion of Socrates in *The Birth of Tragedy*, specifically in the portrait of Socrates as condemning all those who rely on instinct. Socrates replaced instinct by reason. He sought refuge from instinct in reason. But this amounted to adopting a hostile stance toward life itself. The ultimate result was a denial of all those features most characteristic of life, and in particular the result was a dehistoricizing, a denial of becoming: "They think they show their respect for a subject when they de-historicize it, *sub specie aeterni*—when they turn it into a mummy. Philosophers for thousands of years have been turning all the things they handle into concept-mummies; nothing real escapes alive from the grasp of the philosophers. When these honorable idolators of concepts worship something, they kill it and stuff it: they threaten the life of everything they worship. Death, change, old age, as well as procreation and growth are to their mind objections—even refutations. Whatever has being does not become; whatever becomes does not have being" (TI, p. 479).

The result of the Socratic tendency is a twofold negation: of becoming and of sense experience. The result becomes fully evident in Platonism. A supersensible, metaphysical world is erected as true reality in contradiction to this world. This world is understood only in reference to the other "true" world. But then the stage is set for this ultimate reality to be identified with the God of the moral ideal: Christianity, as we heard in *Beyond Good and Evil*, becomes "Platonism for the people."

What then does the death of God mean philosophically? It means that today this metaphysical, supersensible reality, this "true world," has shown itself for what it is, namely, something projected by life itself. And that applies whether this true reality is understood specifically as God, as Platonic Idea, the Kantian thing-in-itself, or Schopenhauer's primal will. Therefore, it no longer gives us the assurance of an external guarantee of our actions and knowledge. The madman asks: "Who gave us the sponge to wipe away the entire horizon? What did we do when we unchained this earth from its sun?" In particular, since truth has always meant correspondence with this "true reality," the question is forced upon us: How is truth now to be understood? That is to say, the death of God poses the task of a new determination of the essence of truth.

E. This-worldly comfort.

The madman asks: "What water is there for us to clean ourselves? What festivals of atonement, what sacred games shall we need to invent?" Here the madman is speaking of getting over the death of God, recovering from it. What is striking is that the madman speaks of festivals and games. Connected to this is something Nietzsche said in the "Attempt at a Self-Criticism" regarding *The Birth of Tragedy*. In that book, Nietzsche's idea of metaphysical comfort played an important role. This comfort remained more or less tied to Schopenhauer's metaphysics of the primal will, hence to a metaphysical reality-in-itself, and hence to the God of the philosophers. Accordingly, from his later perspective Nietzsche rejects this idea. What is needed after the death of God ought not be metaphysical in any sense. With reference to the question of whether metaphysical comfort is needed, Nietzsche says: "Would it not be necessary? No, thrice no! O, you young romantics: it would *not* be necessary! But it is highly probable that it will end that way, that you end that way, namely, 'comforted,' as it is written, in spite of all self-education for seriousness and terror, 'comforted metaphysically'—in sum, as romantics end, as Christians. No! You ought to learn the art of *this-worldly* comfort first; you ought to learn to laugh, my young friends" (BT, p. 26).

Again Nietzsche says: "I do not know any other way of associating with great tasks than *play*" (EH, p. 714). So the madman tells us that what is called for are festivals and games—that is, laughter and play.

F. Transformation into overman.

The madman asks: "Is not the greatness of this deed too great for us? Must not we ourselves become gods simply to seem worthy of it?" Implied is that a great transformation will be required of man as a result of the death of God. Man must become, in a sense, his own God. In other words, man must cease to regard his values as *given*, as imposed on him and guaranteed by God. Man must become his own God to the extent of deliberately giving himself his values. He must become what he is, his own lawgiver. His virtues must be his own; he must be subject *of* rather than subject *to* them: "A virtue must be *our own* invention, *our own* most necessary self-expression and self-defense; any other kind of virtue is merely a danger" (A, §11).

What is the character of this transformation? According to Nietzsche: "The man of faith, the 'believer' of every kind, is necessarily a dependent man, one who cannot posit *himself* as an end, one who cannot posit any end at all by himself. The 'believer' does not belong to himself. Every kind of faith is itself an expression of self-abnegation, self-alienation" (A, §54). The transformation called for is precisely an overcoming of this self-alienation, a returning to one's self, a homecoming. It is a coming into possession of oneself—it is becoming what one is. It is the transformation from man to overman.

G. Beginning of a higher history.

The madman says: "There has never been a greater deed; and whoever will be born after us—for the sake of this deed, he will be part of a higher history than all history hitherto." Very curious! After what superficially appears to be a lament over the death of God, the madman proceeds to say that it is the beginning of a higher history. The death of God means, as we have seen, the devaluation of our values, their own self-negation. This state Nietzsche calls "nihilism." What does nihilism mean? —"That the highest values devaluate themselves. The aim is lacking; 'Why?' finds no answer" (WP, §2).

Yet Nietzsche insists that nihilism is only a "transitional stage" (WP, §7), a "little prelude" (IB, vol. 2, §1209). Nihilism is the beginning of a higher history, the beginning of a revaluation of all values.

H. The shadows of God.

The madman asks: "Do we not hear anything yet of the noise of the gravediggers who are burying God? Do we not smell anything yet of God's decomposition?" The madman answers: "I come too early.... My time is not yet. This tremendous event is still on its way, still wandering—it has not yet reached the ears of man." Thus men do not yet realize the consequences of the death of God. They do not realize that it wipes away the entire horizon, that, to use a Platonic metaphor, it unchains the earth from the sun. Men do not realize that all those beliefs they hold—even the beliefs and institutions they *live*, ones providing the solid ground for all their acts and thoughts—still remain within the compass of God and the moral ideal.

To recognize the death of God does not simply mean to dispense with one item of belief; it means to experience the collapse of everything on the basis of which man has directed himself and understood himself. But man has still to come to this realization. Nietzsche writes: "*New struggles.* After Buddha was dead, people showed his shadow for centuries in a cave—an immense frightful shadow. God is dead: but as the human race is constituted, there will perhaps be caves for millennia yet, in which people will show his shadow. And we—we have still to overcome his shadow!" (GS, §108). Thus it is necessary to seek out and expose all those places where man still lives under the shadow of God. That is the destructive (No-saying) part of Nietzsche's task. Is this perhaps why the madman, knowing full well that God is dead, nevertheless lights a lantern and sets out in search of God?

I. Madness.

Finally, why is this seeker portrayed as a madman? Is it because with the death of God, all foundations crumble, man finds no support and is driven into madness? Or is the madman mad only from the point of view of those who remain in the shadows? Perhaps he is like the prisoner in Plato's allegory of the cave, who, having ascended out of the cave, then returns only to be told by those still in the cave that he has ruined his sight—because he now sees that the shadows are no more than shadows.

VIII. *Thus Spoke Zarathustra*

A. The task of becoming overman.

In Nietzsche's literary remains, he speaks of Zarathustra as follows: "The self-overcoming of Zarathustra as model of the self-overcoming of man—for the sake of the overman" (IB, vol. 2, §1246). Again, in *Ecce Homo*, Nietzsche says of *Thus Spoke Zarathustra*: "Here man has been overcome at every moment; the concept of the overman has here become the greatest reality" (EH, p. 761). And Zarathustra himself, in his very first speech to the people, appears as the teacher of the overman: "I teach you the overman. Man is something that shall be overcome. What have you done to overcome him?" (TSZ, p. 124).

Accordingly, the theme of the overman is at the heart of *Thus Spoke Zarathustra*. And it is clear how Zarathustra teaches the overman, namely, as a task. "The time has come for man to set himself a goal" (TSZ, p. 129). The overman is something to be achieved through man's overcoming of himself, and Zarathustra comes to place upon man the demand for such a self-overcoming. This demand, this task, is the "gift" Zarathustra brings to man.

What is the nature of this task? In general, it is the task of a revaluation of all values. We have already seen something of what that does and does not mean. It does not mean eliminating values or making man oblivious to them. Nor does it mean simply substituting a new set of values, a new moral ideal, for the old collapsed one. Instead, what is involved is a reversal of man's relation to values. Nietzsche proposes not a new set of values but a new kind of relation to values. This new relation of man to values is what Nietzsche thinks through in his theory of the will to power. So in order to enter into *Thus Spoke Zarathustra*, we need to see what is this new relation to values: What is to be achieved by a revaluation, how is it to be achieved, and how does it involve the theory of the will to power?

Let us approach these questions by means of four very important notes from Nietzsche's literary remains. The first note says: "What separates us from Kant just as from Plato and Leibniz is that we believe only in becoming, even with regard to what is spiritual; we are historical through and through. Such is the great revolution" (IB, vol. 1, §621). Let us concentrate on the statement that we are historical through and through. It seems to contradict what Nietzsche said in "On the Uses and Disadvantages of History," where he indicated the necessary limits of the historical sense. In this connection, however, we need to recall an important passage from the essay. Having spoken of the fixing of the limits of a memory of the past, Nietzsche says: "The deeper the roots of man's inner nature, the better will he take the past into himself; and the greatest and most powerful nature will be known by the absence of limits for the historical sense to overgrow and work harm. It would assimilate and digest the past, however foreign, and turn it to sap" (UM, pp. 62–63). This makes it clear that Nietzsche's description of his philosophy as historical through and through—far from contradicting what he said previously—indicates that something exceptional is required for this philosophy: it requires that one have the deepest roots.

In what sense, then, is Nietzsche's thought historical? Perhaps the most important clue is found in another key statement from the literary remains: "We must overcome the past in ourselves" (section 9 of "Explanatory Notes to *Thus Spoke Zarathustra*," included as an appendix to *Twilight of the Idols*, translated by Anthony Ludovici [London: Foulis, 1911], p. 261). Let us try to think through this statement so as to grasp the various senses in which Nietzsche's philosophy is historical.

First, it is historical inasmuch as it is an overcoming of the history that is within us, the past that flows through us, the past running beneath the surface, supporting and forming us. An example would be the past that is folded away in our language. And this overcoming is for the sake of another history, that "higher history" of which the madman speaks in proclaiming the death of God. So Nietzsche's thought is historical inasmuch as it involves the demand that one history be overcome for the sake of another.

But what is the source of this demand? Why is it necessary to overcome the past? The source is simply the past itself. The overcoming is necessary because in the present age, the past (the tradition) has revealed itself as nihilistic, has reached the point at which its inherent negativity has become explicit. So we can also say Nietzsche's thought is historical in the sense that history is what gives it its task of revaluation. In other words, the demand for revaluation arises from the disclosure of our tradition as nihilistic. This disclosure is itself yielded only by the historical unfolding of that tradition to the point of self-negation.

We can combine these two senses in which Nietzsche's thought is historical by saying: history gives to Nietzsche's thought the task of rendering that history ineffective, no longer taken as directive. Yet even if history becomes ineffective, it nevertheless remains as our history. We continue to have it as our past, even if we no longer try to take our directives from it. This points to a still more radical sense of the demand to overcome the past in ourselves, namely, such that past time even loses its character as past, ceases to be there as a past we drag along behind us.

Yet in what sense could the past cease to be past? One sense would be: if it were not only past but also future—that is, if the past recurred. If time were a circle, then the past would be no more past than future. In this connection, then, the demand to overcome the past would be the demand that man comport himself to time as a circle, that he affirm the eternal recurrence of the same. This constitutes the most fundamental sense in which an overcoming of the past is demanded. It is a demand having to do with the eternal recurrence, the central idea of *Thus Spoke Zarathustra*.

From a strictly philosophical point of view, the death of God (the explicit self-negation reached by the tradition) means the collapse of every metaphysical, supersensible reality, every reality-in-itself. To experience the death of God means, philosophically, to experience what was previously taken as true reality to be in fact a lie, an error: "Formerly, alteration, change, any becoming at all, was taken as proof of mere appearance, as an indication that there must be something which led us astray. Today, it is the reverse: precisely insofar as the prejudice of reason forces us to posit unity, identity, permanence, substance, cause, thinghood, being, to that extent we see ourselves somehow caught in error, compelled into error" (TI, p. 482). To experience these as lies is to experience them as invented, as projected by man. It is to experience "being as an empty fiction" (TI, p. 481). It is to experience being (permanence, unity, substance) in opposition to becoming (change, growth, fragmentation) as "projected by thought" (TI, p. 483). The experience of being as a lie, as projected, has two consequences:

First, if being is merely a fiction, merely projected, then there remains only what the tradition took as the world of appearances, the world of becoming. Thus Nietzsche says in the note we just cited that he believes only in becoming—even within the domain of the spirit. And in *The Gay Science*, Nietzsche says that the world is to all eternity chaos and that if we do not so regard it we are still deceived by the shadows of God. This issue is most succinctly stated in "How the true world finally became a fable" (TI, p. 485).

Secondly, we have said already that the tradition, in the self-negating form it assumes today, gives Nietzsche's thought its task. Now we can add: it also discloses the direction in which that task is to be carried out. The point is that to experience being as projected, and specifically to experience our values as projected, is to realize that what previously was taken as something imposed on us is in fact produced by us. But this is already to overcome our self-alienation, already to regain ourselves, already to be on the way toward becoming what we are. Therefore, the overcoming of self-alienation, the revaluation of values, is not something we *accomplish* so much as it is something already set in motion through the experience of the self-destructiveness of the tradition. Nietzsche's thought is historical inasmuch as historical experience, the experience of the death of God, not only gives Nietzsche his task but also sets into motion the execution of that task. Accordingly, nihilism is merely a "little prelude."

The task that would seem to remain, above and beyond the experience of the death of God, the self-negation of the tradition, is only that of making actual this regaining of ourselves. It is to such actualizing that *Thus Spoke Zarathustra* is primarily addressed.

We come now to the third key statement from the literary remains. Since Plato, the nature of philosophy has been determined primarily from its object: philosophy has as its object that which truly is, namely, being (meta-physical realm) as contrasted with becoming (mere realm of appearance and opinion). The question is then: How is the nature of philosophy to be understood once being is experienced as a fiction and there remains only becoming?

Nietzsche's answer was already suggested in *Human, All Too Human*: "But everything has evolved; there are no eternal facts, as there are likewise no absolute truths. Therefore, historical philosophizing is henceforth necessary" (HATH, vol. I, §2). The note from the literary remains goes even further: "Philosophy, in the only way I still allow it, as the most general form of history: the attempt somehow to describe and abbreviate in symbols the Heraclitean becoming, to translate and mummify it, so to speak, into a kind of fictitious way of being" (IB, vol. 1, §636).

The fourth note from the literary remains concerns the problem of truth. We can easily see how the problem arises. For the tradition, truth means correspondence with that which fully is, reality-in-itself, being. So, if now being proves to be a fiction, then what is truth? The note reads: "What constitutes our present situation as regards philosophy is a conviction found in no previous age: we do not have the truth. All earlier men, even the skeptics, 'had the truth'" (IB, vol. 1, §582). What is this conviction? What does Nietzsche mean by saying we do not have the truth?

He does not mean that we simply do not yet possess the truth although we *could* possess it. Nor does he mean simply that we are honest enough to admit our ignorance, to admit that there are truths still to be found—perhaps even truths we will never find. It is not a matter of lacking this truth or that truth, nor even, as in the case of the skeptics, a matter of lacking all truths. It is not a matter of truths but of truth itself, the nature of truth. We do not possess truth for the reason that truth itself has proved to be based on lies; that is, a truth is true precisely by corresponding with a lie, with a fictitious way of being that we project. In different terms, the truth of things (the truth on which, according to our tradition, the truth of propositions rests), the true being of things, has proved to be a lie. So, in experiencing the death of God, truth comes to be experienced as lie; it comes to be experienced as projected, created, by man. Nietzsche's problem is then to understand this projecting, to understand why it is that truth, "the purely invented world of the unconditional and self-identical" (BGE, p. 202), gets projected and even *must* get projected. In other words, granted that man's relation to values (such as truth or being) is creative, what is it that stands behind this creation?

We can anticipate Nietzsche's general answer: this projecting is simply the means by which a living thing institutes order into the chaos of becoming, establishes that permanence and stability without which it could not survive the continual flux of becoming. Recall: "Truth is the kind of error without which a certain species of living being could not live."

This projecting is (in the terms of "Uses and Disadvantages") the means by which a living thing draws a horizon round about itself, a horizon within which it is at home, within which it is in control, able to exercise mastery. It is a horizon of power, a sphere of power. A living thing requires, and must continually seek and provide for itself, a sphere of power: life is will to power.

B. The task of homecoming.

There is a clear parallel between the section called "The Madman" in *The Gay Science* and the Prologue of *Thus Spoke Zarathustra*. In both, a strange man descends on the marketplace and speaks to the people in a striking language full of imagery. In both cases, the man is not understood by the people and realizes he is not understood: they laugh and jeer at him. But, having heard his speech, the people at least understand enough to realize he is a threat. Those who heard the madman stared at him in astonishment. And there is hatred in the stares of those who heard Zarathustra.

Many of the same images occur in the two passages, and if, as Nietzsche says and we already cited, *Thus Spoke Zarathustra* represents a "return of language to the nature of imagery," it is imperative that we attend carefully to this imagery.

We noted that for the madman the sun is such that it no longer allows proper vision and so the madman lit his lantern. Later the sun is mentioned as that from which the earth has been unchained. In the Prologue, Zarathustra's first words are addressed to the sun. Zarathustra interprets his own task by analogy with the sun. In discussing the madman, we interpreted the image of the sun in reference to Plato. In *Thus Spoke Zarathustra*, however, the image of the sun tends to bring out precisely those features that are contrary to Plato's usage: the sun "brings light to the underworld." Platonically speaking, it illuminates the space inside the cave as well as the space outside. And much is made here of the sun's movement. Unlike the sun of Plato, it does not stand fixed in the sky, eternally shining in the same way. Instead, it moves in its circle and produces the eternal recurrence of the cycle of day and night.

Another shared image is that of the earth. The madman is alarmed at the fact that the earth is unchained from the sun and now plunges into the void. But Zarathustra says: "Remain true to the earth." That seems to mean: do not again chain the earth to the sun.

There are other images in common. In "The Madman," lightning and the light of the stars require time before they reach the eyes of man. But in the Prologue, the lightning is the overman ready to flash out of the cloud hovering above man. And a star, a dancing star, is something man can create—provided he has chaos in himself. Furthermore, Nietzsche writes of the night, which the madman says is now coming and about which he is alarmed. But Zarathustra loves the night and loves looking in the face of everything that is sleeping. As for the gravediggers, in "The Madman" they will bury God; in *Thus Spoke Zarathustra*, they bury men. In response to the death of God, the madman speaks of festivals of atonement and sacred games. Zarathustra does not merely speak; as the old saint says, Zarathustra walks like a dancer. Finally, in both passages, there is a death discussed at great length: on the one hand, the death of God; on the other, the death of a man, the tightrope walker.

Despite all the similarity, there is (as some of the parallels already suggest) a subtle difference between the two passages. The difference comes down to this: the madman seeks God, whereas Zarathustra seeks men. In both passages, two basic issues especially stand out: the death of God and the placing of a demand upon man. But they stand out with a different emphasis. The section on the madman is concerned almost entirely with recounting the circumstances and consequences of the death of God. By contrast, Zarathustra mentions the death of God as though it were virtually common knowledge, rather than (as the madman said) something that has not yet reached the ears of man. Zarathustra is surprised, in meeting the saint, that the saint is unaware of God's death: "Could it be possible? This old saint in the forest has not yet heard anything of this, that God is dead!" We might say that, versus the madman, Zarathustra no longer seeks God. Zarathustra has "absorbed" fully the experience of the death of God. He has already passed through that "little prelude" of total devaluation, utter nihilism.

As to the demand, in *The Gay Science* the challenge hurled at man—however weighty it may be—is only mentioned briefly: "Is not the greatness of this deed too great for us? Must not we ourselves become gods simply to seem worthy of it? There has never been a greater deed; whoever will be born after us—for the sake of this deed he will be part of a higher history than all history hitherto." The Prologue, on the contrary, deals with little else besides this demand placed on man—the demand to go under, to overcome oneself for the sake of the overman. The madman tells of the event after which we will be part of a higher history. Zarathustra relates the beginning of this higher history.

So we may express the difference as follows: "The Madman" speaks of nihilism as the destruction of the old; *Thus Spoke Zarathustra* speaks of nihilism in terms of the new beginning. We need to understand this difference, this transition, in order to understand the point at which *Thus Spoke Zarathustra* commences.

Nietzsche provides a clue for understanding this transition from destruction to new beginning, from the madman to Zarathustra, from *The Gay Science* to *Thus Spoke Zarathustra*. The clue is that the final section of Part IV of *The Gay Science* (which was originally the final section of the entire work; Part V was added five years later, in 1887) is virtually identical with the first section of the Prologue of *Thus Spoke Zarathustra*. But there is one difference: in *The Gay Science*, this section carries the title "Tragedy Begins." In other words, the beginning of *Thus Spoke Zarathustra* is the beginning of a tragedy. *Thus Spoke Zarathustra* is a tragedy. The transition from the former work to the latter is a transition from an experience of the collapse of all values, all foundations, to tragedy. Thus the tragedy takes its departure from something like a gaze into the abyss, the fruit of which is the wisdom of Silenus (anything but a joyful wisdom). The transition is what Nietzsche earlier called the birth of tragedy out of the spirit of music. If we note that in later writings Nietzsche designates the synthesis of the Apollinian and Dionysian by the single name "Dionysus," then we can see why he says with respect to *Thus Spoke Zarathustra*: "My concept 'Dionysian' here became the highest deed" and why he calls himself "a disciple of the philosopher Dionysus" (TI, p. 563).

So in order to understand the transition already made at the beginning of *Thus Spoke Zarathustra*, we need to recall what, according to *The Birth of Tragedy*, comes about with the inception of tragedy. Nietzsche sees tragedy as born of two components. Speaking very generally, the Dionysian component is an engagement (by means of the chorus) in the destructiveness of the primal will, the collapse of appearances into the will itself, and the Apollinian component, by its projection of the dreamworld of the scene, is a mirroring of the building up (construction) of individual appearances out of the will. Thus tragedy—as providing the metaphysical comfort saving us from the wisdom of Silenus—is an imitation of the primordial creating-destroying play of the will itself.

In order to apply this conception of tragedy to the context of *The Gay Science* and *Thus Spoke Zarathustra*, one fundamental change is required. With the experience of the death of God, all "reality-in-itself" is destroyed. In particular, the notion of a Schopenhauerian will-in-itself (still present to some extent in *The Birth of Tragedy*) must be rejected. But Nietzsche's rejection of the will as primordial thing-in-itself does not mean he abandons the concept of will as creating-destroying play. He abandons only the empty subject behind this play. In different terms, the will is no longer regarded as a metaphysical reality underlying man's phenomenal existence. Instead, will is precisely this existence itself: man *is* will to power. (The addition, "to power," simply says: as creating-destroying play.) Man *is* the creating of order out of chaos and the dissolving of order into chaos. He is the establishing of a horizon of permanence within becoming *and* an overthrowing of that horizon (self-overcoming). Therefore, tragedy (conceived, as in *The Birth of Tragedy*, to be an imitation of the will) is simply man's imitation of what he is. But to imitate what one is is to engage in becoming what one is. It is to engage in homecoming. Accordingly, *Thus Spoke Zarathustra* is a work of homecoming. It tells of Zarathustra's becoming what he is.

Against this background of a characterization of *Thus Spoke Zarathustra* as a work (or play) of homecoming, we need now to gain some preliminary understanding of what "homecoming" means for Nietzsche—what it means to "become what one is." Specifically, I want to present a series of statements regarding the nature of homecoming and to elaborate them in terms of what Nietzsche says in the Prologue, in works surrounding *Thus Spoke Zarathustra*, and in the self-interpretation found in *Ecce Homo*. These statements will serve also to draw together most of the issues we have been considering.

1. Homecoming proceeds from homelessness.

One can engage in a return home only if one has previously left home. This leaving is exactly what is narrated in the first sentence of *Thus Spoke Zarathustra*: "When Zarathustra was thirty years old, he left his home and the lake of this home and went into the mountains." Why did Zarathustra leave home? The book does not state the reason—at least not directly. A note from the literary remains offers a clue, however; Nietzsche has Zarathustra say: "Among men I was frightened. Among men I desired a host of things, and nothing satisfied me. It was then that I went into solitude and created the overman" (IB, vol. 2, §1213).

Among men Zarathustra was frightened. He was not at home; he lacked the security by which to exclude what is fearful. He lacked the horizon within which to order his desires and satisfactions. Among men—that is, just where he should have been at home—he experienced his homelessness. Presumably, that is why he had to leave his home—because he had already been abandoned by it. More generally, that homelessness from which the homecoming proceeds is the condition Nietzsche describes as nihilism (the devaluation of all value). It is the utter collapse of every foundation, a collapse Nietzsche portrays as the death of God.

This is the homelessness Nietzsche expressed when he wrote in a Dithyramb of Dionysus whose title is repeated as the last line of the poem: *Die Wüste wächst; weh dem, der Wüsten birgt!* ("The wasteland grows; woe to him who harbors wastelands!") (TSZ, p. 417, p. 421).

2. Homecoming proceeds through solitude.

The second sentence of *Thus Spoke Zarathustra* reads: "Here Zarathustra enjoyed his spirit and his solitude and for ten years did not tire of them." Why did Zarathustra retreat into solitude? To be sure, solitude is not simply something subsequent to the experience of homelessness; it already belongs to that experience. Homelessness already drives Zarathustra into solitude. "For a pious man, there is no solitude—we, the godless, have been the first to invent it" (GS, §367).

Yet solitude is not simply a prolongation of homelessness. Instead, something transpires in this solitude—something issues from it, making possible a subsequent return home. In the Prologue, the old saint says to Zarathustra: "No stranger to me is this wanderer; many years ago he passed this way. Zarathustra was he called, but he has changed. At that time, you carried your ashes to the mountains; would you now carry your fire into the valleys?" (TSZ, p. 122). Previously Zarathustra carried his ashes—he was burned out, exhausted, deadened by the experience of nihilism. But now, after his period of solitude, he has new fire, he has somehow recovered. In other words, he has made that transition we described in relating "The Madman" to *Thus Spoke Zarathustra*: a transition from nihilism as the destruction of the old to nihilism as a new beginning. Presumably, this transition has come about solely by meditating on the experience Zarathustra brought with him to the mountain, that is, by fully absorbing the experience of nihilism.

We have seen already something of what results when the experience of nihilism is fully appropriated. To appropriate it means to experience what has hitherto been taken as a value to be in fact only a device for preserving a certain type of life. It means to experience what has been taken as true reality to be a lie, something invented, something projected by man. It means to experience being as "projected by thought."

Accordingly, to experience nihilism in its full depth means to experience all those standards in terms of which things have been taken as real, true, and valuable to be things rooted in life itself, things merely projected by man. It means to experience man as giving himself his standards and values. It means to experience man as his own lawgiver, as the one who draws for himself that horizon within which truth, reality, and value are determined. In short, it means to experience man as will to power.

Because the experience of nihilism issues in an experience of man, a self-experience, it is therefore not just something to be observed at a distance. On the contrary, it must be lived through in oneself. Here we see the "experimental" character of Nietzsche's thought, as he expresses it in *The Gay Science*: "I commend all skepticism which allows me to answer: let us try it! But I wish to hear nothing more of all things and questions which do not allow of experiment. This is the limit of my sense of truth" (GS, §51).

3. Homecoming means to become will to power.

We have seen that from the experience of nihilism, from living through this experience, man comes to be seen as will to power. Yet *Thus Spoke Zarathustra* indicates, by its dramatic character, that homecoming can begin only through what issues from living through this experience, from the ten years of solitude. Thus, homecoming can begin when man is experienced as will to power. Man can set out to become what he is once he has experienced what he is. To become what one is, to experience homecoming, is to become will to power.

4. Homecoming involves a revaluation of all values.

In *Ecce Homo*, Nietzsche speaks of revaluation: "A revaluation of all values: that is my formula for an act of supreme self-examination on the part of humanity, become flesh and genius in me. . . . I was the first to *discover* the truth by being the first to experience lies as lies—smelling them out. My genius is in my nostrils" (EH, p. 326).

We have spoken already of this act of self-examination: it is the one in which Zarathustra was engaged during his decade of solitude. We have seen that it is not merely some sort of introspection, some purely immanent reflection of the self on itself; it is not the Cartesian *cogito*. Already in *Human, All Too Human*, Nietzsche insisted that merely looking into oneself never suffices, because the past flows within us, that is, because we are historical. Thus we have seen that this self-examination (the experience of oneself) is an experience issuing out of an experience of nihilism. It arises when we live through the experience of the self-negation of the traditional ideal—when we "experience lies as lies." What comes from this self-examination is an experience of man as will to power and hence an experience of the demand that man *become* will to power.

5. Homecoming involves a reversal of the nature of truth.

In the passage from *Ecce Homo* quoted earlier, Nietzsche speaks of truth in a striking way: "I was the first to *discover* the truth." This is puzzling in light of what Nietzsche said about truth ever since the early essay "On Truth and Lies." In fact, it would seem to be flatly contradicted by another statement in *Ecce Homo* where Nietzsche speaks of Zarathustra as "one who first creates truth." The problem is that, as we have seen repeatedly, for Nietzsche truth is something created: man as will to power projects those standards by which truth is decided. But, if truth is simply created, then is there any real *discovery* of truth? Recall what Nietzsche said in the essay: "If someone hides a thing behind a bush, seeks it again, and finds it in the same place, then there is not much to praise regarding this seeking and finding."

We can see what is involved here if we consider how Nietzsche says he discovered the truth: not by seeing it, not by an insight, as most philosophers would say. Instead, Nietzsche smelled it and did so by being the first to experience lies as lies, that is, by experiencing truth as something created. So what Nietzsche discovers is not some truth about this or that but rather the truth about truth, the nature of truth. Of course, this too remains questionable: Is the truth about truth also created? Here we must refer to what Nietzsche says of revaluation at the beginning of *Twilight of the Idols*: "A revaluation of all values, this question mark, so black, so tremendous, that it casts shadows back upon the man who sets it forth" (TI, p. 465).

6. Homecoming occurs beyond good and evil, that is, beyond morality.

We have already considered Nietzsche's relation to morality and saw that what he proposes is not simply to present a new set of values, a new morality to replace the old one. Instead, Nietzsche intends a complete reversal of man's relation to values. Whereas man had been the servant of his values, man is now to become their master. That is the revaluation. *Ecce Homo*, as we saw, presents the same idea: "To become what one is, one must not have the faintest notion *what* one is." "No new idols are erected by me."

These statements, to the effect that no new ideals, idols, are to be set up, would seem to contradict something else Nietzsche has been saying, namely, that to become what one is means to become will to power. In other words, Nietzsche seems to be saying that one knows quite well what man is, namely, will to power, and to become what one is means to become this in fact, to assume this character actively. So the problem arises: Is not the idea of the will to power simply a new idol? How can Nietzsche present the idea of the will to power without, in effect, falling back into morality? How can he advocate this idea and yet remain "the first immoralist," beyond good and evil?

To answer, we need to consider more carefully what would be involved in becoming oneself, granted that one is will to power. What would one do? One would assume actively the role one has inadvertently played all along—the role of being one's own lawgiver, being self-legislative, projecting one's own values. But to assume this role actively would amount to refusing to accept any ideal as something externally imposed; it would amount to excluding the possibility of precisely the sort of thing that happened in the tradition: the recoil of values, projected by life, back upon life so as to negate it by way of setting up idols.

That is the "new truth" Zarathustra states in the next to the last section of the Prologue: "An insight has come to me: companions I need, living ones—not dead companions and corpses I carry with myself wherever I want to. Living companions I need, who follow me because they want to follow themselves—wherever I want" (TSZ, p. 135). So, to pose the idea of the will to power is not to erect a new ideal but is rather to affirm life over against every ideal. It is the radical negation of all idols.

7. Homecoming means to become overman.

Zarathustra, on the way of homecoming, speaks of, advocates, and teaches us the overman, as we already heard in Zarathustra's very first speech to the people: "I teach you the overman. Man is something that shall be overcome. What have you done to overcome him?" To become overman is to pass over (beyond) what man has previously been. This transformation is no mere evolution, no mere gradual change in man's beliefs and ways of acting. It is a radical transformation, a reversal of what is most fundamental in man, namely, his relation to values.

Nietzsche describes the overman (and the contrast between mere evolution and radical reversal) by means of the contrast between the overman and the "last man." Who is the last man? Nietzsche says: "No shepherd and one herd! Everybody wants the same, everybody is the same: whoever feels different goes voluntarily into a madhouse" (TSZ, p. 130). Does this mean the last man is simply the moral man, the man still subject to morality? Yes and no. We might say the last man is the one who is still subject to morality but for whom, after the death of God, there is no viable morality. In other words, he is the one who, unlike the overman, is unable to initiate a new beginning from out of the death of God. The last man remains caught up in the destruction of the old, indeed perhaps is not even capable of such destruction: "'What is love? What is creation? What is longing? What is a star?' Thus asks the last man, and he blinks" (TSZ, p. 129).

We have seen that it is in the experience of the death of God as the self-destruction of the ideal—leading to the experience of man as will to power—that Nietzsche finds the directives for a new beginning. It is out of the chaos in ourselves, the chaos brought on by the self-destruction of the ideal, that a new beginning sets in: "I say unto you: one must still have chaos in oneself to be able to bring a dancing star to birth. I say unto you: you still have chaos in yourselves" (TSZ, p. 129). The last man is the one who no longer has this chaos in himself. He is no longer able to despise himself—that is, no longer able to experience the self-destructiveness of the ideal in himself. The last man merely says: "Formerly, all the world was mad" (TSZ, p. 130). But he finds no new beginning thereby. Instead, he blinks.

Of course, these last men are not just at some remote point in the future; they are already present. After the crowd heard Zarathustra's speech, they shouted: "Give us this last man, O Zarathustra! Turn us into these last men" (TSZ, p. 130).

8. Homecoming is self-creation.

To become what one is is not simply to accept some ideal of what one is and then strive to realize that ideal. "I am no seeker. I want to create my sun for myself" (GS, §320). One must create one's own sun, that is, one's own ideal. One must create what one is, create what one is to become in becoming what one is. One must create oneself. Accordingly, homecoming is self-creation; one's self is not something to be simply actualized but something to be *created*.

Yet we must be careful so as not to misunderstand this notion of self-creation. We would tend to regard it as a matter of consciously projecting an ideal and then subordinating all that we are to this ideal. In other words, we would tend to regard self-creation as a kind of self-causation, in the sense of our making ourselves what we are, that is, positing an ideal and then completely reshaping all that we are so we come to be in accord with the ideal. But thereby we remain under the shadows of God, under the power of the theological concept of the *causa sui*—a concept Nietzsche never ceases to condemn. He describes it as "the best self-contradiction that has been conceived so far" (BGE, p. 218). It is, Nietzsche says, the belief that one can "pull oneself up into existence by the hair, out of the swamps of nothingness" (BGE, p. 218). It is in this regard that Nietzsche condemns belief in "freedom of the will" (BGE, p. 218).

Upon a closer look, we can see why self-creation does not have this theological character for Nietzsche. In order to be simply a matter of consciously projecting an ideal and subordinating what we already are to it, we would need to have clearly before consciousness precisely what we are. But Nietzsche insists that for the most part we are unknown to ourselves: consciousness is only a surface. So what then is this self-creation?

9. Homecoming is self-overcoming.

In creating the self, one exercises one's creative power upon what one already is—hence one overcomes what one already is. But this overcoming is not mere negation. It is a creative, overflowing affirmation of what one has already become. So, as we remarked in discussing *Ecce Homo*, to become what one is means to come to be what one has become. But now we must add: it means indeed to be what one has been but to be this *in a new way* and hence is to overcome what one has been. What is this "new way"? It is expressed in *Ecce Homo*: "And this is all my creating and striving, that I create and carry together into unity what is fragment and riddle and dreadful accident" (EH, p. 764). That is precisely what the tightrope walker of the Prologue, the man striding on the rope over man, from beast to overman, could not do. He was unable to accommodate, to take up into his task, the riddle, the accident, namely, the jester who unaccountably appeared and jumped over him and won the race along the rope. Faced with this accident and with his failure, the tightrope walker threw away his balancing pole and fell to his death (TSZ, p. 131). Zarathustra, musing on this event, says: "Human existence is uncanny and still without meaning; a jester can become man's fatality. I will teach men the meaning of their existence—the overman, the lightning out of the dark cloud of man" (TSZ, p. 132).

10. Homecoming requires a going-under.

This notion of going-under recurs throughout the Prologue and is continually played off in Nietzsche's language against going-over and overman. Going-under has at least two senses.

First, one must go under in the sense indicated when Zarathustra compares his task with that of the sun. Zarathustra, we already noted, has "to bring light to the underworld." He must illuminate the underworld; as he said in describing the task of *Human, All Too Human*, he must illuminate the underworld of the ideal—the underworld which, when illuminated, proves to be will to power. So to go under means to experience the death of God all the way through, to the point of experiencing man as will to power.

But there is another meaning. It is also indicated in the Prologue, by Zarathustra saying of himself: "Zarathustra wants to become man again" (TSZ, p. 122). He wants to become man in order to become overman, which is to say that in this transition one becomes what one already is—but in a new way. *The Gay Science* expresses this "new way" as follows: "To 'give style' to one's character—that is a grand and rare art! He who surveys all that his nature presents in its strength and in its weakness, and then fashions it in an ingenious plan until everything appears artistic and rational, and even the weaknesses enchant the eye—he exercises that admirable art" (GS, §290). "We want to be poets of our lives" (GS, §299).

11. Homecoming is affirmation of the eternal recurrence.

The problem is: How can one "give style" to what one has become, "carry it together into unity," unless what one has become is apparent, evident, transparent to consciousness? How can we reshape what we are unless we are conscious of it? Yet Nietzsche insists we have no such consciousness, no such self-transparency.

In *Beyond Good and Evil*, Nietzsche claims that "in every act of the will there is a ruling thought" (BGE, p. 215). It is instructive that he speaks of a *ruling* thought. For, if, in the case of becoming what one is, this thought is to operate effectively, it cannot be a thought which we simply posit and under which we then need to bring what we already are. Rather, it must be a thought which *rules*, which of itself draws together into unity (gives style to) what we have become. In different terms, it would be a thought placing such a "heavy burden" on us as to force us into a self-transformation. This thought is the idea of the eternal recurrence. It is introduced in the penultimate section of *The Gay Science* as originally published (the section identical with the beginning of *Thus Spoke Zarathustra*), immediately preceding the last section, "Tragedy begins." The section introducing the idea of the eternal recurrence is called "The heaviest burden" and reads as follows:

> What if a daimon crept after you into your loneliest solitude some day or night and said to you: "This life, as you live it at present, and have lived it, you must live it once more and also innumerable times; and there will be nothing new in it, but every pain and every joy and every thought and every sigh, and all the unspeakably small and great things in your life must come to you again, and all in the same series and sequences.... If that thought acquired power over you as you are, it would transform you and perhaps crush you; the question with regard to all and everything, 'Do you want this once more, and also for innumerable times?' would lie as the heaviest burden upon your activity! Or, how would you have to become favorably inclined to yourself and to life, so as to long for nothing more ardently than for this last eternal sanctioning and sealing?" (GS, §341)

Nietzsche says that the fundamental idea of *Thus Spoke Zarathustra* is that of the eternal recurrence. The Prologue concludes with Zarathustra's first vision of this idea—not yet as an idea, much less in its power of ruling, but in the distance, overhead, in the image of Zarathustra's animals, the ones that have been with Zarathustra throughout his solitude: "That is what Zarathustra had told his heart when the sun stood high at noon; then he looked into the air, questioning, for overhead he heard the sharp call of a bird. And behold! An eagle soared through the sky in wide circles, and on him there hung a serpent, not like prey but like a friend: for she kept herself wound around his neck" (TSZ, pp. 136–37). Note the serpent *encircling* the eagle, and the eagle flying in recurrent *circles*.

The passage continues: "'These are my animals,' said Zarathustra and was happy in his heart. 'The proudest animal under the sun and the wisest animal under the sun—they have gone out on a search. They want to determine whether Zarathustra is still alive'" (TSZ, p. 137). The proudest animal is the one with the greatest pride in what it is and joyfully affirms what it is—the affirmer of life. The wisest animal is the one with the wisdom which knows not simply a truth but the nature of truth. The animals want to determine whether Zarathustra is still alive: they want to determine Zarathustra's relation to life, whether Zarathustra can affirm life. And they bring the means for this determination: the idea of the eternal recurrence. Zarathustra says: "May my animals lead me!" (TSZ, p. 137).

C. Image-language.

Very few philosophers have thought it necessary, or even appropriate, to discuss laughter, dancing, play. Nietzsche is an exception; not only does he speak of these, but he even does so in a language filled with laughter, a language that dances, a playful language. He says in *Beyond Good and Evil*: "I should actually risk an order of rank among philosophers depending on the rank of their laughter—all the way up to those capable of *golden* laughter. And supposing that gods, too, philosophize—which has been suggested to me by many an inference—I should not doubt that they also know how to laugh" (BGE, pp. 422–23). In *Ecce Homo*, Nietzsche tells us that "Zarathustra is a dancer" (EH, p. 762). And in *Thus Spoke Zarathustra* he says: "I would believe only in a god who could dance" (TSZ, p. 153). Furthermore, Nietzsche claims that "another ideal runs ahead of us . . . : the ideal of a spirit naively playing" (EH, p. 755).

So what kind of thinking is this? What kind of works (or plays) are these? What about *Thus Spoke Zarathustra* in particular? There the playful, dancing character of Nietzsche's writing is quite remarkable, but one could still say of the book: it is a work for thinking, nothing more.

Even so, our attempt to interpret *Thus Spoke Zarathustra* will precisely, in view of the great difficulty of the task, be only an "attempt." In a letter to Carl von

Gersdorff in June 1883, Nietzsche writes: "Do not be deceived by the legendary air of this little book; behind all the plain and strange words stand my *deepest seriousness* and my *whole philosophy*" (SL, p. 213). So to interpret *Thus Spoke Zarathustra* means to interpret Nietzsche's whole philosophy, a philosophy residing, however, *behind* the words and not to be found on the surface. Heidegger says: "Not one thinker has appeared who could stand up to this book's basic thought and to its darkness" (*What Is Called Thinking?*, p. 50). We should take Heidegger's statement as a warning against being deceived by whatever clarity we can attain with respect to this idea, a warning not to expect to find much more than a few pointers into its darkness.

So, again, what kind of book are we dealing with? Recall what we quoted early on, in making it the goal of the course to read and interpret *Thus Spoke Zarathustra*, namely, Nietzsche's statement that "this work stands altogether apart." Thus we have no literary classification under which we can place it. But Nietzsche offers us a clue to ponder. In a letter to Rohde in 1884, Nietzsche declares: "My style is a dance.... In any case I have remained a poet, in the most radical sense of the word" (SL, p. 221). Accordingly, *Thus Spoke Zarathustra* is poetry. But what does that mean?

To say of a book that it is poetry can mean almost anything. One of the few definite things such a book could not be, however, is philosophy. Furthermore, Nietzsche also says: "Perhaps the whole of *Zarathustra* may be reckoned as music" (EH, p. 751). *The Birth of Tragedy* showed that the synthesis of poetry and music is tragedy. So *Thus Spoke Zarathustra* does not just philosophize *about* tragedy, it philosophizes *as* tragedy. Yet what are we to make of this combination of music and poetry, this music-practicing Socrates?

Another clue for understanding Nietzsche's characterization of *Thus Spoke Zarathustra* as poetry is found in claims we already alluded to: "For a genuine poet, metaphor is not a rhetorical figure but a vicarious image that he actually beholds in place of a concept" and "*Thus Spoke Zarathustra* represents a return of language to the nature of imagery."

So the language of this book is an image-language, not a concept-language. Why the image-language? How is it that this language accords with the philosophy expressed in the language? I suggest there are two reasons:

First, Nietzsche understands the contrast between image and concept the way it was understood by Platonism: images remain within and are drawn from the physical, the sensible, whereas concepts refer to something meta-physical. In other words, the relation between image and concept mirrors the relation between the sensible and the supersensible. So, in using an image-language, Nietzsche is advocating the sensible over and against the supersensible. Through the use of an image-language, *Thus Spoke Zarathustra* portrays what it says *in the very way* of saying it. The book asserts *stylistically* what Nietzsche calls being "true to the earth." The language itself asserts what is said in the language: for example, "I beseech you, my brothers, remain true to the earth, and do not believe those who speak to you of otherworldly hopes!" (TSZ, p. 125).

Second, in the contrast between image and concept, Nietzsche also sees a contrast between something that comes upon us, welling up from dark origins, and something we construct consciously and explicitly. He says of Zarathustra: "He overtook me." In the same vein, Nietzsche writes: "A thought comes when 'it' wishes, not when 'I' wish" (BGE, p. 214). The point is that thought, like everything human, has its roots beneath the surface, beneath the level of consciousness, in "instincts," that is, in the will to power. There is an involuntariness about thinking, and that is what poets describe as inspiration: "Everything happens involuntarily in the highest degree but as if in a storm of a feeling of freedom, of being unbound, of power, of divinity. The involuntariness of image and metaphor is strangest of all; one no longer has any conception of what is an image or metaphor and what is not; everything offers itself as the nearest, most rightful, the simplest expression. It actually seems . . . as if the things themselves approached and offered themselves as metaphors. . . . This is *my* experience of inspiration" (EH, pp. 756–57).

D. The central idea of *Thus Spoke Zarathustra*.

According to Nietzsche, "Whatever we have words for, that we have already gone beyond" (TI, p. 530). He says in a letter to his sister in May 1884: "Everything I have written hitherto is foreground; for me the real thing begins only with the dashes. I am dealing with the most dangerous matters; that I meanwhile commend the Germans, in a popular manner, to Schopenhauer or Wagner or think up Zarathustra—these are for me recreation but, above all, hiding places, behind which I can sit down again for a while" (SL, p. 241).

So all of Nietzsche's works, even *Thus Spoke Zarathustra*, are foreground. If we are to attain to the real matters, we must penetrate to the depths beneath the writings. Nietzsche tells Overbeck in April 1884: "I have decided to spend the next five years on an elaboration of my 'philosophy,' the portico of which I have built in my *Zarathustra*" (SL, p. 223). Yet Nietzsche never published this elaboration. It is *not* contained in the books written after *Thus Spoke Zarathustra*. All we have of it is contained in the notes that comprise the literary remains. It is practically impossible to interpret *Thus Spoke Zarathustra* without consulting these notes.

What is the real matter of Nietzsche's thought, to which we gain access by moving through the foreground? So far, we have characterized it in several ways: rebirth of tragedy, homecoming, revaluation, passing over man to the overman. But all of this coalesces in what Nietzsche later declares to be the central idea of

Thus Spoke Zarathustra: the eternal recurrence. What is at issue in the eternal recurrence is a basic transformation of man—a transformation of man's way of comporting himself to time. This transformation is not simply a new view of time; it is instead a transformation of what man is.

Man's relation to time is not merely one relation among others. On the contrary, this relation is central to determining what man is. To transform man is equivalent to transforming human temporality. *Thus Spoke Zarathustra* arrives at this transformation only gradually, although it is on the horizon from the beginning. We need to acquire some sense of the existential dimension of the problem of time—of what could be called the existential ambiguity of time. It is expressed in two odes by Hölderlin.

In general terms, we can put the ambiguity this way: like the primal will of *The Birth of Tragedy*, time tears down and builds up, destroys and creates. Time destroys: we suffer from its ceaseless tearing down, the passing away that is time. Hölderlin (*Poems and Fragments*, bilingual edition, tr. Michael Hamburger [Ann Arbor: University of Michigan Press, 1966], pp. 89–90) writes:

> *Der Zeitgeist*
>
> *Zu lang schon waltest über dem Haupte mir,*
> *Du in der dunkeln Wolke, du Gott der Zeit!*
> *Zu wild, zu bang ist's ringsum, und es*
> *Trümmert und wankt ja, wohin ich blicke.*
>
> *Ach! wie ein Knabe, seh' ich zu Boden oft,*
> *Such' in der Höhle Rettung von dir, und möcht',*
> *Ich Blöder, eine Stelle finden,*
> *Alleserschütt'rer! wo du nicht wärest.*

> The spirit of the age
>
> Too long above my head have you governed there,
>   Wrapped in the thunder cloud, you God of Time!
>   Too desolate and awed the land lies,
>   All that I look at breaks up and totters.
>
> Ah, like a boy I have often cast down my eyes,
>   Seeking refuge from you in some deep cave, and gone searching,
>   Poor craven, for a single place where
>   You, the all-shattering, might be absent.

Man has indeed searched for this "deep cave," this place where "all-shattering" time might be eluded. Plato saw the desire for immortality (escape from time) as inherent in man's most fundamental motive force, Eros. Man experiences the need for permanence, for something abiding, something enduring, and he feels this need precisely in the face of "all-shattering" time, all-undoing time. Nietzsche experienced the destructiveness of time very deeply; he experienced the existential meaning of the fact that one's past is irretrievable.

In the past we made decisions, and then they made us what we are. From a later vantage point, we might see that the decisions were based on self-ignorance, without any real sense of our goals or capacities. But by these decisions we took a certain path, and now we cannot revoke the decisions, cannot undo the fact that they were made, cannot nullify the path already trodden. The possibilities that were once open cannot be brought back—time has carried them away. We are always already in the midst of life, always already set upon a course; we cannot undo what we have become. Nietzsche writes to Overbeck in 1883: "I no longer see *why* I should live for another six months.... I forgo and suffer too much and have come to comprehend, beyond all comprehension, the deficiency, the mistakes, and the real disasters of my whole past intellectual life. It is too late to make things good now; I shall nevermore do anything that is good. What is the point of doing anything?" (SL, p. 210).

If time carries away our possibilities, still we can say that, in another respect, time grants us our possibilities. These grow beneath the surface and are yielded up unaccountably: a thought comes when *it* wishes. Nietzsche says that "one collects from everything one sees, hears, lives through." But this chaos within us requires the ordering that only time can bring: "The organizing 'idea' that is destined to rule keeps growing deep down" (EH, p. 710).

What we are and what we are capable of—these are yielded by our past and not only by our individual past but by the whole past of our tradition, which "continues to flow within us in a hundred waves." Our past yields up possibilities precisely to the extent that this chaos comes under an organizing idea. How does it do so? It is not something we can consciously effect. The idea needs to grow deep down. What is involved? One element involved—the main element—is suffering: "This is the most profound conception of suffering: the form-giving forces are in painful collision" (WP, §686). "The discipline of suffering, of *great* suffering—do you not know that only *this* discipline has created all enhancements of man so far?" (BGE, p. 344). "How profoundly human beings can suffer almost determines their order of rank.... Profound suffering makes noble" (BGE, p. 410). Finally, there is the cryptic remark in *Ecce Homo*: "What does not kill a man makes him stronger" (EH, p. 680).

So in the end is Nietzsche brought back to a dreary, pessimistic view of human life? If the course of life is inherently strewn with suffering, do we not return to a wisdom which is anything but a "gay science," the wisdom of Silenus?

The answer is no. We can see why from what Nietzsche says about suffering in *On the Genealogy of Morals*: "What really arouses indignation against suffering is not suffering as such but the senselessness of suffering" (GM, p. 504). Thus the question is how man gives meaning to his suffering. Must he negate life in order to endure his suffering? Or is he able ("strong enough") to affirm life despite suffering, to affirm his suffering as integral to life, even to will the eternal recurrence of his suffering? Let us refer to a second ode by Hölderlin (*Poems and Fragments*, pp. 148–49):

Lebenslauf

Größers wolltest auch du, aber die Liebe zwingt
All uns nieder, das Leid beuget gewaltiger,
 Doch es kehret umsonst nicht
  Unser Bogen, woher er kommt.

...

Alles prüfe der Mensch, sagen die Himmlischen,
Daß er, kräftig genährt, danken für Alles lern',
 Und verstehe die Freiheit,
  Aufzubrechen, wohin er will.

Course of life

More you also desired, but love forces down
 Every one of us, and grief bends with still greater power;
  Yet our arc not for nothing
   Returns whence it began.

...

A man shall try out everything, thus say the heavenly ones,
 So that strongly nurtured he shall learn thankfulness for everything
  And understand the freedom
   To set forth whithersoever he wants.

E. *Thus Spoke Zarathustra* as tragedy.

Nietzsche says: "The most suffering animal on earth invented for itself—laughter" (WP, §990). Yet, as we noted, the last section ("Tragedy begins") of *The Gay Science* is identical with the beginning of *Thus Spoke Zarathustra*. Accordingly, *Thus Spoke Zarathustra* is tragedy (poetry plus music). What sort of tragedy? And how related to laughter? In the first place, this book is a work for thinking; it is the portico of Nietzsche's whole philosophy. So it is a tragedy that is also a work of philosophy. It is the product of an "artist-philosopher," a music-practicing Socrates. (There is still the question of exactly how art and philosophy are to be brought together.) Second, *Thus Spoke Zarathustra* is not a tragedy meant to provide metaphysical comfort. In his "Attempt at a self-criticism," Nietzsche poses the question of whether the tragic person of today has need of metaphysical comfort. Nietzsche, as we already quoted, is adamant in his answer: "No, thrice no! . . . No! You ought to learn the art of *this-worldly* comfort first; you ought to learn to laugh, my young friends." And Nietzsche has Zarathustra say: "So learn to laugh away over yourselves! Lift up your hearts, you good dancers, high, higher! And do not forget good laughter. This crown of him who laughs, this rose-wreath crown: to you, my brothers, I throw this crown. Laughter I have pronounced holy; you higher men, learn to laugh!" (TSZ, p. 407).

Thus Spoke Zarathustra is a tragedy that has to do with laughter. It is different from those tragedies loved by the men who "search lustfully for sufferers" (TSZ, p. 167). Its goal is not to provoke pity in the face of human suffering. Instead, it is a tragedy for those of whom Nietzsche speaks in "On reading and writing": "You look up when you feel the need for elevation. And I look down because I am elevated. Who among you can laugh and be elevated at the same time? Whoever climbs the highest mountains laughs at all tragic plays and tragic seriousness" (TSZ, p. 152–53). According to Nietzsche, "There are heights of the soul from which even tragedy ceases to look tragic" (BGE, p. 232). *Thus Spoke Zarathustra* is a tragedy to which laughter belongs; it is a tragedy that is also a comedy.

A tragedy has a hero. Nietzsche even says: "Around the hero everything turns into a tragedy" (BGE, p. 280). Zarathustra is the hero of Nietzsche's tragedy. But Zarathustra is not only the hero; he is also the advocate of the hero: "By my love and hope I beseech you: do not throw away the hero in your soul! Hold holy your highest hope!" (TSZ, p. 156).

Who is Zarathustra? What most fundamentally distinguishes him? In *Ecce Homo*, Nietzsche explains that he uses the name because his Zarathustra is precisely the opposite of the Persian Zarathustra (Zoroaster). Speaking of the Persian Zarathustra, Nietzsche says: "He was the first to consider the fight of good and evil the very wheel in the machinery of things: the transposition of morality into the metaphysical realm, as a force, cause, and end in itself, is *his* work. . . . Zarathustra created this most calamitous error, morality; consequently he must also be the first to recognize the error" (EH, p. 327).

Why? Why is it that the one who created morality (as metaphysics) must be the one who recognizes it as error and destroys it? The reason is that morality is not destroyed by anything external but only by itself. That is to say, it promotes the ideal of truthfulness until finally the lie involved in that ideal becomes unbearable: morality destroys itself, is its own self-overcoming. Speaking of himself, Nietzsche says: "Am I understood? The self-overcoming of morality, out of truthfulness; the self-overcoming of the moralist, into his opposite—into me—that is what the name of Zarathustra means in my mouth" (EH, p. 784).

Accordingly, Zarathustra's situation is the point where the moral ideal comes to self-negation, self-overcoming. In other words, his situation is that of nihilism. That is why Zarathustra says the greatest experience one can have is the "hour of the great contempt" (TSZ, p. 125), the time when one is able to condemn radically one's happiness, reason, virtue. Yet Zarathustra is not only the embodiment of nihilism. He is also the bringer of a counterideal, such as has been entirely lacking hitherto.

In what way does Zarathustra bring a counterideal? —By being the teacher of the eternal recurrence. That is the most fundamental answer to the question, "Who is Zarathustra?" He is the teacher of the eternal recurrence. Accordingly, the idea of the eternal recurrence is the fundamental conception of *Thus Spoke Zarathustra*. In the section "On the convalescent," Zarathustra's animals proclaim: "For your animals know well, O Zarathustra, who you are and must become: behold, *you are the teacher of the eternal recurrence*—that is your destiny" (TSZ, p. 332). Zarathustra *is* the teacher of the eternal recurrence. But he also must *become* this teacher—that is, he must become who he is. *Thus Spoke Zarathustra* is the drama of Zarathustra's becoming who he is, the drama of his homecoming.

Many questions arise here, ones we should perhaps let remain open for now. What kind of teaching is this? Is it a new conception of the cosmos? or of man? Or is it perhaps not a conception at all in the usual sense? How is this teaching to be taught by Zarathustra? What form does the teaching take? Most striking is that Zarathustra does not teach it by providing a "clear" exposition and proof. Instead, he teaches by means of a "return of language to the nature of imagery." Also, his teaching takes the form of a tragedy that is also a comedy. Why? What does this idea have to do with tragedy and comedy? Furthermore, to whom does Zarathustra teach his teaching? Does he indeed teach it first to himself? But how can he, unless he already knows it? What is required in order to be taught this teaching? Finally, what does this teaching, which is scarcely mentioned in early parts of the book, have to do with the many other matters Zarathustra speaks of, such as marriage, women, children, values, creation, and knowledge?

F. Images in the Prologue.

Let us begin by considering some of the images occurring in the Prologue.

1. Home. The very first words of the Prologue are these: "When Zarathustra was thirty years old, he left his home and the lake of his home and went into the mountains" (TSZ, p. 121). The image of home points to *Thus Spoke Zarathustra* as a drama of homecoming. This drama begins with Zarathustra *leaving* home, because at home he experienced the most profound homelessness.

2. Solitude. "Here he enjoyed his spirit and his solitude and for ten years did not tire of them" (TSZ, p. 121). The image of solitude indicates a man without God, man in the condition of utter nihilism.

3. Dawn. "But at last a change come over his heart, and one morning he rose with the dawn, stepped before the sun, and spoke to it" (TSZ, p. 121). The image of the dawn, which in *Ecce Homo* is identified with revaluation, signifies the bringing of a counterideal, namely, the teaching of the eternal recurrence.

4. Sun. The image of the sun is linked to the sun of Plato and represents the metaphysical. Yet the sun addressed by Zarathustra is one that goes "behind the sea" and "brings light to the underworld" (TSZ, p. 122), that is, to the cave. Also, the sun is connected to Apollo. "Phoebus," one of the epithets of this god, means "brilliant," "shining," and Apollo was considered the sun god. Zarathustra proposes to imitate the sun. Thus the Apollinian is brought into play right from the beginning.

5. Eagle and serpent. Zarathustra's animals are the eagle (image of pride) and the serpent (image of wisdom). At the end of the Prologue, these animals give Zarathustra his first sign of the eternal recurrence: the eagle flies in circles with the serpent wound around him in a circle. Zarathustra says: "May my animals lead me!" His animals are to lead him to become who he is, namely, the teacher of the eternal recurrence. How are the animals able to do this? Is it perhaps because, as Zarathustra says, they "have innocence" (TSZ, p. 166)?

6. Earth. There is an additional image at least as important as the foregoing. It is the image of the earth. When Zarathustra appears as the teacher of the overman, he says: "Behold, I teach you the overman. The overman is the meaning of the earth. Let your will say: the overman *shall* be the meaning of the earth! I beseech you, my brothers, remain true to the earth, and do not believe those who speak to you of otherworldly hopes!" (TSZ, p. 125). This image of the earth occurs again in the Prologue: "I love those who do not first seek behind the stars for a reason to go under and be a sacrifice, but who sacrifice themselves for the earth, that the earth may some day become the overman's" (TSZ, p. 127).

This image harbors two main issues. First, the earth is contrasted with the "other world," the metaphysical world. We have already referred to the passage in *Twilight of the Idols* where Nietzsche tells "how the true world finally became a fable." The passage stresses that the abolition of the true world does not leave the earth untouched: "The true world—we have abolished it. What world has remained? The apparent one perhaps? But no! With the true world we have also abolished the apparent one" (TI, p. 486). The point is that as long as the other world is taken as the "true world," then this world, the earth, is understood in terms of it, namely, as a mere shadow of it. But once the other world is abolished, this world is no longer an "apparent" one. The earth is "set free" but thereby also becomes a problem. As we heard the madman ask: "What did we do when we unchained this earth from its sun? Whither is it moving now? . . . Is there any up or down remaining? Are we not straying as through an infinite nothing?" With the destruction of the metaphysical world, that is, with the advent of nihilism, the earth is set free, set loose, and thereby deprived of coordinates such as up or down. In other words, the domain of the sensible becomes problematic in a radically new way.

The passage from *Twilight of the Idols* about the true world becoming a fable concludes as follows: "Noon; moment of the briefest shadow; end of the longest error; high point of humanity; *incipit Zarathustra*" (TI, p. 486). Accordingly, *Thus Spoke Zarathustra* begins with the unchaining of the earth from the sun, with the setting free of the earth. And Zarathustra himself begins by beseeching men to remain true to the earth and by proclaiming the meaning the earth is to have: "The overman shall be the meaning of the earth." So the revaluation does not replace God with man but with the earth: "Once the sin against God was the greatest sin; but God died, and these sinners died with him. To sin against the earth is now the most dreadful thing" (TSZ, p. 125).

The second main issue regarding the image of the earth can be seen in Zarathustra's speaking of modern man's ground, which "is still rich enough" but someday will be "poor and domesticated." Zarathustra goes on: "I say unto you that one must still have chaos in oneself to be capable of giving birth to a dancing star" (TSZ, p. 129). This expresses something about the earth, not as such, but as it is in man, as man's ground. Man's ground must be chaos. But what is that chaotic ground which bursts forth so as to generate something which shimmers like a dancing star? *The Birth of Tragedy* called it the Dionysian. So, if Apollo enters in the image of the sun, Dionysus enters in the image of the earth.

G. First stage of homecoming: the camel.

Thus Spoke Zarathustra is the drama of Zarathustra's homecoming. This involves three stages, presented in the Prologue in terms of homelessness, solitude in the mountains, and return from the mountains. Zarathustra has already passed through the initial two stages when the work opens, but much of the First Part is a reiteration of the three stages. They are presented in the opening section of First Part in the images of camel, lion, and child and again in the last section of that Part in the images of high noon, evening, and new morning.

The image of the camel involves two related senses. First, it signifies the stage at which mankind is loaded down with a burden. Historically, it is the entire era of morality and religion, an era that is only now coming to an end. But, second, this stage is not merely a past era of history at which the philosopher can gaze without being involved in it himself. It is a past still flowing within him: "Not only the reason of millennia, but their madness too breaks out in us. It is dangerous to be an heir" (TSZ, p. 189).

Granted that the philosopher is already involved in the past, how should he relate to it? He must, as we already saw, "overcome the past in himself." Yet if he is to overcome it, he—unlike the men of that era—must feel the burden *as* a burden. The philosopher must take on what is most difficult, must shoulder the full weight of the burden of morality and religion. So the philosopher is a camel in a different sense than were all previous men: whereas they were loaded down with the burden without feeling its weight (that is, without recognizing it as a burden), the philosopher takes on the burden of feeling this burden in its full weight.

Thus the image of the camel portrays simultaneously the first stage of mankind and the first stage of philosophy (that is, the first stage of Zarathustra's becoming who he is). It is primarily with respect to philosophy that Zarathustra describes the burden in the first section. He asks: What is most difficult? One answer he suggests is: "parting from our cause when it triumphs" (TSZ, p. 138). The reference is presumably to the cause of Wagnerian music, which Nietzsche championed in *The Birth of Tragedy* as bringing about a new beginning, an overcoming of nihilism. By abandoning this cause (recognizing that Wagnerian music is itself nihilistic), Nietzsche came to experience more profoundly the weight of the burden and the difficulty of throwing it off. Another difficult thing is "being sick and sending home the comforters and making friends with the deaf, who never hear what you want" (TSZ, p. 138).

The initial sections of the First Part deal primarily with the stage of the camel.

1. "On the teachers of virtue." They are distinguished by the fact that they speak well of sleep; from them one can learn to sleep well. That is to say, from them one learns to escape from waking life; one stays awake only in order to be able to sleep (just as the Christian endures this life only for the sake of the next). Furthermore, the best sleep is "without dreams." It is sleep in which all bonds to waking life are severed, sleep from which even Apollo (the dream god) is banished. So from these teachers one learns to escape from life. How does one make this escape? "And when night comes I guard well against calling sleep. For sleep, the master of the virtues, does not want to be called. Instead, I think about what I have done and thought during the day.... Weighing such matters and rocked by forty thoughts, I am suddenly overcome by sleep, the uncalled, the master of the virtues.... Verily, on soft soles he comes to me, the dearest of thieves, and steals my thoughts" (TSZ, p. 141). So how are those who learn from the teachers of virtue led into sleep? —Not directly, but by musing on the past. A certain way of being related to the past, to time, is at the root of the escape.

Zarathustra, having listened to the teachers of virtue, then draws his conclusion: "Their time is up. And not for long will they stand like this: soon they will lie down. Blessed are the sleepy ones, for they shall soon drop off" (TSZ, p. 142).

Zarathustra does not elaborate, but we recall from the Prologue that he is one of those whom these men avoid, for he stays awake at night: "He was used to walking at night and loved to look in the face of all that slept" (TSZ, p. 134).

2. "On the afterworldly." This section begins by bringing the philosopher's (rather than mankind's) peculiar experience of the burden into prominence: "At one time Zarathustra, too, cast his delusion beyond man, like all the afterworldly" (TSZ, p. 142). Immediately, however, Nietzsche introduces the ironic twist that distinguishes Zarathustra from the afterworldly. The afterworld projected by Zarathustra is not that of the afterworldly; it is not a perfect being that would represent a "counterconcept," an opposite, of life. What Zarathustra projects is not a God standing beyond time and beyond suffering. Zarathustra is more consistent: rather than projecting a God who is the opposite of the conditions that impelled man to create him, Zarathustra projects a God who mirrors the human condition that gave rise to the projection. What Zarathustra projects is a God who resembles the primal will of *The Birth of Tragedy*, a suffering and tortured God who created the world in order to look away from himself and to experience a kind of oblivion, a drunken joy. So it is human suffering that is the root of the afterworld. But it is not simply suffering: "It was suffering *and* incapacity that created all afterworlds" (TSZ, p. 143). It is suffering and the incapacity for overcoming it that constitute the origin of the afterworld: "Weariness that wants to reach the ultimate with one leap, with one fatal leap, a poor ignorant weariness that does not want to want any more: this created all gods and afterworlds" (TSZ, p. 143).

Such is the man who is overcome by suffering, who is like the "preachers of death." They "encounter a sick man or an old man or a corpse, and immediately they say, 'Life is refuted'" (TSZ, p. 157). This man no longer wants to want, to will, to live; in the face of suffering, he is unable to affirm life.

Zarathustra has lived through all this but has done so to the point of having overcome it. He has overcome his suffering: "What happened, my brothers? I overcame myself, the sufferer; I carried my own ashes to the mountains; I invented a brighter flame for myself. And behold, then this ghost fled from me" (TSZ, p. 143). Zarathustra overcame his suffering—the ghost (God, the afterworld) fled, disappeared. Zarathustra learned a new pride, the one of remaining true to the earth. He learned a new will—the will that affirms life in the face of suffering, that affirms and loves even the suffering—the will capable of *amor fati*: "A new pride my ego taught me, and this I teach men: no longer to bury one's head in the sand of heavenly things, but to bear it freely, an earthly head, which creates a meaning for the earth. A new will I teach men: to *will* this way which man has walked blindly, and to affirm it, and no longer to sneak away from it like the sick and decaying" (TSZ, p. 144).

3. "On the despisers of the body." Zarathustra speaks of those who suffer but are unable to overcome their suffering: they are in a condition of not being able to get over their suffering. Rather than overcoming it, "having done with it," their memory of it becomes "a festering wound." This condition is one of *resentment*. Unable to come to terms with their suffering, they vent their resentment on something else. They see in the body the source or locus of the suffering, and it is against their body that they turn. They become despisers of the body.

In contrast, Zarathustra *advocates* the body. Consciousness (soul, the "little reason"), which in these men turns against the body, is not something autonomous, not master of itself. Instead, there is something beneath the surface of consciousness, something Zarathustra calls "the prompter of its concepts," the "great reason"—namely, the body. "An instrument of your body is also your little reason, my brothers, which you call 'spirit,' a little instrument and toy of your great reason" (TSZ, p. 146). It is the "great reason" that *prompts*, is at the root of, the despiser's resentment. The body is turned against itself: "Even in your folly and contempt, you despisers of the body, you serve your self [your great reason]. I say unto you: your self itself wants to die and turns away from life. It is no longer capable of what it would do above all else: create beyond itself" (TSZ, p. 147).

What are we to understand here by "body"? We can say at least that just as the earth is freed from being regarded as a shadow of the otherworld, so the body is freed from being understood negatively in terms of the soul—for example, as the prison of the soul. Only with the death of God does the body actually become a problem in its own right. When Nietzsche speaks here of the body, he is not proposing a simple materialism, for that would merely invert the metaphysical order. Instead, he calls the body the "great reason." The problematic character of the body is also indicated at the very beginning of this section: "'Body am I, and soul'—thus speaks the child. And why should one not speak like children? But the awakened and the knowledgeable say: body am I entirely, and nothing else; soul is only a word for something about the body" (TSZ, p. 146). Which of these is Zarathustra? The old saint says that Zarathustra "has become a child" (indeed the final stage is the child) and that Zarathustra "is an awakened one" (TSZ, p. 123).

* * *

To return to the image of the camel, we see that this beast of burden represents the first stage of mankind, in which man is encumbered with a heavy load and life is turned against itself. At bottom, Nietzsche finds here resentment and, associated with it, a relation of man to time and to suffering. It is clear that in the case of the philosopher, the stage of the camel is necessary: "The difficult and the most difficult are what his strength demands" (TSZ, p. 137). Yet, with respect to mankind as a whole, one could easily receive the impression that this stage was only a disastrous error which would better have been avoided. But that is not so. This stage was necessary for man to become what he is. Accordingly, Nietzsche says: "Even the blunders of life have their own meaning and value" (EH, p. 710).

Indeed the first stage was based on errors, but only through those errors has man become what he is: "Without the errors which lie in the assumption of morality, man would have remained an animal" (HATH, vol. I, §40). Or again, Nietzsche says: "It seems that all great things first have to bestride the earth in monstrous and frightening masks in order to inscribe themselves in the hearts of humanity with eternal demands" (BGE, pp. 192–93). Finally, according to Nietzsche:

> Man has been bound with many chains in order that he might forget to comport himself like an animal. And indeed he has become more gentle, more intellectual, more joyous, and more meditative than any animal. But now he still suffers from having worn his chains so long, having been so long without pure air and free movement. These chains, however, are, as I keep repeating, the ponderous and significant errors of moral, religious, and metaphysical ideas. Only when the disease of these chains is overcome is the first great goal reached—the separation of man from the brute. At present we stand in the midst of our work of removing the chains. (HATH, vol. II, pt. 2, §350)

H. Second stage of homecoming: the lion.

At the beginning of *Thus Spoke Zarathustra*, we are told that Zarathustra left his home and went into solitude. In other words, homecoming, the way to the overman, leads through solitude. Yet solitude is not simply one step along the way; instead, it pertains to the entire way as such. Nietzsche indicates that in *Ecce Homo*: "My humanity is a constant self-overcoming. But I need solitude—which is to say, recovery, return to myself, the breath of a free, light, playful air. My whole *Zarathustra* is a dithyramb on solitude or, if I have been understood, on *cleanliness*" (EH, p. 689).

Thus Spoke Zarathustra is a dithyramb, a hymn to Dionysus. It is a Dionysian celebration of solitude (return to self), which requires cleanliness—that is to say, it requires that one cleanse, purify, oneself of all the delusions and mistakes that "still dwell in our body" (TSZ, p. 189). *Thus Spoke Zarathustra* is a Dionysian purification rite.

In different terms, the flight into solitude involves throwing off the burden with which man (as camel) has been loaded down. At its simplest level, that burden is the moral ideal, and to throw it off requires that one fully appropriate the death of God. The flight into solitude is a flight into nihilism. Yet also, as we have already begun to see, there is something else more fundamental than the moral ideal, something providing the ground for it, namely, man's relation to time.

So, at a more fundamental level, the load needing to be thrown off is the burden of time itself. This would require a new relation to time, and that relation is what is at issue in Zarathustra's fundamental teaching, the eternal recurrence.

To throw off the burden is to become light: "Butterflies and soap bubbles and whatever in man is of their kind seem to know most about happiness" (TSZ, p. 153). Furthermore, to become light is to be able to dance: "I would believe only in a god who could dance.... Now I am light, now I fly, now I see myself beneath myself, now a god dances through me" (TSZ, p. 153).

It is with the stage of the lion that the burden is thrown off and there occurs a flight into solitude. We need to ask: (1) How is spirit able to throw off the burden so as to become a lion? (2) What is the task confronting the lion? (3) What are the dangers confronting the lion? (4) How is spirit led to the final metamorphosis, from lion to child?

1. How to become a lion.

We have seen that the first stage, at which man is laden with the burden of the moral ideal, was necessary in order for man to become more than a pack animal. As Nietzsche summarizes in *The Will to Power*, "We ought to be most profoundly thankful for what morality has done hitherto, but now it is no more than a burden which may prove fatal" (WP, §404).

Nietzsche says with respect to the philosopher, who must take on this burden and feel its weight, that it is what the philosopher's *strength* demands. The question is: How does it happen that man, having been laden with the burden, is not simply exhausted by it but rather eventually is made capable of throwing it off? How does it happen that, by having borne the burden, he gains the strength to throw it off? In what way was man formed by the burden so as finally to gain this strength?

We have already seen a general answer to this question in our consideration of the Christian-moral ideal. This ideal involves an inherent negativity, expressed succinctly in a section called "On priests." According to Zarathustra: "As corpses they meant to live" (TSZ, p. 204). In other words, the priests affirmed life, they made it livable, they escaped the pessimism of Silenus, only by negating life, only by turning against it, only by positing God as the "counter-concept to life" and the moral ideal as the denial of life. Eventually, however, this negativity becomes explicit. Zarathustra says, again talking about priests: "Once when the sea cast them about, they thought they were landing on an island; but behold, it was a sleeping monster. False values and delusive words: these are the worst monsters for mortals. Long does calamity sleep and wait in them. But eventually it comes and wakes and eats and devours whatever built huts upon it" (TSZ, p. 203).

This says that the effect of the inherent negativity is the ideal eventually coming to negate itself. That is the self-overcoming of morality. It is to this self-negation, which in our age has become explicit, that Zarathustra refers in speaking of "Preachers of death": "'Life is only suffering,' others say, and they do not lie. See to it, then, that *you* cease! See to it, then, that the life which is only suffering ceases!" (TSZ, p. 157).

Zarathustra also refers to the specific way the self-negation takes place. In "On enjoying and suffering the passions," he speaks of the *necessary* war among the virtues, of jealousy among the virtues: "Virtues too can perish of jealousy. Surrounded by the flame of jealousy, a person will in the end, like the scorpion, turn his poisonous sting against himself. Alas, my brother, have you never yet seen a virtue deny and stab itself? Man is something that must be overcome; therefore you shall love your virtues, for you will perish of them" (TSZ, p. 149).

This passage is referring especially to truthfulness. It is a virtue erected as an ideal, but precisely thereby we come eventually to the point where we can no longer tolerate the lie involved in the ideal, namely, the lie in the denial that lies are necessary for life. So the effect of the ideal is to give the man under it the very means of negating it, of overcoming it. That is why the philosopher needs to take on the burden and feel its full weight. Thereby he obtains the means for throwing it off. Yet, for moral man to overcome the ideal is to overcome himself, to overcome man, to move in a direction beyond man toward the overman, to *go under* as man. For moral man, it means to die, and everything depends on one's dying, as Zarathustra says, at the right time (TSZ, p. 183).

2. The task of the lion.

Once the strength is gained for throwing off the burden, the camel has changed into the lion. What is the task confronting him? His task is to carry through the radical destruction of the ideal, that is, to free himself entirely from it. He sets out to *fight* his last god.

According to Nietzsche, "the free man is a warrior" (TI, p. 542). The lion is the warrior portrayed in "On war and warriors," the one who is "forerunner" (and so is not the final stage) of "the saints of knowledge" (TSZ, p. 159). The lion sets out to fight the "great dragon": "Who is the great dragon that the spirit will no longer call lord or god? 'Thou shalt' is the name of the great dragon. But the spirit of the lion says, 'I will.' 'Thou shalt' lies in his way, sparkling like gold, an animal covered with scales; and on every scale shines a golden 'thou shalt.' Values, thousands of years old, shine on these scales" (TSZ, p. 138).

The lion's task is to destroy those values which take the form of a "thou shalt," that is, the values imposed on man as a command. He does this for the sake of an "I will." Yet he only prepares the way for the "I will"; he does not achieve it. "To a good warrior, 'thou shalt' sounds more agreeable than 'I will'" (TSZ, p. 160). Even though the lion finds only illusion in the old "thou shalt," he is still not at the level of the "I will." He still receives his highest thought as a "thou shalt." Zarathustra says: "Your love of life shall be love of your highest hope; and your highest hope shall be the highest thought of life. Your highest thought, however, you should receive as a command from me—and it is: man is something that shall be overcome" (TSZ, p. 160).

3. Dangers.

There are two principal dangers confronting the lion. He is able to contend with the first. But the second surpasses his ability and requires a final metamorphosis.

The first danger derives from the fact that the lion's "No-saying" is not accomplished simply by his rejection of the Christian God and Christian morality. We saw this portrayed in the response of those who heard the madman: at first they laughed and joked, then they stared at him in amazement, although none of them believed in God. So more is required for the No-saying than mere atheism. In *On the Genealogy of Morals*, Nietzsche insists that even atheism is no antithesis to the ascetic idea but "only one of the latest phases of its evolution" (GM, p. 596). The reason is that the ascetic ideal has been so built into the foundations of our culture and into ourselves that only the greatest effort can suffice to free us: "Alas, all this delusion and all these mistakes still dwell in our body; they have there become body and will" (TSZ, p. 188).

In order to free ourselves from the moral ideal, we must free ourselves from ourselves, overcome ourselves: we must die. Nietzsche says that in order for a man to gain this freedom from what determines the current epoch, "He must first of all 'overcome' this epoch in himself" (GS, §380). That is the task of becoming untimely.

Therefore, it does not suffice merely to renounce Christian religion and its morality. Speaking of the Church, Nietzsche says: "Today it alienates rather than seduces. Which of us would be a free spirit if the Church did not exist? It is the Church and not its poison that repels us. Apart from the Church, we, too, love the poison" (GM, p. 472). The "No-sayer" must free himself from the poison also, from the "shadows of God."

When the support of the ascetic ideal (that is, God) comes to be removed, the needs that created it (ultimately, the incapacity of the sufferer) do not simply disappear: "It seems to me that the religious instinct is indeed in the process of growing powerfully—but the theistic satisfaction is refused with deep suspicion" (BGE, p. 256). The needs, however, continue to be served by the various instruments forged by the ascetic ideal, instruments still "hanging on" after the death of God.

Zarathustra names some of these "shadows of God":

(i) In "On chastity," Zarathustra points to the slaying of the senses, and to this he opposes the "innocence of the senses" (TSZ, p. 166).

(ii) Zarathustra refers to the "love of the neighbor" and says it is actually "your bad love of yourselves. You flee to your neighbor from yourselves and would like to make a virtue out of that. But I see through your 'selflessness'" (TSZ, p. 172).

(iii) Zarathustra points to work, the so-called blessings of work. "All of you to whom furious work is dear, as is whatever is fast, new, and strange, you find it difficult to bear yourselves; your industriousness is escape and the will to forget yourselves" (TSZ, p. 158).

Not only do instruments like these continue to operate, but man easily comes to attach himself to substitutes for God, new idols able to provide support for man's own self-negation. Foremost among the new idols is the state. Nietzsche says the state is a "sin against customs and rights." He contrasts the state with a people (*Volk*): "It was creators who created peoples and hung a faith and a love over them: thus the creators served life. It is annihilators who set traps for the many and call these traps the 'state': the annihilators hang a sword and a hundred appetites over the many" (TSZ, pp. 160–61). Zarathustra says of the state: "Everything about it is false" (TSZ, p. 161).

Culture is another, connected, idol. For Nietzsche, "culture is, before all things, the unity of artistic style in every expression of the life of a people." But such a unity of style requires creators who configure a people and hang over them, as Zarathustra says, their "tongue of good and evil" (TSZ, p. 161). It requires men who do not either just enslave ("hang a sword") or merely satisfy the appetites of the populace without configuring a coherent culture. It requires something other than technocrats who do nothing but find ways of satisfying people's appetites.

The principal way a unity of artistic style is concretely established (and a people formed) is by institutions. A section of *Twilight of the Idols* is called "Critique of modernity." Nietzsche's critique is that modern man is not capable of genuine institutions, has lost "the instincts out of which institutions grow."

> In order that there may be institutions, a kind of will is necessary, an instinct or imperative, one which is anti-liberal to the point of malice: the will to tradition, to authority, to responsibility for centuries to come, to the solidarity of chains of generations, forward and backward *ad infinitum*. When this will is present, something like the *imperium Romanum* is founded. . . . The whole of the West no longer possesses the instincts out of which institutions grow, out of which a future grows: perhaps nothing antagonizes its "modern spirit" so much. One lives for the day, very fast, very irresponsibly: precisely this is called "freedom." That which makes an institution is despised, hated, repudiated: one fears the danger of a new slavery the moment the word "authority" is even spoken out loud. (TI, p. 543)

So, to return to the main issue, various "shadows of God" linger on even after the death of God. Nietzsche asks: "When will all these shadows of God cease to deceive us?" (GS, §109). The task of the lion is to say no to all these shadows of God and become radically free of them. Yet they are so intertwined with everything around us and within us that to say no to them means to "speed into the desert," the wasteland, where there is nothing to sustain us. In other words, it is to flee into solitude.

Accordingly, in section after section, Zarathustra mentions the need for this flight. For example, in the section called "On the flies of the market place," he says: "Flee, my friend, into your solitude! I see you dazed by the noise of the great men and stung all over by the stings of the little men. . . . Where solitude ceases, the market place begins. . . . Far from the market place and from fame happens all that is great: far from the market place and from fame the inventors of new values have always dwelt. Flee, my friend, into your solitude" (TSZ, p. 163).

Or again, in Zarathustra's celebration of friendship over against love of the neighbor, solitude is the real issue. As regards love of neighbor, "Your bad love of yourselves turns your solitude into a prison" (TSZ, p. 173). But friendship, rather than being an escape from solitude, is rather in service to it: "Are you pure air and *solitude* and bread and medicine for your friend?" (TSZ, p. 169). Zarathustra even says: "You would have to create your friend and his overflowing heart out of yourselves" (TSZ, p. 173).

Who is this friend that one would create out of oneself? Is Nietzsche speaking only of friendship in the usual sense of a relation between two people, or is something quite different the more fundamental issue here? Who is this friend one would create out of one's solitude for the sake of that solitude?

Let us review some of the curious remarks about the friend:

(i) "What is the face of your friend anyway? It is your own face in a rough and imperfect mirror" (TSZ, p. 168). So the friend is an image of oneself.

(ii) Zarathustra recommends love of the friend rather than of neighbor and characterizes love of the friend as a love of the farthest and the future, a love higher than the love directed toward human beings. So the friend is not a human being but rather is something removed, something future in which we see an image of ourselves.

(iii) The friend is not the overman; instead, he is "the festival of the earth" and "an anticipation of the overman." So the friend is something that celebrates earth *and* something that heralds the advent of the overman, calls forth the overman.

4. "I teach you the friend in whom the world stands completed, a bowl of goodness—the creating friend who always has a completed world to give away. And as the world rolled apart for him, it rolls together again in circles for him, as the becoming of the good through evil, as the becoming of purpose out of accident" (TSZ, p. 174).

What is this image that calls forth the overman, the image in which the world stands completed, that is, in which the flux of becoming is surpassed? What is this image in which becoming is surpassed without the world that has rolled apart remaining in that state or, in other terms, without the metaphysical dualism of truth and appearance? What is the image in which the world rolls together in *circles*? It is the image of the eternal recurrence. The friend is the image of the eternal recurrence.

This image is what "saves" solitude, which, as Zarathustra says, prevents the I and me from falling too deep in conversation, "prevents the conversation of the two from sinking into the depth" (TSZ, p. 168). Yet for Zarathustra at this point the friend remains a ghost to which he still must give *his* flesh and bones: "This ghost that runs after you, my brother, is more beautiful than you; why do you not give him your flesh and your bones?" (TSZ, p. 173).

* * *

We arrive now at the second danger confronting the lion, the danger that surpasses the powers of the lion. Nietzsche says that even the liberated spirit—even the man freed from the shadows of God—must still "purify himself." What is this purification rite, and why is it necessary? In "Of the tree on the mountainside," Nietzsche indicates the danger from which the purification rite is meant to deliver man: "But this is not the danger of the noble man, that he might become one of the good, but a churl, a mocker, a destroyer. Alas, I knew noble men who lost their highest hope. Then they slandered all high hopes. Then they lived impudently in brief pleasures and barely cast their goals beyond the day. . . . Do not throw away the hero in your soul! Hold holy your highest hope!" (TSZ, p. 156).

The same is presented in different terms in "On the way of the creator." However essential it is to free oneself from God and his shadows, this freedom *from* is insufficient. It must become the way to a new freedom *for*:

> Alas, there are so many great thoughts which do no more than a bellows. They puff up and make emptier. You call yourself free? Your dominant thought I want to hear, not that you have escaped from a yoke. Are you one of those who had the *right* to escape from a yoke? There are some who threw away their last value when they threw away their servitude. Free *from* what? As if that mattered to Zarathustra! But your eyes should tell me brightly: free *for* what? Can you give yourself your own evil and your own good and hang your own will over yourself as a law? (TSZ, p. 175)

In order to see the genuine issue here, let us return to the question of solitude and try to grasp it more fundamentally. In *The Gay Science*, as already noted, Nietzsche explicitly connects solitude with the death of God: "For a pious man, there is no solitude—we, the godless, have been the first to invent it." So, with the death of God, man is able to be really alone with himself.

This aloneness means, most fundamentally, that in the experience of the death of God, man discovers the all-too-human roots of everything previously taken to be transcendent: the moral ideal, the metaphysical world, every thing-in-itself. That is to say, man experiences the destruction of all transcendence. He comes to see the transcendent as merely *posited* by man himself. Hence, man is radically alone: "Only man places values in things, and he does so in order to preserve himself. He alone created a meaning for things, a human meaning" (TSZ, p. 171).

Yet if man creates the meaning of things (creates even the concept of thing) in order to preserve himself, then these meanings do not actually belong to the things and thus are not truths but rather lies which man forgets are lies. They are false. That is the conclusion threatening the lion: "But the time will come when solitude will make you weary, when your pride will double up and your courage gnash its teeth. And you will cry, 'I am alone!' . . . Even what seems sublime to you will frighten you like a ghost. And you will cry, 'All is false!' There are feelings which want to kill the lonely. And if they do not succeed? Well, then they themselves must die. But are you capable of this—to be a murderer?" (TSZ, p. 175).

The danger is that man will be brought to radical skepticism and that in its wake man will cease to create beyond himself, will become eventually the last man, whose ground is poor and is domesticated. So these feelings must die, the ground must be preserved. What is this murder that must be committed if the lion is to withstand the threat? It is a murder producing the kind of death Zarathustra describes in the section "On free death": "Thus I want to die myself that you, my friends, may for my sake love the earth more; and to earth I want to return that I may find rest in her who gave birth to me" (TSZ, p. 185).

It is a death that is a return to the earth. For, as Zarathustra tells the youth in "Of the tree on the mountainside": "The more man aspires to the height and light, the more strongly do his roots strive earthward, downward, into the dark, the deep—into evil" (TSZ, p. 154). This death, however, like every free death, is for the sake of life. Thus it is at the same time a birth—the birth of a child: "The child is innocence and forgetting, a new beginning, a game [play], a self-propelled wheel, a first movement, a sacred 'Yes.' For the game [play] of creation, my brothers, a sacred 'Yes' is needed: the spirit now wills its own will" (TSZ, p. 139).

With the birth of the child, the spirit wills its own will in such a way as to return to the earth. In other words, with the birth of the child, solitude is redeemed in the love of the eternal recurrence. It is to this "new beginning" that we must now turn.

I. Final stage of homecoming: the child.

In the section "On the famous wise men," Zarathustra says: "Spirit is the life that itself cuts into life. With its own agony it increases its own knowledge. . . . You know only the spark of the spirit, but you do not see the anvil it is nor the cruelty of its hammer" (TSZ, p. 216). Nietzsche portrays the way of spirit in the image of the three metamorphoses. We have seen at the stages of the camel and lion how life itself "cuts into life." In both cases, the "agony" ("death") is related to the self-negation of the moral ideal: the agony of taking on and feeling its full weight and the agony of throwing it off and having to flee into the desert, into solitude. We arrive now at the final metamorphosis: the birth of the child.

Zarathustra says: "To be a child who is newly born, the creator must also want to be the mother who gives birth and be the pangs of the birth-giver" (TSZ, p. 199). The question is: How, in the birth of the child, does life cut into life? What is the agony here? And how, through this agony, does spirit increase its knowledge?

The birth of the child is not just one issue among others—it is *the* issue of *Thus Spoke Zarathustra*, and all others are subordinated to it. That is indicated, externally, by what happens at the beginning, middle, and end of the work: at each of these crucial places, Zarathustra is related to a child. At the beginning, the old saint describes Zarathustra as a child. At the end of the Second Part, Zarathustra is told by his "stillest hour" that he must "yet become as a child." And the Fourth Part ends with Zarathustra proclaiming that his children are near.

More importantly, there is an internal connection between the character of *Thus Spoke Zarathustra* as a tragedy and the fact that its central issue is the birth of the child. Such is already indicated by the title of Nietzsche's first book, which names the theme as the *birth* of tragedy out of the spirit of music. In other words, tragedy has to do with birth—so that to speak of tragedy requires speaking of its birth and of that from which it is born. It is even clearer in Nietzsche's account of tragedy: most fundamentally, for Nietzsche, tragedy is the play of creation and destruction, of tearing down and building up, of birth and death. It is the play of a birth to which death belongs integrally. In the terms of *Thus Spoke Zarathustra*, it is a play that is both a going-over and a going-under. So the image of the birth of a child expresses the essence of tragedy. Accordingly, *Thus Spoke Zarathustra*, as a play on the birth of a child, not only is a tragedy but also enacts the essence of tragedy; it is a tragedy about tragedy. So, to interpret the final metamorphosis is to interpret *Thus Spoke Zarathustra* as a whole. The birth of the child will be our sole theme from this point on.

Let us now try to gain a more adequate view of the whole, taking our departure from our previous characterizations. *Thus Spoke Zarathustra* is a tragedy. But it is not simply a tragedy; instead, it involves some curious dualities. In the first place, it is also a work of philosophy and indeed is the entrance hall to Nietzsche's entire philosophy. And it not only *is* a tragedy but also brings to light the essence of tragedy. Furthermore, it attains a certain distance from tragedy in the usual sense, the distance necessary in order to be able to laugh at tragedy. So it is not only a tragedy but also a comedy.

In its simplest form, this duality appears in the fact that what is at issue (birth of a child) is both spoken about and enacted (undergone). That is to say, *Thus Spoke Zarathustra* incorporates two interrelated dimensions: word and deed. We must now clarify the main articulations in each of these dimensions.

We will begin with what is *said* about the child. Several different levels of speech are involved:

1. A play of images, much of which is allegorical: for example, the three metamorphoses.
2. Songs sung at crucial junctures in the Second, Third, and Fourth Parts. The songs are especially important inasmuch as tragedy is born out of the spirit of music.
3. Dreams and their interpretations—for instance, "The child with the mirror" (TSZ, pp. 195-97) and "The soothsayer" (TSZ, pp. 245-49). These are important since tragedy is related to dreams and to the dream god, Apollo.
4. Theoretical formulations given in *Thus Spoke Zarathustra*, which, however, always retain a close connection with the dramatic character and image-play of the work.
5. Formulations of the same issues at a more strictly theoretical level in other works, especially in *The Will to Power*. These formulations, however, are problematic in view of the destruction of Socratism announced in *The Birth of Tragedy*.

Our interpretation will begin at the level of the play of images and then will move back and forth amid these various levels. At one point (the theory of the will to power) we will need to remain for some time at the level of the theoretical formulations. Yet we must be careful not to assume that this is a "higher" level.

In addition, it is essential that our interpretation be carried out in view of the overall structure of *Thus Spoke Zarathustra*:

Prologue
{ Zarathustra left his home
{ Zarathustra went into solitude } Recalled
{ Zarathustra descends to man (at dawn)
  Zarathustra speaks:
    (1) To people in the marketplace (= last men)
    (2) To tightrope walker ("dead man"—unable to cross over—death without birth)
      Noon comes for Zarathustra (vision of the eternal recurrence in the form of his animals)

First Part
    Zarathustra seeks companions:
        (1) Speaks of three metamorphoses (camel, lion, child)
        (2) Recounts stages of camel and lion
        (3) Speaks of noon, evening, new morning
    Zarathustra returns to solitude. Anticipates two later meetings with his friends:
        (1) When they have denied him
        (2) To celebrate the great noon

Second Part
    Child comes to Zarathustra (in dream)
    Zarathustra leaves his cave (before dawn) and returns to his friends, and speaks to them
    Night comes for Zarathustra (he sings "The Night Song," "The Dancing Song," "The Tomb Song")
    Zarathustra leaves his friends ("The Stillest Hour")—must yet become a child

Third Part
    Zarathustra's wandering
    Zarathustra returns home (to his solitude)
    Zarathustra sings "The Other Dancing Song" and "The Yes and Amen Song"
    (Zarathustra loves eternity, mother of the child)

Fourth Part
    Higher men come to Zarathustra's cave
    Celebration of evening (midnight—"The Drunken Song")
    Zarathustra's morning ("My children are near")

Against this background, let us move from word to deed, that is, to the second dimension, the *enactment* of the birth of the child. We will begin with the structure of the play of images. A major factor determining that structure is the progression: from camel to lion to child. But there is not merely a single linear progression through these stages in the course of the work. Instead, the threefold progression occurs on three occasions, and these correspond to past, present, and future.

1. Past. At the beginning of the Prologue, Zarathustra is the one who goes through the stages. And the first two stages are merely recounted. The work properly begins with the initiation of the final metamorphosis; the first two stages are already past.

2. Present. In the course of the book, Zarathustra himself goes through the three stages. Noon corresponds to the end of the Prologue, night to the middle of the Second Part, and morning to the end of the Fourth Part.
3. Future. Zarathustra's companions go through the first two stages, and the work ends by looking to the future when the companions capable of the final metamorphosis will come to Zarathustra.

Thus the problem of time (and time is a problem for man because of its dispersion into three dimensions) is interwoven with that of the progression which culminates in the birth of the child.

We see this interweaving again in the First Part. Zarathustra begins by speaking of the progression as one from camel to lion to child. Then he recounts the first two stages and thus comes to the point at which the child appears on the horizon. Then (at the end of the First Part, after the section on death) Zarathustra presents the same progression but in different terms, in temporal terms: noon, evening, morning. In fact, the question of the birth of the child and the question of time are not merely interwoven; they are one and the same question. This sameness is already indicated dramatically in the Prologue: Zarathustra's pupil, the tightrope walker, turns out to be one who cannot cross over the rope between beast and overman; when he tries to do so he falls to his death. Accordingly, in the case of the tightrope walker, there is *mere* death, not a death from out of which something (the child) is born. Then it is exactly when Zarathustra is musing on having become a "gravedigger," on seeing only death and not birth, that the sign comes to him: in the form of his animals (eagle circling, with the serpent wound about), he obtains his first vision of the eternal recurrence. And Zarathustra says: "May my animals lead me!" It is an image of the eternal recurrence leading beyond death to the birth of the child.

Because of the repetition of the three-fold progression within *Thus Spoke Zarathustra*, the dramatic time structure of the work is complex. For example, Zarathustra himself goes through the progression twice. He has already gone through the first two stages at the beginning of the Prologue; they are already past. Then how is it that he goes through them again in the course of the work? In different terms, how is it that at the beginning of the work the stages of noon and evening are past *as well as* future for Zarathustra?

The answer is obvious: it is because noon and evening return every day. They recur; there is an eternal recurrence. Thus the structure of the work reflects the central idea: the overcoming of the difference between past and future in the vision of the eternal recurrence. Accordingly, there is an identity between the beginning and the end of the work. At both points, the child approaches against the background of the previous two stages. In other words, the work as a whole is a great circle.

Yet it is not simply a circle. Something happens in the work that is not recalled at the beginning, namely, Zarathustra's friends passing through the metamorphoses. And at the end it is not *a* child but children that approach. The end is not only Zarathustra's transformation into a child but also the metamorphosis of his friends into children.

Much of the complexity in the structure of the work derives from the way Zarathustra's own metamorphosis is intertwined with the metamorphosis of those who learn from him. This intertwining has its ground in the fact that Zarathustra is the *teacher* of the eternal recurrence. For him to become who he is, he must become this teacher. And that requires that he first teach this teaching to himself.

Not only must Zarathustra have the teaching in view (have the vision of the eternal recurrence) but also must appropriate it and let himself be transformed by the appropriation. Furthermore, to teach himself he needs to sink into conversation with himself, that is, withdraw into solitude. Thus we see in the structure of the work that each stage of metamorphosis through which Zarathustra passes is correlated with a return to solitude. In particular, this teaching of himself reaches its fulfillment in the last half of the Third Part, after Zarathustra's final return to the solitude of his cave.

Let us note again how many typically Platonic images are used here by Nietzsche—used with an inversion of their Platonic meaning. For example, Zarathustra finds solitude in his cave, whereas for Plato the cave represents the "marketplace" where solitude is impossible, at least if there is to be a just city. Also, whereas for Plato the movement from the cave is an ascent, for Nietzsche it is a descent.

Nevertheless, this descent from the cave to the marketplace is necessary, because Zarathustra is a teacher, because he must teach others: Zarathustra must descend to man. This task is expressed from the beginning: Zarathustra tells the old saint that he, Zarathustra, loves man and is bringing men a gift. Yet this gift is one that will transform man, will bring about a reversal. Already in §1 of the Prologue, Zarathustra tells the sun: "I would give away and distribute, until the wise among men find joy once again in their folly, and the poor in their riches" (TSZ, p. 122). This is even more powerfully expressed in that section ("Upon the blessed isles") of the Second Part when Zarathustra speaks to his friends: "But my fervent will to create impels me ever again toward man; thus is the hammer impelled toward the stone. O men, in the stone there sleeps an image, the image of my images. Alas, that it must sleep in the hardest, the ugliest stone!" (TSZ, p. 199). Zarathustra then goes on to tell how his hammer will chip away pieces of the stone to reveal what is most beautiful, the overman.

So Zarathustra has a dual task: to teach himself and to teach man. This duality is reflected in the continual tension between Zarathustra's ascent to the solitude of his cave and his descent to men. The tension persists until the Fourth Part. What we find then is that Zarathustra has taught others to the point that he no longer has to descend to them. Instead, they now come up to his cave and sing with him the same song he sang in his solitude at the end of the Third Part: "The drunken song."

J. The child in the First Part of *Thus Spoke Zarathustra*.

Let us now consider, at the level of the play of images, what is said about the child in the First Part. There are two primary image-plays pertaining to the child.

The first occurs in the section on the three metamorphoses. Zarathustra provides a series of images descriptive of the child, as we have already seen. The child is innocence and forgetting, a new beginning, a game, a self-propelled wheel, a first movement, a sacred "Yes." We need to consider each of the images.

1. "The child is innocence and forgetting, a new beginning." The image of a "new beginning" unites the other two images. A new beginning is a radical break with what has preceded and has come to its end. This break is portrayed in the first two images: innocence and forgetting.

The image of forgetting indicates the radical character of the break: what has preceded is not simply abandoned, but every trace of it is removed—forgotten. But what has preceded? Spirit as child has been preceded by spirit as lion and camel. Spirit has preceded itself, so that what it abolishes (forgets) is itself. Zarathustra says in "On the way of the creator": "You must wish to consume yourself in your own flames: how could you wish to become new unless you had first become ashes!" (TSZ, p. 176).

The other image, innocence, indicates what it was that determined the spirit in its previous form—what therefore needs to be forgotten—namely, morality, which loaded man down with guilt. Thus the child is to be beyond good and evil. But what was it, in turn, that determined this morality which the child must surpass? Most fundamentally, it was resentment against suffering; it was the spirit of revenge. Accordingly, Zarathustra says: "For man to be delivered from revenge, that is for me the bridge to the highest hope, a rainbow after long storms" (TSZ, p. 211). So, most fundamentally, the innocence of the child signifies deliverance from revenge.

2. A new beginning is not only a break with the old but is also the start of something new. This "something new" is expressed in the remainder of the images.

The child is a game; the child is play. The next sentence tells us what kind: a play of creation. It is as such that the child wins redemption from suffering and resentment: "Creation—that is the great redemption from suffering, a life's growing light" (TSZ, p. 199).

What is that play of creation through which one gains redemption from suffering and escapes the life-negating pessimism of Silenus? It is the creative play belonging to tragedy and intertwined with the play of destruction. Zarathustra says: "Indeed, there must be much better dying in your life, you creators" (TSZ, p. 199).

Another important passage speaking of play occurs in the section called "The great health" of *The Gay Science*. Nietzsche says: "Another ideal runs on before us, a strange, tempting ideal, full of danger . . . : the ideal of a spirit that plays naively (involuntarily and from overflowing abundance and power) with everything hitherto called holy, good, inviolable, divine" (GS, §382).

Nietzsche then goes on to say it is perhaps with this ideal of play "that the great seriousness really begins, that the real question mark is posed for the first time, that the destiny of the soul changes, the hand moves forward, the tragedy begins" (GS, §382). What is especially significant is that play (creation) is called an ideal. Accordingly, with the advent of the child, a new ideal is posed.

3. The character of this ideal is expressed by the next image: the child is a self-propelled wheel. What does the wheel refer to?

In the first place, it refers to the circle joining man's creative activity to that which he creates, that which, prior to the death of God, was taken to be beyond man, transcendent, in-itself. This relation of creator to created is a circle because the created is what provides man the foundation from which to create further. Nietzsche expresses this circle in the concept of self-overcoming.

The wheel is self-propelled because there is nothing beyond it, no in-itself, that could determine man's creative play. To take play, understood in terms of a self-propelled wheel, as an ideal is to recognize what man creates *as* something created. Thus it is to overcome the alienation of man from what he creates, the alienation fostered by the tradition, which placed beyond man a "true world," a world of the "in-itself."

For man to posit this ideal signifies his reclaiming as his own the previously unrecognized products of his creativity. It means, according to the first section of *The Gay Science*, for the comedy of existence to become conscious of itself. The First and Second Parts of *Thus Spoke Zarathustra* frequently allude to the return out of such alienation:

(i) In "On the gift-giving virtue," Zarathustra says: "Alas, there has always been so much virtue that has flown away. Lead back to the earth the virtue that flew away, as I do—back to the body, back to life, that it may give the earth a meaning, a human meaning" (TSZ, p. 188).

The "virtue that has flown away" refers to the values from which man has been alienated, which have been taken as transcendent, imposed on man, rather than understood as his own creation. Zarathustra now demands that they be led back to the earth, to life—that is, recognized as man's own creative products.

Zarathustra also demands that such virtue "give the earth a meaning." In other words, having been created by man, these values in turn reflect back on man so as to promote and enhance his creativity rather than rob him of it, as did the ascetic ideal.

(ii) The same theme is expressed in the Second Part, in "On the virtuous." Zarathustra refers to the origination of "virtue" from oneself, as one's own creation: "That your virtue is your self and not something foreign, not a skin or cloak—that is the truth from the foundation of your souls, you who are virtuous" (TSZ, p. 206).

Again Zarathustra refers to a new kind of relation to values. Values, having arisen from man, are no longer to fly away and rob man of his creativity but are to reflect back on his creativity: "Your virtue is what is dearest to you. The thirst of the ring lives in you: every ring strives and turns to reach itself again" (TSZ, p. 206).

(iii) Finally, in the Second Part, in "Upon the blessed isles," Zarathustra takes up the same theme: "God is a conjecture; but I desire that your conjectures should not reach beyond your creative will. Could you *create* a god? Then do not speak to me of any gods" (TSZ, p. 197). The demand here is that what is created be recognized *as* created and be created accordingly: "And what you have called world, that shall be created only by you. Your reason, your image, your will, your love shall thus be realized" (TSZ, p. 198). So we can understand why Zarathustra says in the last part of the characterization of the child: "He who had been lost to the world now conquers his own world" (TSZ, p. 139).

The new ideal expressed in the images of the play of creation and the self-propelled wheel is not simply a new set of values to be posited in place of the old set. Instead, the new ideal is *the positing itself* (the play). In "On the thousand and one goals," Zarathustra says: "To esteem [evaluate] is to create. Hear this, you creators! Esteeming is itself of all esteemed things the most estimable treasure" (TSZ, p. 171). Such creating play, such "evaluating," is exactly what Nietzsche calls will to power. And thus he says of the child: the spirit now wills its own will.

The child is a "first movement." Of what? —Presumably of that self-propelled wheel Zarathustra has just mentioned. With the advent of the child, the self-propelled wheel is set in motion for the first time (in its proper motion). Yet, if the wheel is self-propelled, why is it necessary for it to be *set* in motion? To say it is self-propelled means that what is created provides the foundation for further creative activity. That is what Nietzsche is referring to in speaking of man creating "beyond himself"—that is, man creating beyond that creation he has already given to himself as a foundation.

Nietzsche says, however, that the great danger of nihilism is that man will cease to create beyond himself: "All beings so far have created something beyond themselves. Do you want to be the ebb of this great flood?" (TSZ, p. 124). Why does nihilism harbor this danger? It is because with nihilism all foundations collapse. All foundations of the kind that man has previously required disappear. The "true world" finally becomes a fable.

In terms of the image, the self-propelled wheel approaches a state of rest (which, if realized, would yield the "last man"). So something is needed in order to reinitiate its self-propelling movement. What is required is a vision of another wheel that is self-propelling, a wheel that is an image of the first wheel. What is required is another wheel whose movement can be "imparted" to the self-propelled wheel of play.

4. This other wheel is the eternal recurrence, expressed in the final image, the only one Zarathustra repeats: the child is "a sacred 'Yes.'" How does the child say "Yes" to, for example, suffering, so as to attain innocence in the sense of deliverance from that spirit of revenge which always says "No" to suffering? The child says "Yes" to the suffering by willing its eternal recurrence. In *Ecce Homo*, Nietzsche says the idea of the eternal recurrence is the "highest formula of affirmation that is at all attainable" (EH, p. 751). It is the appropriation of this "formula," the appropriation of the idea of the eternal recurrence, that brings about the new beginning, the birth of the child. Accordingly, the two issues (the birth of the child and the eternal recurrence) are one and the same.

K. Marriage and women.

In the First Part of *Thus Spoke Zarathustra*, the second play of images dealing with the child revolves around the issues of marriage and women.

The section "On child and marriage" ties marriage to the overman. "Marriage: thus I name the will of two to create the one that is more than those who created it" (TSZ, p. 182). Zarathustra then says that the will to marriage should be a longing to attain the overman. So the child is to be the overman, the one for whose sake man goes under. (Thus the next section is "On free death.") What is required of man for such a marriage?

Zarathustra says: "Are you a man entitled to wish for a child? Are you the victorious one, the self-conqueror, the commander of your senses, the master of your virtues? This I ask you. Or is it the animal and need that speak out of your wish? Or loneliness? Or lack of peace with yourself?" (TSZ, p. 181). So such a marriage requires a man who has achieved that victory, that conquest over the old values (and over himself as formed by those values) which is the task of the spirit as lion.

Who is the woman involved in this marriage? Who is to marry the creator? In "On little old and young women," Zarathustra is carrying a little truth given him by an old woman, a little truth as troublesome as a child. This truth is: "You are going to women? Do not forget the whip!" (TSZ, p. 179).

Who is this woman whom creative man must tame with the whip? Zarathustra says something about her when he recounts what he said to the old woman about women: woman is a riddle to be solved by the creator. "Everything about woman is a riddle, and everything about woman has one solution, and that is pregnancy" (TSZ, p. 178). Woman is also related to danger and play: "A real man wants two things: danger and play. Therefore, he wants woman as the most dangerous plaything" (TSZ, p. 178). So woman is riddle, danger, play, and something whose solution (redemption) lies in her being tamed and informed by creative man.

Yet these are exactly the terms in which Nietzsche described life itself, the Dionysian substratum of life, in *The Birth of Tragedy*. And in *Ecce Homo*, Nietzsche says: "May I venture the surmise that I *know* women? That is part of my Dionysian dowry" (EH, p. 722). This identity of the woman becomes explicit in "The dancing song." The woman Zarathustra loves is *life*: "Deeply I love only life" (TSZ, p. 221). But Zarathustra adds that there is another woman, one who is even angry with him because of his love of life. This other woman is his "wild wisdom": "But that I am well disposed toward wisdom, and often too well, is on account of her reminding me so much of life" (TSZ, p. 221).

This play of images is again taken up in the Third Part of *Thus Spoke Zarathustra*, especially in "The other dancing song" and "The seven seals, or, the yes and amen song." In these places, Zarathustra says seven times: "Never yet have I found the woman from whom I wanted children, unless it be this woman I love: for I love you, O eternity!" (TSZ, pp. 340–43). So the woman who is to give birth to the overman is *life* and is *eternity*: eternal life. How does she give birth? "In a real man a child is hidden—and wants to play. Go to it, women, discover the child in man! . . . Let your hope be: may I give birth to the overman" (TSZ, p. 178).

So woman can give birth to the child by discovering, drawing out, the child in man; in other words, woman is not only wife but also midwife. Eternal life draws the child out of man. So it is through his love of eternal life that man becomes child (that is, overman).

What does eternal life mean? The term is radically ambiguous. It might mean life in an afterworld—the kind of thing man is led to love because of his resentment against this life. (Zarathustra speaks of resentment in the section "On the adder's bite," which stands between the section on women and the section of the child and marriage.) Or it might mean the eternity of *this* life—its eternal recurrence. In the latter case, the wisdom that man would love and that would resemble life would presumably be a wisdom able to see life in the image of the eternal recurrence.

L. The child in the Second Part of *Thus Spoke Zarathustra*.

The image of the child appears at the very beginning of the Second Part; the first section is "The child with the mirror." This section is as important for the Second Part as is the section on the three metamorphoses for the First.

At the end of the First Part, Zarathustra had announced he was leaving his friends. But he promised he would return to them: "And only when you have all denied me will I return to you" (TSZ, p. 190). This promise is used as the heading for the Second Part, which tells of this return. Yet Zarathustra returns to his friends only in the second section ("Upon the blessed isles"). In the first section, he is in solitude in his cave and speaks only to himself. What he tells himself is why he must return to his friends, why he must descend from the solitude of his cave. He can tell this to himself, however, only because it has been told to him—in a dream. His "dialogue" with himself is an interpretation of what has come to him in a dream. It is a response to what has been given him by the dream god Apollo.

So it is Apollo who draws Zarathustra beyond the stage of noon characteristic of the First Part. The god of light draws him toward evening, toward darkness.

What appears in the dream? —Not the evening, that is, the lion, but rather that for the sake of which Zarathustra will endure the night, namely, morning, the child. What is announced in the dream is the dawn: it is "before dawn" when he awakes from his dream. And, whereas at Zarathustra's noon the dawn was announced only in the sign given to him when he looked at his animals, now his animals *look at him* and are amazed "for, like dawn, a coming happiness lay reflected in his face" (TSZ, p. 195).

Zarathustra recounts his dream to himself. In the dream, a child came to him carrying a mirror and asked him to look at himself in it. But when Zarathustra looked into the mirror, he cried out and his heart was shaken, "For it was not myself I saw but a devil's grimace and scornful laughter" (TSZ, p. 195). So in the dream the child gives Zarathustra the means of seeing himself. Zarathustra is to see himself in the sense of measuring his own image against the image of the child. But the image Zarathustra sees does not measure up to the image of the child. What he sees is thus not himself as he really is. A disparity exists between image and original. Accordingly, Zarathustra still needs to become who he is.

Who is Zarathustra? He is the teacher of the eternal recurrence. He can become this only by advocating his teaching against those who endanger it. Thus Zarathustra interprets his dream as follows: "Verily, all too well do I understand the sign and admonition of my dream—my teaching is in danger" (TSZ, p. 195).

So Zarathustra sets out on his way from noon to evening by returning to his friends, ones who are now poised against him because of what has happened to his teaching. And when ("Upon the blessed isles") he begins to speak to them, it is, as he says, afternoon.

Again we see how Zarathustra's own passage through the three metamorphoses is interwoven with the passage of his friends. Zarathustra is drawn toward the eternal recurrence and toward his friends. The unity of these two movements was already indicated by the fact that the description of the friend in the First Part turned out to be, at the most fundamental level, a description of the eternal recurrence.

Nevertheless, before Zarathustra sets out, he speaks further to himself regarding the descent about to commence: "From silent mountains and from thunderstorms of suffering my soul rushes into the valleys" (TSZ, p. 196). Zarathustra's descent is one from silent mountains, from the solitude of his cave. What is it about his solitude that requires him to leave it? Zarathustra explains: "Too long have I belonged to loneliness; thus I have forgotten how to be silent. Mouth have I become through and through" (TSZ, p. 196). So in the silence of his cave Zarathustra has forgotten how to be silent. He is like that hermit ("On the friend") who needs a friend in order that the I and the me do not sink too deep into conversation, so deep that the hermit no longer hears, no longer receives, but only speaks, only gives.

What is it that Zarathustra now needs to hear and receive? He said his soul rushes into the valleys from thunderstorms of suffering. Then he added: "Let all who suffer be my physicians" (TSZ, p. 196). So it is the sound of suffering that he must now hear; it is to suffering that he must open himself. In other words, he still needs to face up to the problem of suffering, face up to this *enemy*. Yet Zarathustra goes to his enemies not passively but in order to hurl his spear at them: "How grateful I am to my enemies that I may finally hurl it!" (TSZ, p. 196). In different terms, Zarathustra becomes receptive only in order to *give* more abundantly. He will relearn silence only in order to enrich his speech: "I want to plunge my speech down into the valleys" (TSZ, p. 196). So what comes with Zarathustra's descent is a new way of speech: "New ways I go, a new speech comes to me. Like all creators, I grow weary of the old tongues. My spirit no longer wants to walk on worn soles" (TSZ, p. 196).

We need to consider this new speech. It determines much of what happens in the Second Part. Specifically, we need to ask: Of what does Zarathustra speak when this new speech comes to him? And what is the character of this new speech? With respect to these two questions, we must keep in view the metamorphoses that are underway: the metamorphosis into the lion and at the same time a prefiguring of the final metamorphosis into the child.

Of what does Zarathustra speak? The general answer is already given by Zarathustra's reflection on his descent. Zarathustra descends in order to face up to suffering and hurl his spear at it. Accordingly, what he speaks of is suffering. Nevertheless, he first speaks of *redemption* from suffering. In "Upon the blessed isles," Zarathustra declares his teaching*s* (though not yet *the* teaching), and at the center of these is his claim that *creation* is the great redemption from suffering: redemption from suffering comes only when the will wills itself.

Zarathustra then speaks of the opposite of redemption from suffering, namely, absorption in the spectacle of suffering. He calls this absorption "pity." Pity is the comportment toward suffering that sees in it only something negative and objectionable. Nietzsche describes the man of pity in *The Gay Science*: the one who "does not reflect that there is a personal necessity for misfortune—that terror, want, impoverishment, midnight watches, adventures, hazards, and mistakes are as necessary to me and to you as are their opposites; yea, to speak mystically, the path to one's own heaven always leads through the voluptuousness of one's own hell" (GS, §338).

The title of this section of *The Gay Science* already points out the essential opposition: "The will to suffering and those who pity." The man of pity stands at the opposite pole from Zarathustra, such that "The return home" of the Third Part of *Thus Spoke Zarathustra* presents pity as the "greatest danger" (TSZ, p. 297). Indeed, over against the man of pity, Zarathustra describes himself as "the advocate of suffering" (TSZ, p. 328), the one who speaks for suffering, who says "Yes" rather than "No" to suffering.

Zarathustra stresses the destructive character of pity: "And what in the entire world has caused more suffering than the folly of those who pity?" (TSZ, p. 202). The destructiveness lies in the relation to resentment. In *The Gay Science*, §338, Nietzsche says that pity divests suffering of its properly personal character. It separates suffering from its involvement in life and in the enhancement of life. Pity isolates suffering and places it at the distance needed for resentment against suffering to arise. Zarathustra stresses that the resentment released by pity may even be vented upon the one who pities: "Having seen the sufferer suffer, I was ashamed for the sake of his shame, and when I helped him, I transgressed grievously against his pride. Great indebtedness does not make men grateful, but vengeful; and if a little charity is not forgotten, it turns into a gnawing worm" (TSZ, p. 201). Indeed, the devil tells Zarathustra: "God is dead; God died of his pity for man" (TSZ, p. 202). But Zarathustra himself says: "All great love is even above all its pity; for it still wants to create the beloved" (TSZ, p. 202).

Having spoken of pity and resentment, Zarathustra speaks next of priests—those whose "spirit was drowned in their pity" (TSZ, p. 204), those who want to make another suffer because they have suffered too much, those who vent their resentment against suffering upon their fellow man. The priest—more generally, the Christian-moral ideal—represents the embodiment of that pity and resentment which Zarathustra mentioned in the previous section.

Zarathustra next speaks of "the virtuous"—of the way virtue has been poisoned by the ideal that fosters pity and resentment, of the way virtue has poisoned even the souls of the best with such words as "reward, retribution, punishment, and revenge in justice" (TSZ, p. 208). In fact, virtue has polluted not only the soul but *all things*. It has robbed all things of their innocence. Zarathustra says of the virtuous: "They have lied reward and punishment into the foundation of things" (TSZ, p. 205). This lie they tell is metaphysics—the projection of the afterworld, the "true world."

Zarathustra next expresses his nausea at the form life has assumed by being shaped according to resentment as an ideal. He calls this form of life "the rabble": "Life is a well of joy; but where the rabble also drinks, all wells are poisoned" (TSZ, p. 208). Zarathustra is nauseated not because life requires hostility and death (suffering) but because it requires even the rabble—the "small man." This nausea will prove to be one of Zarathustra's greatest dangers.

Zarathustra then addresses those who advocate the rabble—"the preachers of equality"—whose clamor for equality is only a way of taking revenge on those to whom they are not equal: "'We shall wreak vengeance and abuse on all whose equals we are not'—thus do the tarantula-hearts vow. 'And will to equality shall henceforth be the name for virtue; and against all that has power we want to raise our clamor!'" ("On the tarantulas," TSZ, p. 212).

Finally, in the section "On the famous wise men," Zarathustra speaks of how even thought has been poisoned by this ideal, how even the famous wise men have remained servants of the people, of the rabble. The wise men have fallen short of the metamorphosis from camel to lion, that metamorphosis in which (as Zarathustra says here) life itself cuts into itself.

Our second question asked about the character of the new speech. Much of this speech is a "No-saying," that is, the speech of the lion. Indeed, at the end of the section "On the famous wise men," Zarathustra speaks of the lion-will and identifies it with "The will of the truthful." So it is the speech of the truthful, that is, of the spirit which, on account of its truthfulness, denounces lies. In this respect, the speech is not different in character from that of the First Part.

Nevertheless, it was the child, not the lion, who brought this new speech to Zarathustra. The reference to the child (a new beginning, innocence) is evident inasmuch as Zarathustra first speaks of redemption (Yes-saying) and only then proceeds to his No-saying. More generally, the speech of the lion is in service to the arrival of the child. That is, concretely, there can be found in this speech an anticipation of the speech of the child.

What is to be the speech of the child? What is it anticipated as being? It is to be a speech of *beauty* (a beautiful speech that itself attends to beauty). That was indicated already in "On priests": "Naked would I see them: for only beauty should preach repentance" (TSZ, p. 204).

Most important in this connection is the opposition between beauty and truth. As Heidegger sees it, this opposition is a "raging discord" (*Nietzsche*, vol. I [New York: Harper & Row, 1979], p. 211). The lion, the hero, is the truthful spirit. Nevertheless, Zarathustra says: "But just for the hero the *beautiful* is the most difficult thing. No violent will can attain the beautiful by exertion. A little more, a little less: precisely this counts for much here and matters most of all" ("On those who are sublime," TSZ, p. 230).

For the lion (hero), the beautiful is the most difficult thing—in fact, so difficult that the hero must be overcome, must be made to abandon the soul: "He must still discard his heroic will" (TSZ, p. 230). "For this is the soul's secret: only when the hero has abandoned the soul is it approached in a dream by the over-hero" (TSZ, p. 231). That means the spirit must abandon truthfulness (and specifically the truthfulness which must declare lies to be lies) *for the sake of beauty*, for the sake of the dream in which beauty can appear. In the terms of *The Birth of Tragedy*, the spirit must abandon the Socratic for the sake of the Apollinian.

Yet we know from *The Birth of Tragedy* that the Apollinian reaches its fulfillment only when it is born out of the Dionysian. This suggests the second feature of the child's speech: it is to be music. That was indicated in an anticipatory way by the speech of the lion at the beginning of the Second Part. Zarathustra says of the priests: "They would have to sing better songs for me to have faith in their Redeemer" (TSZ, p. 204). It is also indicated by Zarathustra's anticipation of his meeting with his friends: "Indeed, you too will be frightened, my friends, by my wild wisdom; and perhaps you will flee from it, together with my enemies. Would that I knew how to lure you back with shepherds' flutes! Would that my lioness, wisdom, might learn to roar tenderly!" (TSZ, p. 197).

It is vitally important to note that once Zarathustra has carried through his No-saying and has spoken finally ("On the famous wise men") of how the spirit of resentment has poisoned even thought, once, as he says, night has arrived, he then *sings*. His songs are "The night song," "The dancing song," and "The tomb song."

In the middle of the Second Part of *Thus Spoke Zarathustra*, night does arrive, and then Zarathustra sings. His three songs are an anticipation of those other songs that will mark the advent of the child. In other words, Zarathustra's passage into night anticipates the passage to dawn for the sake of which night is endured. Yet these songs of the Second Part are not the songs of the dawn. Especially in the first song, what Zarathustra sings about is night; indeed, that song is called "The night song." We need to consider Zarathustra's songs in some detail.

M. The night song.

Here we find one of the purest image-plays of the entire work. What kind of play with images is involved here? We might characterize it by appealing to Merleau-Ponty ("On the phenomenology of language," in *Signs* [Evanston, IL: Northwestern University Press, 1964], pp. 90–91), who describes creative speech as one that "coherently deforms" the already available means of expression, purposely throws the existing language out of joint. Creative speech makes words disjoin, lose their usual connections and affinities, so as to rejoin them in a novel way and thereby say something that has not been said before. Accordingly, creative speech does violence to the already established language. It puts together words that do not belong together, letting them collide. But it is precisely in this collision, which throws a whole system out of joint, that something new is said.

It is just such violence that Nietzsche is practicing in "The night song" (TSZ, pp. 217–19). To be sure, the images there are almost commonplace. On the surface, it even seems Nietzsche has failed to observe one of the most elementary principles of poetic composition, namely, the avoidance of a blatant mixing of metaphors. Yet what we have in this poem is *not* an uncritical mixing of metaphors. It is even questionable whether we do justice to Nietzsche's song by regarding any image here as a metaphor (something sensible signifying something beyond the sensible). The very notion of metaphor is already, as Heidegger says, a metaphysical notion (*The Principle of Reason* [Bloomington: Indiana University Press, 1996], p. 48). In any case, "The night song" involves no mere confused mixing of images but rather a violence that lets images collide. It is through this collision of disparate images that something decisive is said. So we need to attend primarily to those points of collision.

There are four main images in the song. Each is played off against a kind of opposite, and the four divergent sets of images are played off against one another:

night—light
fountain—well
lover—revenger
warmth—ice.

Already we see something curious: the opposites are not the precise opposites. The precise opposite of night is day, not light; the opposite of love is hate, not revenge; the opposite of warmth is cold, not ice. And what about the opposition between fountain and well? The opposite of a fountain is some arid place, whereas a well is merely water within the earth versus water flowing out of it. At least this is clear: Nietzsche's very choice of opposites harbors a kind of disruption of established connections.

The song begins by introducing the images of night and fountain: "Night has come; now all fountains speak more loudly. And my soul too is a fountain." Zarathustra's soul is a fountain; all fountains speak more loudly; therefore, Zarathustra's soul speaks more loudly. Otherwise expressed, Zarathustra is still "mouth through and through," even more so than when the child came into his dream and when Zarathustra spoke to his friends in the afternoon. Thus Zarathustra has not yet learned silence; he has not yet learned to listen, to receive.

Later in the song, Zarathustra declares: "There is a cleft between giving and receiving: and the narrowest cleft is the last to be bridged." Zarathustra still needs to bridge this cleft. Yet he calls it the *narrowest* one. Why is it so? What could be more radically opposed than giving and receiving? Do we not have here (in contrast to the other opposites) a simple, straightforward opposition? Not at all. In fact, Zarathustra's giving is one that is also a taking away, and it is a giving whereby he gives something to himself: thus it is a kind of receiving. Precisely for that reason, Zarathustra is unable to receive in the other sense, receive something from another: "I do not know the happiness of those who receive; and I have often dreamed that even stealing must be more blessed than receiving. This is my poverty, that my hand never rests from giving."

After the opening line, "The night song" continues by juxtaposing night and lover: "Night has come; only now all the songs of lovers awaken. And my soul too is the song of a lover." The songs of lovers awaken; Zarathustra's soul is the song of a lover; therefore, Zarathustra's soul awakens. In what sense? What is it that awakens in his soul? The next verse of the song provides the answer: "Something unstilled, unstillable, is within me; it wants to be voiced. A craving for love is within me; it speaks the language of love."

So Zarathustra *craves* to be a lover—but he *is* not a lover. Zarathustra's night song is not the song of a lover. It is a song of one who craves love but is not able to love. Zarathustra's craving "speaks the language of love" but does not in fact sing a lover's song.

Presumably Zarathustra is not able to love because he has not found his beloved. Why not? Zarathustra answers this question through a collision of images. In the darkness of night, Zarathustra has failed to find his beloved, *not* because he lacks the light with which to search for her but rather precisely because he *is* light:

> Light am I; ah, that I were night! But this is my loneliness, that I am girt with light. Ah, that I were dark and nocturnal! How I would suck at the breasts of light! And even you would I bless, you little sparkling stars and glowworms up there, and would be overjoyed with your gifts of light.

Night has come, but Zarathustra has not himself become night. That is why he is not able to love, to open himself up to another, to receive sustenance from another, to overcome or redeem his solitude. Zarathustra must still become night in order to be able to love, in order to bridge the cleft between giving and receiving. That is confirmed in the section of *Ecce Homo* discussing *Thus Spoke Zarathustra*. Nietzsche quotes "The night song" in its entirety and provides a short commentary. He describes this song as "the immortal lament at being condemned by the overabundance of light and power, by Zarathustra's sun-nature, not to love" (EH, p. 762).

So Zarathustra is not able to love, to find his beloved, because he is light. But what kind of "because" is this? In other words, what is Zarathustra's "sun nature," and how does this nature condemn him not to love?

The next part of the song begins: "But I live in my own light; I drink back into myself the flames that break out of me." Zarathustra speaks here of how he lives; he speaks of life. For Nietzsche, life does not refer to one aspect of man alongside other aspects (such as thought and will). Instead, life is Nietzsche's word for man as such—for what the modern tradition calls "subject," "subjectivity." So it is a stage of subjectivity as such that Zarathustra is describing here.

The fundamental characteristic of subjectivity at this stage is expressed in Zarathustra's statement: I live in my own light. In other words, the subject, by itself, provides the illumination necessary in order for it to live, to be a subject. The subject is the source of this illumination (creator of values); it gives itself its illumination. It is its own sun. At this precise point, Zarathustra speaks of his poverty, namely, that he only gives and does not know the happiness of those who receive. And he adds: "Oh, darkening of my sun! Oh, craving to crave! Oh, ravenous hunger in satiation!"

The sun imagery is resumed later in the song—resumed in order to bring out the contrast already suggested, the one between Zarathustra (who lives in his own light) and those who have their illumination provided by a sun. This sun is the one that, since Plato, has been an image of the supersensible, the meta-physical, being-in-itself, God. Zarathustra says: "Many suns revolve in the void: to all that is dark they speak with their light—to me they are silent."

This is then one way man can be night; he can let himself be passively spoken to by the sun rather than bringing forth his own light. But this way is not open to Zarathustra, for night has come, God is dead. *Thus Spoke Zarathustra* began with Zarathustra speaking to the sun rather than being spoken to by it.

Let us return to the main statement: "But I live in my own light; I drink back into myself the flames that break out of me." Note the collision of images: he drinks the flames. The image of drinking invokes an image introduced at the beginning: Zarathustra said his soul is a fountain. In terms of the present statement, it is a fountain drinking back into itself what flows out of it. So it is a self-sustaining fountain that requires no source beyond itself for the water (or fire) flowing out. It does not require anything like a well to supply it with what issues forth.

The image of flames also invokes the light imagery of the first part of the sentence. We know subjectivity is its own source of illumination. Presumably, however, it brings forth this illumination in order to illuminate something. What would then be brought back to the subject would be a knowledge of things as they are. But what does Zarathustra bring back? Precisely the illuminating flames themselves or, in other words, the realization that there is nothing but the illuminating, that there are no beings-in-themselves which subjectivity would illuminate, that being is a fallacy and a vapor. What is brought back is a realization that subjectivity does not simply illuminate but rather brings things forth, creates them. This realization is exactly what constitutes the consummation of nihilism!

It is a painful realization. What Zarathustra drinks back are *flames*. As a realization that brings pain, it provokes resentment and fosters a spirit of revenge. Zarathustra says:

> I should like to hurt those for whom I shine. . . .
> Such revenge my fullness plots: such spite wells up out of my solitude.

Zarathustra, unable to love, is threatened by resentment. What is required of him in order to escape this threat? As he said in the First Part, he must still purify himself by consuming himself in his own flames. That is, he must put forth light to the point that he ceases to be the source of light. He must become nocturnal, must learn to receive.

Near the end of the song, Zarathustra again draws the contrast between himself and the nocturnal ones. Now he introduces the images of warmth and ice:

> Oh, it is only you, you dark ones, you nocturnal ones, who create warmth out of that which shines. It is only you who drink milk and refreshment out of the udders of light.
> Alas, ice is all around me, my hand is burned by the ice. Alas, thirst is within me that languishes after your thirst.

Note again the collision of images: night and light are colliding with images of warmth and ice. Furthermore, the nocturnal ones alone manage to secure warmth. In other words, the night is warm and the day cold. Also, Zarathustra is *burned* by ice.

Beside these curiously mixed images, Zarathustra introduces the image of drinking and its opposite, thirst: Zarathustra languishes after the thirst of the nocturnal, whose thirst is satisfied by milk and refreshment. Yet, as we saw, Zarathustra cannot become one of these nocturnal ones to whom a sun still shines, for night has arrived. Zarathustra cannot satisfy his thirst by drinking milk from the udders of light. With what can he then satisfy his thirst? And from what source is he to drink? Zarathustra identifies the source: "Night has come: now my craving breaks out of me like a *well*." It is from a well that he is to drink. The light by which he is to be warmed is not, in fact, something light but something dark—a well. What will he drink from this well? Water, or perhaps wine?

N. The dancing song.

This song differs from the earlier one inasmuch as the song proper is enclosed between two other sections in which Zarathustra speaks directly (TSZ, pp. 219–22). Thus there are three parts:

1. indication of what occasions the song,
2. the song itself,
3. indication of the result of Zarathustra's singing this song.

1. Zarathustra walks through the forest one evening in search of a well. It is still night, and Zarathustra goes searching for that well about which he sang at the end of "The night song." What does Zarathustra find? —Not the well, but rather a green meadow where girls are dancing. He is pleased with them and urges them to continue dancing: "God's advocate am I before the devil. But the devil is the spirit of gravity. How could I, you lightfooted ones, be an enemy of godlike dances? Or of girls' feet with pretty ankles?"

So what Zarathustra finds is not the well but a "commentary" on his search for the well. A well is something from which to drink so as to gain refreshment for dancing, but it is also something one can fall into. It is a place where the "spirit of gravity" can drag one down to death. Indeed, philosophers are famous for falling into wells and being ridiculed for it by young girls. The ambiguity of a well is central to "The dancing song."

Zarathustra says he is God's advocate! He does not say which god he advocates, except that it is a god whose opposite is the spirit of gravity. Zarathustra proceeds to tell the dancing girls about the god he advocates: "Indeed, I am a forest and a night of dark trees. But one who is not afraid of my darkness will also find rose slopes under my cypresses. And he will find the little god girls like best. Beside the well he lies, still, with his eyes shut. Verily, in bright daylight he fell asleep."

Zarathustra calls himself "a night of dark trees." This indicates the transition that has been made since the night song: now Zarathustra has *become* night. That he has done so suggests he has found the well. Yet at the beginning we were told Zarathustra was in search of the well. The crucial point is that he was searching for it in the forest and he tells the girls that he *is* a forest. In other words, he is searching for the well *in himself*. And he has found it in the sense that he now knows where to look for it—in himself. That is confirmed by his further remarks to the girls: Zarathustra is a forest; under his trees one can find the little god lying beside the well; so, the well also lies under the trees, within Zarathustra.

Who is this little god Zarathustra advocates? The god is eventually identified as Cupid, that is, Eros. Zarathustra says this god fell asleep in "bright daylight." Recall that in "The night song" Zarathustra was unable to love because he was light. Now, at night, the god awakens, and it is the prospect of dancing that awakens him. Accordingly, Zarathustra is singing a song for Cupid's dance, a dancing song that also mocks the spirit of gravity. It turns out to be a song about Zarathustra's own love. Zarathustra has become night. He has found his beloved and now opens himself up to her. In contrast to "The night song," Zarathustra does now sing the song of a lover.

2. The song itself begins by identifying Zarathustra's beloved: "Into your eyes I looked recently, O life!" Later he adds: "Deeply I love only life." The song immediately proceeds to indicate the danger to which Zarathustra exposes himself by opening himself up, by looking into the eyes of life. It is the same danger already suggested in the image of a well into which one could be dragged down by the spirit of gravity. Zarathustra says: "And into the unfathomable I then seemed to be sinking."

The German word here rendered as "unfathomable" is *unergründlich*, meaning that its *ground* cannot be found. But that is exactly how Nietzsche refers to life as primal will in *The Birth of Tragedy*: groundless, abyssal. What, according to that book, is the result of looking into the eyes of life, gazing into the abyss? The result is terror and ultimately the hatred of life as expressed in the wisdom of Silenus.

The song continues: "But you pulled me out with a golden fishing rod." That is to say, life itself (not something beyond life, something meta-physical) saved him from the consequences of gazing into the abyss. What is the "golden fishing rod"? Presumably it has something to do with tragedy, since that is what saves man from the wisdom of Silenus.

Zarathustra now sings of how life laughed mockingly when he called her unfathomable. He tells how she rejected those attributes men give her (profound, faithful, eternal, mysterious) and how she insists that humans have simply projected on her their own attributes. The question raised here is one of the most difficult in Nietzsche's thought. In *The Birth of Tragedy*, life (its Dionysian substratum) is understood in the framework of Schopenhauer's metaphysics as thing-in-itself. Yet, with the death of God, any such "true being," any thing-in-itself, becomes a "fable," recognized as not being-in-itself but something projected by man. The question is then: If the Dionysian can no longer be understood as being-in-itself, does that mean it undergoes the same fate as the metaphysical world of Platonism and Christianity? Must it be regarded as simply projected by man? In terms of the song, does man simply present life with his own virtues, his own attributes, ones originating from him? Or, in terms of the night song, does man remain, even in reference to this well ("life is a well"), a self-sustaining fountain?

That is what life tries to make Zarathustra believe. But he says he never believes her when she speaks this way. Why does Zarathustra not believe her? He does not really say. Perhaps he does not yet actually know.

In the next section of the song, Zarathustra discourses not with life but with his "wild wisdom":

> And when I talked in confidence with my wild wisdom, she said to me in anger, "You will, you want, you love—that is the only reason you *praise* life." Then I almost answered wickedly and told the angry woman the truth; and there is no more wicked answer than telling one's wisdom the truth.

What is this "truth" Zarathustra almost told his wisdom? It is a truth contradicting what his wisdom has said: he is not attached (in love with) life *because* he wills and wants and loves. Why not? —Because willing, wanting, loving are always intertwined with their opposites: that is, preeminently with suffering. Thus, they no more justify praise of life than condemnation of life; they provoke hatred of life as much as love of life. Zarathustra says: "Deeply I love only life—and verily, most of all when I hate life."

That is the monstrous ambiguity. Life (and also wisdom whom Zarathustra loves only when she reminds him of life) is a well of joy *and* a well of suffering. It is because joy is so intertwined with suffering that the danger of falling into the abyss (succumbing to the spirit of gravity) is so great.

In the conclusion of the song, it is this threat which approaches once more: "Ah, and then you opened your eyes again, O beloved life! And again I seemed to myself to be sinking into the unfathomable." This time there is no mention of the golden fishing rod.

In the short section following the song, the threat becomes a question. Zarathustra refers again to night: "The sun has set long ago." That is, the consummation of nihilism has arrived. All goals, all "whys," by which Zarathustra might be attached to life are lacking. Furthermore, Zarathustra has himself become night and so cannot even give binding goals and whys to himself. So nothing remains to bind him to life, whereby something unknown and thoughtful approaches Zarathustra, namely, the question: "Are you still alive, Zarathustra?" In other words, is Zarathustra capable of being bound to life?

Finally, the same question is asked in different terms: "Why? What for? By what? Whither? Where? How? Is it not folly still to be alive? Alas, my friends, it is the evening that asks thus through me. Forgive me my sadness. Evening has come; forgive me that evening has come."

O. The tomb song.

The last part of "The dancing song" (the part in which Zarathustra expresses his question) concludes with these words: "Thus spoke Zarathustra." In the next section, which is entirely a song, "The tomb song" (TSZ, pp. 222–25), Zarathustra *sings* the same question. Indeed, almost the entire song is a singing of this question. Specifically, Zarathustra sings the question of his attachment to life by singing of that which most of all threatens to separate him from life, that from which he suffers most deeply, namely, time and its "it was," the transiency of time.

Zarathustra sings of the tombs of this youth. His past is buried—in the sense suggested when he says: "Once I possessed you, and you still possess me." That expresses the essential duality: on the one hand, his past is dead and buried, solidified into an "it was." It is irretrievable. Zarathustra refers to this when he speaks to his enemy (namely, time):

> What is all murder of human beings compared to that which you have done to me? What you have done to me is more evil than any murder of humans; you have taken from me the irretrievable.

So the past is irretrievable, or, as Zarathustra later says: the will cannot will backwards. On the other hand, the past still possesses him. It has shaped him and continues to do so. It shapes him, but he is not able to shape it.

Zarathustra goes on to sing of his own—that is, Nietzsche's own—past. But then the song concludes with an allusion to the way this greatest danger, the suffering from time itself, is to be overcome: "Indeed, in me there is something invulnerable and unburiable, something that explodes rock: that is *my will*." How is the will capable of exploding that rock which the past has become? How is the will able to will backwards, to redeem the past? Zarathustra does not yet say. He only sings: "Hail to thee, my will! And only where there are tombs are there resurrections."

P. Metaphysics.

We have seen that a great deal of what is at issue in *Thus Spoke Zarathustra* converges on the problem of will. The new ideal, presented in the image of the child, is that of will willing itself. Also, according to the tomb song, that which is capable of breaking the tombs of the past (hence releasing man from the most fundamental resentment—against time) is the will. So we need to consider this issue, starting with the general context, one of utmost importance for determining the bearing of Nietzsche's thought on contemporary philosophizing.

The general question providing the context is that of Nietzsche's relation to metaphysics. In order to pose this question, let us appeal to the Aristotelian conception of metaphysics, a conception that determines what metaphysics means for the entire tradition. Aristotle characterizes first philosophy (what the tradition calls metaphysics) as a science dealing with τὸ ὄν ᾗ ὄν. The all-determining question of metaphysics is: τί τὸ ὄν; In *Twilight of the Idols*, Nietzsche answers the question by calling being an empty fiction. Along with this answer, Nietzsche refers to a thinker who is premetaphysical, Heraclitus.

What is the significance of Nietzsche's answer to the metaphysical question? What does the answer say regarding the relation of his thought to metaphysics? The fact that it *is* an answer to the metaphysical question suggests Nietzsche's thought is metaphysical, belonging to the tradition of Western metaphysics. But the kind of answer it is indicates that Nietzsche's thought marks the *end* of this tradition. For the tradition, the very possibility of metaphysics derives from the questionableness of being, from being presenting itself as something to be questioned. For Nietzsche, however, being is emptied of its questionableness: being is not only a fiction but an *empty* fiction. So Nietzsche's thinking constitutes that metaphysical thinking in which metaphysics is brought to its end. Nietzsche develops metaphysics to the point at which it is emptied, ended. Nietzsche's thought is the destruction of metaphysics from within metaphysics itself. As Heidegger says, Nietzsche is "the last metaphysician" (*Nietzsche*, vol. III [New York: Harper & Row, 1987], p. 8).

Here we arrive at the most important question for the contemporary interpretation of Nietzsche. It is a question over which Nietzsche's greatest interpreters disagree. It is, in effect, a question whose answer determines what Nietzsche can offer to contemporary thought. The question amounts to this: Is Nietzsche no more than the last metaphysician, or is there also in his thought a new beginning that moves decisively beyond metaphysics? Does Nietzsche remain captive to the metaphysical tradition he destroys, or does he accomplish an overcoming of metaphysics?

In order to get our bearings, we need to consider briefly the view of Heidegger, since he was the one who decisively posed the question. In calling Nietzsche "the last metaphysician," Heidegger means that Nietzsche's thinking takes the form of a metaphysics in which metaphysics is "reversed in its essence" (*Nietzsche*, vol. IV, p. 148). According to Heidegger, Nietzsche's thinking represents "the historical moment in which the essential possibilities of metaphysics are exhausted" (*Nietzsche*, vol. IV, p. 148). In different terms, Heidegger means that in Nietzsche's thought the entire metaphysical tradition is collected and brought to fulfillment, such that an encounter with Nietzsche's thought constitutes in effect an encounter with the entire tradition. And because Nietzsche is the *last* metaphysician, there arises through his thinking the need for another beginning that would leave metaphysics behind.

Yet, for the most part, Heidegger does not regard Nietzsche as having accomplished such a new beginning. Nietzsche's thought, as the end of metaphysics, remains nevertheless a form of metaphysics. That is, Nietzsche's thought, while embodying the final reversal in the essence of metaphysics, remains itself caught up in that which it reverses. Heidegger characterizes Nietzsche's entanglement in metaphysics in three different ways:

1. Nietzsche's thought takes up only the *Leitfrage* (the "guiding question," the question of the essence of beings: What are beings?) and completely fails to develop the *Grundfrage* (the "basic question," the question of being: What is being itself?). And because Nietzsche fails to pose the question of being, he also fails to pose the genuine question of truth—that is, truth remains for Nietzsche the truth of knowledge.

2. Heidegger characterizes Nietzsche's thought as the consummation of the modern age. Specifically, Heidegger maintains that Nietzsche's theory of the will to power is "the most extreme development of that theory of Descartes according to which all truth is grounded on the self-certainty of the human subject" (*Nietzsche*, vol. IV, p. 86). In this connection, Heidegger makes his famous remark that in Nietzsche's teaching regarding the overman, "Descartes celebrates his highest triumph" (*Nietzsche*, vol. IV, p. 28).

3. Heidegger describes Nietzsche's thought as a *mere* reversal of Greek thought, specifically a reversal of Platonism. It is *merely* a reversal because it remains imprisoned in that which it reverses. In other words, Nietzsche simply reverses the Platonic order of rank between the supersensible and the sensible but remains within the compass of the Platonic (metaphysical) distinction.

So for Heidegger, Nietzsche is no more than the last metaphysician. Heidegger returns to this conclusion again and again. Nevertheless, there are a few passages in Heidegger's vast study of Nietzsche that seem to suggest something like a positive seed of a new beginning in Nietzsche's thought—or at least seem to leave the question open. Let us consider two such passages:

1. The first passage occurs at the end of an essay ("Who Is Nietzsche's Zarathustra?") where Heidegger refers to the possibility that Nietzsche's idea of the eternal recurrence "conceals something unthought which at the same time stands outside of metaphysical thinking" (*Nietzsche*, vol. II [New York: Harper & Row, 1984], p. 233). Although this statement is more positive, nevertheless it says that what might be beyond metaphysics in Nietzsche's thought is *not* thought by Nietzsche—it remains unthought in what he has thought.

2. A more important passage occurs near the end of Heidegger's lecture series on "The will to power as art" in a chapter called "Nietzsche's overcoming of Platonism" (*Nietzsche*, vol. I, pp. 200–210). There Heidegger comments in detail on that section of *Twilight of the Idols* bearing the title "How the true world finally became a fable." Heidegger focuses on Nietzsche's insight into the fact that the destruction of the supersensible world ("true world") does not leave the apparent world standing. The apparent world can be the apparent one only as the opposite of the true world. In Nietzsche's words: "With the true world we have also abolished the apparent one." Heidegger suggests that here Nietzsche no longer merely reverses the terms of the Platonic distinction. When the sensible is no longer the apparent one, then "Platonism is first overcome, that is, turned

around in such a way that philosophical thought is turned out of it" (*Nietzsche*, vol. I, p. 201). Yet Heidegger regards this possible overcoming of Platonism as having been initiated by Nietzsche only at the end of his work and so *after Thus Spoke Zarathustra* (*Twilight of the Idols* was written three years later, in 1888, Nietzsche's final productive year). Nietzsche might have initiated a genuine overcoming of metaphysics in his last writings but gave only a preliminary indication of it. For the most part, in Heidegger's view, Nietzsche was merely the last metaphysician.

If we focus on that section of *Twilight of the Idols* where Heidegger sees Nietzsche coming closest to initiating a new beginning, we note something curious: the section concludes with the words *Incipit* Zarathustra ("*Thus Spoke Zarathustra* begins"). That means Nietzsche regards the overcoming of metaphysics initiated by this section as situated not at the end of his thought but prior to *Thus Spoke Zarathustra* and as providing the point from which that book begins. More generally, we find throughout Nietzsche's writings an interplay between the destruction of the tradition and a new beginning served by this destruction. In the terms of *Thus Spoke Zarathustra*, the fulfillment comes not with the lion but with the child.

So there is a conflict between Heidegger's interpretation of Nietzsche and Nietzsche's own self-interpretation. It is in view of this conflict that Eugen Fink poses the question of Nietzsche's relation to metaphysics. In Fink's words, the question amounts to "whether Nietzsche is only a reversed metaphysician—or whether with him there is announced a new primordial experience of being." Fink then takes issue with Heidegger by seeing in Nietzsche's idea of the eternal recurrence the elements of a new beginning. Fink concludes: "It is a one-sided interpretation to take the will to power as Nietzsche's basic formula for being and to see therein an extreme position of the modern metaphysics of subjectivity. . . . This interpretation with which we still must concern ourselves, because it is the Nietzsche-interpretation of the greatest living thinker, perhaps touches only the 'metaphysical' in Nietzsche, only his unwilling dependence on the history which he strove to overcome; but it does not touch the will to power in its inner relation to the eternal recurrence" (*Nietzsches Philosophie*, p. 178).

Fink goes on finally to propose that this question—whether Nietzsche remains wholly a captive of metaphysics or whether he moves beyond it—is the central question of every Nietzsche interpretation.

Let me situate our own approach to the question. We have had this duality (destruction of the tradition versus a new beginning) in view almost from the start. For, we took our bearings from the book in which it is most transparent, *The Birth of Tragedy*. There the duality appeared in terms of the self-destruction of Socratism versus the rebirth of tragedy (a music-practicing Socrates). Also we have tried to see how the duality remains basically intact in *Thus Spoke Zarathustra* and how, specifically, the problem of nihilism is a broadening and deepening of the problem of Socratism. We viewed *Thus Spoke Zarathustra* as itself an attempt at that rebirth of tragedy called for in *The Birth of Tragedy*. We have devoted our efforts to *Thus Spoke Zarathustra*. We have good reason for doing so, if we want to focus on a new beginning in Nietzsche—or at least want to see whether a new beginning really occurs there and in what sense. For, in *Ecce Homo*, Nietzsche himself refers to *Thus Spoke Zarathustra* as "The Yes-saying part" of his task and contrasts it specifically with the later works. It is presumably in the "Yes-saying part" that we are to find the new beginning—provided it is to be found at all.

If we are to gain some insight into the overcoming of metaphysics in Nietzsche, we must see—more precisely than we have up to now—how Nietzsche brings metaphysics to its conclusion. We must thereby refer to later writings and the literary remains, but even then we will do well to take our bearings as much as possible from *Thus Spoke Zarathustra*.

It is in the theory of the will to power that Nietzsche brings metaphysics to its end. So we need to understand that theory and also try to see whether it already involves Nietzsche in a new beginning or whether (as Fink suggests) only the further idea of the eternal recurrence does so.

The question of metaphysics is the question of being: τὶ τὸ ὄν; In modern metaphysics, this becomes the question of subjectivity. For Descartes, the *cogito* becomes that in reference to which every being must be certified in its being. Leibniz explicitly puts forth the *cogito* as that model in reference to which substance as such (every being) is to be understood. Kant regards the objectivity of objects as constituted by the subject; objectivity, that which makes a being a being, has its ground in the subject. Therefore, to ask about being is to ask not about substance (as in Aristotle) but about the subject. According to Hegel, "Substance is essentially subject." To ask about being is to ask about the being of the subject, the ground of the being of all objects. In turn, to ask about the being of the subject is to ask about the subject's relation to itself, since that is what uniquely characterizes the subject, its relatedness to itself. German Idealism understands this relation to self as self-consciousness, and it is thereby that the subject is the ground of the being of objects. Fichte is explicit: all consciousness rests on self-consciousness.

Nietzsche's position within this general movement of modern metaphysics is indicated already in the First Part of *Thus Spoke Zarathustra*. In "On the Afterworldly," Nietzsche speaks of the afterworld, the "true world," of Platonism and of Christianity: "But 'that world' is well concealed from humans—that dehumanized inhuman world which is a heavenly nothing; and the belly of being does not speak to humans at all, except as a human" (TSZ, p. 144). That means being speaks to us only as something human, only in terms of its relation to man, to subjectivity. All being-in-itself (dehumanized being) is "well concealed" from man—in fact, completely concealed, since it is nothing.

The issue is developed more explicitly in the literary remains: "'Things that have a constitution in themselves'—a dogmatic idea with which one must break absolutely" (WP, §559). Nietzsche goes on to explain why it is a dogmatic idea: "That things possess a constitution in themselves apart from interpretation and subjectivity is a quite idle hypothesis: it presupposes that interpretation and subjectivity are not essential, that a thing freed from all relationships would still be a thing" (WP, §560). Finally, he says in a later section: "We possess the concept 'being,' 'thing,' only as a relational concept" (WP, §583), thus only in terms of the relation to subjectivity.

So all being is being in relation to subjectivity—being is being *for* a subject. That is precisely the issue in one of Zarathustra's peculiar statements to his friends residing on the blessed isles. He speaks to them of God (God as representative of being-in-itself): "God is a conjecture; but I desire that your conjectures should be limited by what is thinkable. Could you *think* a god? But this is what the will to truth should mean to you: that everything be changed into what is thinkable for man, visible to man, palpable by man. You should think through your own senses to their consequences" (TSZ, p. 198). We will see how the theory of the will to power involves an attempt to think through the senses to their consequences.

In the section "On the afterworldly," Zarathustra continues: "Verily, all being is difficult to prove and difficult to induce to speak. Tell me, my brothers, is not the strangest of all things proved most nearly? Indeed, this ego and the ego's contradiction and confusion still speak most honestly of its being—this creating, willing, valuing ego which is the measure and value of things" (TSZ, p. 144).

This passage says the ego is the measure and value of things. The ego is that through which things are measured in their being, that by which their being is determined. In other words, the being of things not only has reference to subjectivity but is even *projected* by subjectivity (being is a fiction). *Twilight of the Idols* makes that explicit: "Man posited 'things' as 'being,' in his image, in accordance with his concept of the ego as a cause. Small wonder that later he always found in things only what he had put into them" (TI, p. 495). Man posits the being of things and does so in terms of his concept of the ego, his concept of himself, his relation to himself. So, as in German Idealism, the subject's relation to itself is the ground of its relation to an object.

The passage also says that all being is difficult to prove and to induce to speak. Why? —Because what being says is only the echo of our own voice: we find in things not being, but rather only what we have put there. This issue is the same as the one in the night song, where the one who lives in his own light drinks back into himself only his own flames. What then is the strangest of all things that is proved most nearly? Presumably it is the fact that being cannot be proved at all (skepticism). But that is not quite proved, for there is one thing which does speak: the ego. Only the being of subjectivity speaks; all other being is a fiction mirroring the being of subjectivity. In other words, all other being has its ground in subjectivity.

Yet how does the ego speak? It does so in terms of its contradiction and confusion—that is, in terms of its *relation to itself*. And, as such, it proves to be a creating, willing, valuing ego. Let us take our clue from this description and try to elaborate a more systematic view of Nietzsche's conception of subjectivity. Let us consider the subject in turn as willing, as creating, and as valuing.

1. The subject as willing.

We have seen already that one of the names Nietzsche uses for subjectivity is "life." It is especially in this connection that he speaks of subjectivity as will—indeed not simply as will but as will to power. He says in "On self-overcoming": "Where I found the living, there I found will to power" (TSZ, p. 226). In *Beyond Good and Evil*, Nietzsche is even more explicit: "Life itself is will to power" (BGE, p. 211).

In describing subjectivity as will to power, there is first of all a negative intent. Nietzsche wants to deny that subjectivity is certain other things. One such denial is already evident in the passage from "On the Afterworldly." Zarathustra says that the ego speaks honestly of its being, and then he adds: "And this most honest being, the ego, speaks of the body" (TSZ, p. 144). This bodily character of the subject is also addressed in "On the despisers of the body." There Zarathustra distinguishes between the "great reason" (body, self) and the "little reason" (spirit), and he says: "Behind your thoughts and feelings, my brother, there stands a mighty ruler, an unknown sage, whose name is self. In your body he dwells; he is your body" (TSZ, p. 146). In negative terms, this means subjectivity is not identical with consciousness. Consciousness is only a "surface": "The greater part of our intellectual activity goes on unconsciously" (GS, §333).

To say that subjectivity is not identical with consciousness or that the subject is bodily does not mean resorting to a simple materialism that would make man a thing among other things. The body is not a mere thing, a mere chunk of matter. If it were, Nietzsche could not say: "There is more reason in your body than in your best wisdom" (TSZ, pp. 146–47). Instead, Nietzsche's point is that there is much in the subject that is *beneath* the surface, there is a wealth within the subject that remains concealed, the subject is not self-transparent.

In this connection, Nietzsche repeatedly attacks the Cartesian *cogito*, that is, the belief in the possibility of grasping oneself fully and adequately in an act of thinking, the belief that in reflection the subject has immediate certainty of itself:

> When I analyze the process that is expressed in the sentence "I think," I find a whole series of daring assertions that should be difficult, perhaps impossible,

to prove; for example, that it is I who think, that there must necessarily be something which thinks, that thinking is an activity and operation on the part of a being who is thought of as a cause, that there is an "ego," and, finally, that it is already determined what is to be designated by thinking, that I *know* what thinking is. For if I had not already decided within myself what it is, by what standard could I determine whether that which is now happening is not perhaps "willing" or "feeling"? In short, the assertion "I think" assumes that *I* compare my state at the present moment with other states of myself which I know, in order to determine what it is; on account of this retrospective connection with further "knowledge," it has no immediate certainty for me. (BGE, p. 213)

So even the presumed immediate certainty of oneself as a thinking being has its roots beneath the level of conscious transparency.

On the positive side, how does Nietzsche understand self-consciousness? That is, to what extent can man become conscious of himself? *The Gay Science* raises that question and suggests there is a relationship between the development of self-consciousness and the necessity for communication. In other words, it is only as a social animal that man learned to become conscious of himself, and his self-consciousness, as tied to communication, is also tied to speech, language.

Therefore, self-consciousness develops only in the framework of society and language (Nietzsche is here close to Hegel). Nietzsche draws this conclusion: "Consequently each of us, in spite of the best intention of understanding himself as individually as possible, and of 'knowing himself,' will always just call into consciousness the non-individual in him, namely, his averageness" (GS, §354).

The other principal denial involved in Nietzsche's description of subjectivity as will to power is that the subject is not to be regarded in terms of the traditional concept of substance. The subject is not a kind of subject-thing behind our actions, thoughts, and decisions. The subject is not an agent behind the scenes causing what happens on the stage, not a "free" subject in the sense of being able to remain aloof, untouched, unaffected, uncompromised. Nietzsche radically rejects such notions of freedom and causality.

In *On the Genealogy of Morals*, Nietzsche makes that point with an example: just as we tend to separate lightning from its flash and take the flash as an action by a subject (the lightning), so we tend to separate man from his actions and place him behind them as their cause: "But there is no such substratum; there is no 'being' behind the doing, effecting, becoming. The 'doer' is merely a fiction added to the deed—the deed is everything" (GM, p. 481).

In *The Will to Power*, Nietzsche refers to the same issue. He speaks of the will in the sense of this sort of substantial agent and even says: "There is no such thing as 'will'" (WP, §671). We might suspect Nietzsche is going beyond the metaphysical tradition here. But that is not the case. He is only reiterating the critique of substance initiated by Kant and developed in German Idealism. Nietzsche is saying the same as Fichte: being is a derived concept; the positive concept is *activity*.

So Nietzsche is denying that the subject is substance and, as we discussed first, denying that the subject is identical with consciousness. These two denials are related. That the subject is not substance means there is not something behind the actions of the subject, no doer behind the doing, no "depth dimension" beneath the subject. Yet the other denial (of the subject as consciousness) means that Nietzsche indeed is inserting another depth dimension beneath subjectivity. To say the subject is not identical with consciousness means consciousness is merely a surface, or, in other words, there is something (a depth) of which it is a surface. This new depth dimension is described in the First Part of *Thus Spoke Zarathustra* as "bodily." We will see that it bears other names, such as "earth" and the "Dionysian."

2. The subject as creating.

One sense of this creating is suggested in "On the despisers of the body": "Always the self listens and seeks. It compares, overpowers, conquers, destroys. It controls, and it is in control of the ego too" (TSZ, p. 146). The activities of the subject are summed up in its controlling. The creating that belongs to the self is a controlling, a commanding. *Beyond Good and Evil* is explicit: the will "is above all an affect and specifically the affect of command" (BGE, p. 215).

Thus the subject is a commanding, a mastering, a gaining power over. Nietzsche speaks of the will as "the will from multiplicity to simplicity, a will that ties up, tames, and is domineering and truly masterful" (BGE, p. 349). Or again, he says that the will's "power to appropriate the foreign stands revealed in its inclination to assimilate the new to the old, to simplify the manifold" (BGE, p. 350). Thus, willing appropriates, and its creating is an ordering of chaos, a gaining of mastery, of power. It is precisely in this sense that Nietzsche calls it "will to power." Power is not just some "object" after which the will strives, not something to which willing can be directed. Instead, power expresses the very nature of willing: will to power is will *as* overpowering.

What is it that the will overpowers, overcomes? The answer is provided in "On self-overcoming": "And life itself confided this secret to me. 'Behold,' it said, 'I am that which must always overcome itself'" (TSZ, p. 227). So what the will to power overcomes is *itself*: its willing is a willing beyond itself, a creating beyond itself. "A man who wills commands something within himself that renders obedience or that he believes renders obedience. But now let us notice what is strangest about the will—this manifold thing for which people have only one word: . . . we are at the same time the commanding and the obeying parties" (BGE, p. 216).

The structure of this "manifold thing" (the will) as self-overcoming is elaborated in several places. For example, in *Beyond Good and Evil*, Nietzsche stresses the duality involved: in willing there is a state "away from which" and a state "toward which." This same duality is expressed in *Thus Spoke Zarathustra* in the images of birth and death, creation and destruction. It is because the will intrinsically involves such duality that Zarathustra repeatedly claims whoever would be a creator must also be an annihilator.

The character of the duality is most clearly elaborated in the section "On the tarantulas": "Life must overcome itself again and again. Life wants to build itself up into the heights with pillars and steps; it wants to look into vast distances and out toward stirring beauties: therefore it requires height. And because it does so, it requires steps and contradiction among the steps and the climbers. Life wants to climb and to overcome itself climbing" (TSZ, p. 213). So life requires the passage into heights, a surpassing, a movement beyond itself. Nietzsche's usual term for this element in willing is "enhancement." But the movement toward the heights requires the steps on which one ascends. That is to say, it requires that a firm basis be established from which to ascend, even though the goal is to overcome such steps (life overcomes itself in climbing). Nietzsche's usual term for this element, the firm basis, is "preservation": something must be established, preserved, instituted, as a basis from which the overcoming proceeds.

This is then the fundamental structure of the will to power: a dynamic duality of preservation and enhancement.

3. The subject as valuing.

In the section on "How the true world finally became a fable," Nietzsche traces the history of metaphysics. The last stage (at which he says his *Zarathustra* begins) is that of the death of God, the consummation of nihilism. Then Nietzsche says the true world has been abolished and with it the apparent one as well. We have noted that the apparent, sensible world can no longer be a mere image of true being, if true being has collapsed. So how is the sensible world to be understood? Nietzsche answers in *The Will to Power*: "The apparent world is a world viewed according to values—ordered and selected according to values—in this case according to the viewpoint of utility with regard to the preservation and enhancement of the power of a certain species of animal" (WP, §567). So the world of appearances is a world viewed and ordered according to values, and values, Nietzsche suggests, are related to preservation and enhancement. Let us then try to come to terms with what Nietzsche means by value.

Valuating or evaluating is something belonging fundamentally to life, to the will to power. In "On a thousand and one goals," Nietzsche says: "No people could live without first evaluating" (TSZ, p. 170). Yet evaluating does not mean simply to estimate or judge things in relation to a presupposed set of values or standards. Instead, it means more fundamentally to *posit* those values themselves: "Verily, men gave themselves all their good and evil. Verily, they did not take it, they did not find it, nor did it come to them as a voice from heaven. Only man placed value in things to preserve himself—he alone created a meaning for things, a human meaning. To evaluate is to create.... Through evaluating alone is there value, and without evaluating, the nut of existence would be hollow" (TSZ, p. 171). So values presuppose evaluating (creating) rather than being presupposed by it. "Life itself forces us to posit values" (TI, p. 490).

Therefore, values are posited by the will to power. But, as so posited, they are correlative to the viewpoint or perspective from which they are posited. That has an important consequence: since it is in terms of values that the world is viewed, ordered, interpreted, or, in other words, given its character, then this character is always relative to a viewpoint. That is Nietzsche's notion of "perspectivism." He says the world "has no meaning behind it but *contains* countless meanings—'perspectivism'!" (WP, §481). Or again, he says: "The perspective therefore decides the character of the 'appearance'" (WP, §567).

What defines this viewpoint or perspective? How is it related to the values posited from it? Nietzsche says: "It is our needs that interpret the world" (WP, §481). "The values of a human being betray something of the structure of his soul and betray the place where his soul finds its conditions of life, its true needs" (BGE, p. 407). So the viewpoint in relation to which values are posited is defined in terms of the needs or conditions of life. But what kind of conditions are involved?

Nietzsche is quite explicit about the character of the conditions: "The viewpoint of value is the viewpoint of the conditions of preservation and enhancement for complex forms of relative life-duration within the flux of becoming" (WP, §715). So the conditions determining the viewpoint are the ones of preservation and enhancement. In turn, these conditions determine the character of the values posited: "In valuations are expressed conditions of preservation and enhancement" (WP, §507).

In summary, values are that in terms of which the world is ordered, viewed, interpreted. Values are posited by the will to power in function of conditions, needs, pertaining to that will to power, specifically pertaining to its needs with regard to preservation and enhancement. So the positing of values is the way the will to power supplies its most basic needs, the way it guarantees the fulfillment of those fundamental conditions without which it could not exist as will to power. In the terms of *The Birth of Tragedy*, the positing of values is the means by which life secures its own continuation.

The idea of two fundamental types of needs or conditions of life is present almost from the beginning of Nietzsche's thought, although the idea never fully emerges in any of the published works. It is already indicated at the end of the early, unpublished essay "On Truth and Falsity." The only difference is that in this essay Nietzsche draws the distinction between these two types of conditions as a distinction between two types of men rather than as a duality within every man. First is the "rational man," the one engaged in constructing the framework of ideas that grant life stability, permanence, order. Nietzsche then contrasts him with the "intuitive man" or artist. The artist throws metaphors into confusion, shifts the boundary stones of the framework of ideas, throws it out of joint. The artist uses the order, provided by the rational man, only as a scaffolding for a movement beyond, for an overcoming.

The contrast just mentioned is in turn a development of the one already drawn in *The Birth of Tragedy* between Socrates and Dionysus, between knowledge, truth (the preservation condition) and art (enhancement). Furthermore, the problem of understanding how these two basic needs (and their corresponding values) belong together in every individual (rather than pertaining to different types of individuals) is the problem of how Socrates and Dionysus belong together. At its highest point, the problem of the will to power is the same as the one of a music-practicing Socrates. And this is precisely the problem the Greeks failed to solve. Their failure is what made possible the unlimited dominance of Socratism (metaphysics). Thus in the problem of the will to power, Nietzsche has returned to a problem that arises prior to metaphysics. In the theory of the will to power, Nietzsche not only is the last metaphysician but also occupies a position prior to (outside of) metaphysics.

Q. Knowledge and truth.

One aspect of the duality constitutive of the will to power has to do with the preservation condition, the establishment of permanence, stability, order. Already in "On Truth and Falsity," Nietzsche linked this function to the intellect and knowledge. The intellect is described as a "means for preservation," and knowledge described in terms of the way it establishes order and stability. So, to understand the will to power, we need to look briefly at Nietzsche's conception of knowledge and truth. We will base ourselves on the literary remains, but our goal is to return to *Thus Spoke Zarathustra* and follow it beyond the point we have reached (that is, beyond the songs of the Second Part).

Nietzsche remarks: "Perhaps no one yet has been truthful enough about what truthfulness is" (BGE, p. 283). What would it mean to be truthful about truthfulness? If we think through this issue, we might see how questionable the question of truth actually is.

Suppose I ask: What is truth? Suppose I try to discover what truth is. Then I am trying to discover the truth about truth. But in order to set about trying to discover the truth about anything, I must already know what truth is. The question of truth thus presupposes its own answer. Therefore, it is a question involving a risk. It is a risky question, one threatening to break down, to recoil upon itself, to undercut its own foundation, to bite its own tail. Such an eventual recoil is what Nietzsche sees as involved in the character of Socratism, specifically as bringing an end to Socratism itself and generating the need for tragedy. In taking up the problem of truth, part of Nietzsche's intention is to bring Socratism (metaphysics) to its end—so as to prepare the way for tragedy, that is, for *Thus Spoke Zarathustra*.

Let us then confront that most questionable question: What is truth? In the tradition, truth means correspondence. Truth is a mark of knowledge or judgment. A judgment is true if it corresponds with things *as they are*. But for Nietzsche there are no such things, no things as they are, no things-in-themselves. There is only the world of appearances, a world shaped and ordered by us. Beyond this, we can speak only of chaos. In other words, if we try to "think away" what we have added (regularity, structure, order, permanence), we can speak only of the chaos of becoming. And with such chaos, knowledge can have nothing to do: "The character of the world in a state of becoming as incapable of formulation, as 'false,' as 'self-contradictory.' Knowledge and becoming exclude each other" (WP, §517).

Thus Nietzsche is maintaining what was argued again and again in Greek philosophy: there can be no knowledge of sheer becoming, flux, chaos. Instead, knowledge (the very possibility of correspondence) requires a degree of order, structure, relative permanence. Nietzsche prefaces the passage just quoted by saying: "In order to think and infer, it is necessary to assume beings; logic handles only formulas for what remains the same. . . . 'Beings' are part of our perspective" (WP, §517). He says much the same in *Thus Spoke Zarathustra*: "Everything permanent—that is only a parable. And the poets lie too much" (TSZ, p. 198). Nietzsche concludes that "what can be thought must certainly be a fiction" (WP, §539). In other words, truth (knowledge) involves correspondence only with what the subject has itself created: "There must first of all be a will to make knowable, a kind of becoming must itself create the deception of beings" (WP, §517).

Against this background, we can now understand Nietzsche's very curious definition of truth: "Truth is the kind of error without which a certain species of life could not live" (WP, §493).

First, truth is a kind of error. That is, truth means correspondence, not with things-in-themselves but with the fictions we ourselves create. If we measure such truths against the traditional definition of truth, then they are precisely errors. Truth in Nietzsche's sense is error in the traditional sense.

Second, truth is something without which we could not live. Truth is a way of meeting essential conditions of life, such as the need for permanence. After defining truth, Nietzsche says: "The value for *life* is ultimately decisive" (WP, §493). Thus knowledge is a way the will to power fulfills a basic condition necessary for it to exist as will to power, the condition of stability, permanence, order.

How does knowledge fulfill this condition? In general, it does so by simplifying and determining the chaos. In knowing, we take possession, appropriate, gain mastery over, the chaos of sensations. We assimilate the chaos; we order and structure it in a way that puts it at our disposal, makes it familiar, makes it such that we can contend with it. *The Gay Science* clearly formulates this conception of knowledge: "What do the people really understand by knowledge? What do they want when they seek 'knowledge'? —Nothing more than that something strange be traced back to something known. And we philosophers—have we really understood anything more by knowledge? . . . is our need of knowing not just this need of the known? Is it not just the will to discover in everything strange, unusual, or questionable something which no longer disquiets us?" (GS, §355).

The same conception is expressed often and elaborated in *The Will to Power*: "In our thought the essential feature is the fitting of new material into old schemata (Procrustes' bed), the making-equal of what is new" (WP, §499). "Not 'to know,' but rather to schematize—to impose upon chaos as much regularity and form as our practical needs require. In the formation of reason, of logic, of categories, *need* has been the standard: the need, not 'to know,' but rather to subsume, to schematize, for the purpose of intelligibility and calculation. . . . No preexisting 'idea' was here at work, but rather utility, that only when we see things coarsely and made equal do they become calculable and manageable to us" (WP, §515).

Proceeding now from this general conception, we need to work out Nietzsche's view of the full structure of knowledge. Knowing is a determining, a schematizing, an assimilating of the new to the old and familiar. If, in particular, we regard knowing as schematizing, we can then distinguish two constituents: first, the elements that become schematized, placed under the schemata, and second, the schemata themselves. In an act of knowing, the schemata are presupposed. Knowledge consists simply in bringing the elements under the already available schemata. But this process presupposes another more fundamental one, namely, a process in which the elements have been *made* such that they can be placed under the schemata, a process in which they have been appropriately formed and shaped.

What is required for that? What is required to make the multiplicity of sensations capable of being brought together under a schema, such as being taken as pertaining to one and the same enduring thing? Nietzsche's answer is that what is to be schematized must undergo an *equalizing*: "All thought, judgment, perception, considered as comparison, has as its precondition a 'positing of equality' and earlier still a 'making equal'" (WP, §501).

The point is that to bring a mass of sensations together under a schema is to view the sensations as the same, to disregard their differences. But in order to view them as the same, posit them as equal, I must already have formed them in the way they are to be viewed. "Before there is 'thought,' there must have been 'invention.' The *construction* of identical cases, of the appearance of sameness, is more primitive than the *knowledge* of sameness" (WP, §544). Or again, Nietzsche speaks of that "older function . . . which must have been active much earlier, which makes cases identical and similar which are in themselves dissimilar. . . . There could be no judgment at all if a kind of equalization were not practiced within sensations. . . . Before judgment occurs, the process of assimilation must already have taken place" (WP, §532).

So what is required, as standing behind all knowledge, is an equalizing of things that are unequal. Knowledge thereby presupposes a "fundamental falsification" (WP, §512). Let us look closer at this equalizing process at the basis of knowledge. It is important to see that it is not purely arbitrary.

Equalizing is always an equalizing in some particular respect or other. If we are given a multiplicity of elements, they can in principle be made equal in many different respects. According to Nietzsche, however, the elements are not equalized in just any respect; instead, they are equalized in such a way as to make possible their schematization. They are equalized in reference to the schemata under which they are subsequently to be brought. That means the schemata are already operative prior to the explicit schematization. The whole process of equalizing (falsifying) that precedes the actual schematizing (the knowing as such) is already guided by the schemata. Therefore, not only the knowing process but also the prior process of equalizing depend essentially on the schemata.

What are these schemata? They are what the tradition calls categories (fundamental determinations of things). They are that in terms of which we order the world of appearances. They are what Nietzsche calls *values*. As such, they are posited, created, by the will to power: "It is we who created the 'thing,' the 'identical thing,' the subject, attribute, activity, object, substance, form" (WP, §521). So if we find our world to be one of substances, things, of relative permanence and order, it is because we have made it such: "The world seems logical to us because we have made it logical" (WP, §521).

This creating is not arbitrary. It is a creating required by the will itself, a creating dictated by the fundamental needs of life as will to power, a creating that serves precisely to fulfill these needs: "The inventive force that invented categories labored in the service of our needs, namely, our need for security, for quick understanding on the basis of signs and sounds, for a means of abbreviation" (WP, §513). This is of course what Nietzsche calls more generally the preservation condition, the need for permanence, order, stability.

Clearly we have here a very traditional account of knowledge: first, knowledge as subsumption under categories (ideas); second, categories as constitutive of the empirical world; and third, categories as referred back to subjectivity as their ground. It is thus that Heidegger and others see in Nietzsche's theory of the will to power only the work of the last metaphysician. They are indeed correct if Nietzsche's analysis is taken straightforwardly, thus as basically the same kind of enterprise as Kant's in *The Critique of Pure Reason*. But is that the appropriate way of taking it? Is there perhaps something else going on behind the scenes? Nietzsche writes: "A critique of the faculty of knowledge is senseless: how should a tool be able to criticize itself when it can use only itself for the critique?" (WP, §486). In other words, what we have just seen Nietzsche doing is *senseless*. We need to ask: Does perhaps its very senselessness constitute its significance for what is really at issue here? Is Nietzsche's Kantian-like critique perhaps one in which logic does bite its own tail?

Nietzsche's Analysis of Knowledge

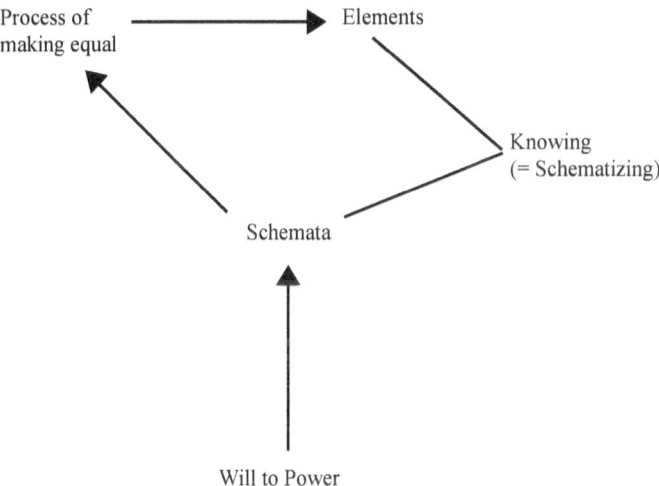

R. Night.

The central event of *Thus Spoke Zarathustra* is the birth of the child. The child is the one who wills his own will, who is capable of a sacred "Yes-saying." The child is one who is able to bind himself to life, to say "Yes" to life—in contrast to the man of the ascetic ideal, who says "No" to life and seeks to escape from life to an afterlife. What makes it possible for a man to bind himself to life? In the most general terms, man can bind himself to life insofar as he is able to let himself be bound by the idea of the eternal recurrence. Accordingly, the birth of the child coincides with Zarathustra's coming to be bound by the idea of the eternal recurrence, by his teaching of this idea to himself. That event is also portrayed in the image of dawn. But dawn is preceded by night, and we can understand the dawn only if we understand what happens in the night. So let us try to draw together and make more explicit all we have learned about the night. Then we will be able to see what is really at issue in the dawn, in the birth of the child—that is, we will be able to take up the final and most difficult issue, the idea of the eternal recurrence.

The most important indications regarding night are provided in the songs of the Second Part. In effect, they present an outline of the main stages passed through in the course of the night:

1. Zarathustra lives in his own light ("The night song").

2. Zarathustra consumes himself in his own flames (becomes nocturnal). This is the point of transition between "The night song" and "The dancing song."

3. Zarathustra seeks and finds, within himself (in his life), ambiguity and the danger of falling into the unfathomable.

4. The last stage is the question: How can Zarathustra be bound to life? "The tomb song" specifies what threatens to separate Zarathustra from life, what must be overcome, namely, resentment against time and its "it was."

We need to elaborate these stages in terms of the theory of the will to power. Before that, however, we need to see that this sequence of stages corresponds to another such schema, the one already at play in *The Birth of Tragedy*:

1. Socratism. This corresponds to the spirit that lives in its own light, since what is decisive for Socratism is the order of intelligibility (light) projected in advance as support for the uncovering activity of Socratic man. In other words, Socratic man wants to live solely in accord with the reasons he uncovers (projects) behind things.

2. The self-destruction of Socratism (logic bites its own tail). This stage corresponds to Zarathustra's consuming himself in his own flames, that is, becoming nocturnal (the advent of nihilism).

3. The gaze into the Dionysian abyss. This results once Socratism comes to its point of self-destruction. This "gaze into the eyes of life" harbors the danger of falling into the unfathomable, succumbing to the pessimistic wisdom of Silenus.

4. The result is the need for tragedy. It is needed in order for us to be saved from the wisdom of Silenus, to be bound to life rather than to the life-negating wisdom.

In terms of the will to power, these stages are the self-destruction of Socratism, the priority of art over truth, and the sublime man.

Socratism (the spirit that lives in its own light) is the issue in Nietzsche's discussion of knowledge within the framework of the will to power. Nietzsche's analysis puts Socratism at issue by tracing all order, structure, reasons, intelligibility (being-in-itself) back to its ground in subjectivity. All of the intelligibility on which Socratic man would base himself collapses into subjectivity. To that extent, what Nietzsche carries out is basically the same as what Kant accomplishes in the first Critique, namely, a demonstration of subjectivity as the ground of objectivity. The comparison with Kant is important, because in *The Birth of Tragedy* it was precisely Kant whom Nietzsche saw as bringing Socratism to the point where its logic bites its own tail. So Nietzsche is taking up the Socratic project, in its modern epistemological form, not in order to ground or affirm it but rather so as to bring it to the point where its logic bites its tail. Nietzsche's intention can be seen in his statement that precisely the kind of critique of knowledge in which he is engaged is "senseless." It undercuts itself. What it uncovers conflicts with the very project of an unlimited uncovering. We can see the conflict in two ways:

First, what is uncovered is a subjectivity intrinsically opaque to itself, not a pure consciousness but a bodily one "of the earth." That is to say, the uncovering serves to point out a radical concealment, a radical nonintelligibility, at the very foundation of existence and the world. It points to precisely that which had to be covered over as a condition of the very possibility of the Socratic project.

Second, Nietzsche's critique of knowledge reveals that the "will to truth" (the allegiance to truth as the highest value, the all-determining value for Socratism) is not ultimate but instead rests on a deeper foundation, one covered up by Socratism. Thus the very condition of possibility of the Socratic uncovering is itself a covering up of its own "motivation."

What is this deeper foundation? In the most general terms, it is life as will to power. The will to truth as a projection of structure and order is a way the will to power fulfills its existential need. This issue is expressed in *Thus Spoke Zarathustra*, Second Part, at the beginning of the section "On Self-Overcoming":

> "Will to truth"—you who are wisest give this name to that which impels you and fills you with lust?
>
> A will to the thinkability of all beings: that is what *I* call your will. You want to *make* all being thinkable, for you doubt with well-founded suspicion that it is already thinkable. But it shall yield and bend for you. Thus your will wants it. It shall become smooth and serve the spirit as its mirror and reflection. That is your whole will, you who are wisest: a will to power. (TSZ, p. 225)

So Nietzsche's critique of knowledge is an attempt to complete the turning of Socratism back upon itself; it is an *enactment* of the self-destruction of Socratism. It is an invocation of nihilism.

The spirit of this critique is perhaps best expressed by Zarathustra's shadow, which says to him: "Too often, verily, did I follow close on the heels of truth; so she kicked me in the face. Sometimes I thought I was telling lies, and behold, only then did I hit the truth. Too much has become clear to me: now it no longer concerns me" (TSZ, p. 386).

S. Priority of art over truth.

Let us look more carefully at the outcome of Nietzsche's consideration of knowledge. Nietzsche interrogates knowledge by trying to uncover the conditions of its possibility, with knowledge understood as schematizing. What are the conditions? Prior to knowledge, there must be a projecting (creating) of schemata (categories, values), and in addition the chaos of sensations must be formed accordingly. In other words, what Nietzsche discovers beneath the epistemological subject (beneath the activity of knowing) is a creative subject with its existential needs and perspectives. In terms used in earlier works, what Nietzsche discovers beneath the knowing subject is the creative artistic self. Beneath the knower, Nietzsche discovers the artist (who creates and forms). With respect to the theory of the will to power, this entails that fundamentally all projection of values is the work of the artist in us. Therefore, all projection of values is fundamentally directed to the fulfillment of the need of the artist, namely, the enhancement-need, the need to create beyond oneself, to overcome oneself. Even the values by which permanence is established are directed toward the fulfillment of the enhancement-need.

Thus the two sides of the will to power are not simply coordinate. Instead, all value projection is a function of the enhancement-need. The preservation-need is subordinate to it. Establishment of permanence is, properly speaking, only for the sake of enhancement (willing beyond oneself, self-overcoming). The will to truth is therefore *in service to* the will to power as self-overcoming.

Accordingly, Nietzsche says that the will to power "wishes to preserve itself only indirectly. It actually wishes to surpass itself" (WP, §488). Nietzsche explains: "Life is founded upon the premise of a belief in enduring and regularly recurring things; the more powerful life is, the wider must be the knowable world to which we, as it were, attribute being.... Man projects his drive to truth, his 'goal' in a certain sense, outside himself as a world that has being, as a metaphysical world, as a 'thing-in-itself,' as a world already in existence. His needs as creator invent the world upon which he works, anticipate it; this anticipation (this 'belief' in truth) is his support" (WP, §552).

So Nietzsche's discussion of the will to power leads to a priority of art over truth: "Art is more valuable than truth" (WP, §853, IV). We have seen already that Nietzsche defines truth as a kind of error (falsification, instituting of permanence) by which the preservation-need is satisfied. Now Nietzsche goes further: the will to power is essentially a willing beyond itself, an enhancement. Truth is what accords with this enhancement: "The criterion of truth lies in the enhancement of the feeling of power" (WP, §534).

Previously we would have expected Nietzsche to say that the criterion of truth resides not in enhancement but in preservation. Now he is saying that, since the fulfillment of the preservation-need is properly in the service of enhancement, it is in enhancement that we find the criterion of truth. Thus a category is true to the degree that the permanence it establishes serves for the enhancement of power, serves the will's self-overcoming.

T. The sublime man.

The foregoing issues are elaborated in the Second Part of *Thus Spoke Zarathustra*, in the section "On Those Who Are Sublime." Nietzsche describes a man who is sublime, solemn, "an ascetic of the spirit": "As yet he has not learned laughter or beauty. Gloomy this hunter returned from the woods of knowledge. He came home from a fight with savage beasts; but, out of his seriousness, there also peers a savage beast—one not overcome" (TSZ, p. 229).

This man returned *gloomy* from his hunt for knowledge. His gloom is related to the outcome of that hunt. The same is expressed in the Fourth Part in the section "On the Magician," where this "ascetic of the spirit" is discussed. There he is characterized by the magician as one "who at least turns his spirit against himself, the changed man who freezes to death from his evil science and conscience" (TSZ, p. 368). Also, in "The leech," this same type of man expresses himself by saying: "I go to the ground. . . . A hand's breadth of ground suffices me, provided it is really ground and foundation. A hand's breadth of ground—on that one can stand" (TSZ, p. 362).

How then to understand this hunt for the ground, a hunt from which the sublime man returns gloomy? Such a hunt for ground on which to stand is characteristic of Socratism. It is the hunt Nietzsche enacts in his "critique of knowledge." The ground to which Nietzsche comes back is himself as artist. That is, beneath knowledge and its "objects," he discovers (as ground) his own creativity. The result is, in the first instance, skepticism, a lack of any guarantee whatever that his knowledge and its objects involve anything but mere fiction. Indeed, these come to be seen merely as serving for the fulfillment of certain existential needs. Furthermore, even this knowledge about knowledge cannot sustain itself. The situation is comparable to that of the skeptic who claims to know that there is no knowledge. The critique is in the end senseless.

Zarathustra says regarding the sublime man: "He subdued monsters, he solved riddles. But he must still redeem his own monsters and riddles, changing them into heavenly children" (TSZ, p. 230). His own "monsters and riddles" we can take to mean his own creativity—and indeed it is a monster and a riddle within the sphere of knowledge. It explodes this sphere; it is the riddle on which Socratism founders.

The question then becomes: What is required in order to redeem the creativity, to change it into a heavenly *child*? What is required for the birth of the child? The passage says of the sublime man: "As yet he has not learned laughter or beauty." He must still learn beauty—he is in need of art. More specifically, he needs to take up a different kind of relation to those illusions (appearances) which he has discovered to be projected only by his own creativity. He needs to be related to these illusions in a way that takes them not in terms of the concepts of truth and being but in terms of the concept of beauty. He needs an artistic rather than a metaphysical relation.

Nietzsche draws the contrast in *Twilight of the Idols*. Having spoken of the metaphysical distinction between the "true" and "apparent" worlds as symptomatic of decadence, he goes on to say: "That the artist esteems appearance higher than reality is no objection to this proposition. For 'appearance' in this case means reality *once more*, only by way of selection, reinforcement, and correction" (TI, p. 484). In other words, the artistic relation to illusions is such that we find in them not a negation of life but an incitement to life. "Where is beauty? It is where I must will with all my will, where I want to love and perish that an image may not remain a mere image" (TSZ, p. 235).

So the sublime man returns gloomy because he has discovered that his truths are lies and that lies are even necessary for life. "That lies are necessary in order to live is itself part of the terrifying and questionable character of existence" (WP, §853, I). But the artist is not crushed, not made gloomy, by the necessity of lies and illusions. He delights in illusion. Art is "the good will to illusion" (WP, §853, III). It is from this good will (joy) that the laughter (which the sublime man has not yet learned) will issue forth. So the sublime man's hunt for knowledge leads into a self-destructive skepticism and pessimism in the sphere of knowledge. Art is his redemption from that condition: "Art is the redemption of the man of knowledge—the redemption of those who see the terrifying and questionable character of existence, who want to see it, the men of tragic knowledge" (WP, §853, II). Here is evident the connection with *The Birth of Tragedy*; Nietzsche is speaking of what he earlier called the gaze into the Dionysian abyss. It is the gaze resulting from the collapse of the Socratic search for knowledge. It is insight into truth—not in the Socratic sense but in the Dionysian sense. "'How much truth can a spirit *endure*, how much truth does a spirit dare?'—This became for me the real standard of value" (WP, §1041). What results is the need for a means of *enduring* this Dionysian truth, the need for a means of redemption from the pessimistic wisdom of Silenus, that is, the need for art. "We have art in order not to perish from the truth" (WP, §822).

Thus art for Nietzsche is the decisive countermovement against the nihilism that would separate man from life. Art is what harbors the possibility of man's being bound again to life, being faithful to the earth: "Art and nothing but art! It is the great means of making life possible, the great seduction to life, the great stimulant of life. Art as the only superior counterforce against all will to the denial of life, as that which is anti-Christian, anti-Buddhist, anti-nihilist par excellence" (WP, §853, II).

U. Philosophy and art.

If we grant that Nietzsche enacts a self-destruction of Socratism, then the philosophy issuing from this destruction is clearly not to be understood in terms of the Socratic ideal. In other words, Nietzsche's philosophy is not an attempt at a fundamental uncovering of intelligibility in the Socratic sense. It is not an attempt to uncover first causes and principles, not an ascertaining of ultimate truth in the Socratic sense, not a metaphysics. That is clear in *The Will to Power*: "The ascertaining of 'truth' and 'untruth,' the ascertaining of facts in general, is fundamentally different from creative positing, from forming, shaping, overcoming, willing, such as is of the essence of philosophy" (WP, §605). On the contrary, the character of Nietzsche's philosophy is to be understood as corresponding to the task he already enunciated in *The Birth of Tragedy*: a rebirth of tragedy out of the ashes of science.

Accordingly, Nietzsche's philosophical activity is more nearly akin to art than to theoretical activity in the Socratic sense. At its most fundamental level, Nietzsche's philosophy wants to be regarded primarily in terms of its affinity with art. That is why his tragedy, *Thus Spoke Zarathustra*, is the center of his work and is that to which everything else remains in a sense preliminary. And that is also why in *Beyond Good and Evil* he says of the "philosophers of the future" that "their 'knowing' is a creating" (BGE, p. 326).

This affinity to art is indicated by Nietzsche in many places. "In the main I agree more with the artists than with any philosopher hitherto" (WP, §820). "Those Greeks were superficial—out of profundity. And is not this precisely what we are again coming back to, we daredevils of the spirit who have climbed the highest and most dangerous peak of present thought and looked around from up there—we who have looked *down* from there? Are we not, precisely in this respect, Greeks? Adorers of forms, of tones, of words? And therefore—*artists*?" (NCW, p. 683). Finally, Nietzsche says in *The Birth of Tragedy* and repeats in *The Will to Power*: "Art represents the highest task and the truly metaphysical activity of this life" (BT, p. 31–32; WP, §853, IV).

What is the artistic activity in which Nietzsche's philosophy culminates? According to *The Birth of Tragedy*, it should, as tragedy, be a projection of an Apollinian image from out of that Dionysian insight arising with the destruction of Socratism. The result of this projection, this renewal of tragedy, should be to bind man to the creative-destructive play of life itself, that is, to make possible a "Yes-saying" to life.

V. The eternal recurrence.

The Apollinian image in Nietzsche's tragedy is the idea of the eternal recurrence. What kind of image is this, and how is it capable of binding man to the play of life? The dawn, the birth of the child, is Zarathustra's teaching the idea of the eternal recurrence to himself. That is the sense in which the idea of the eternal recurrence is the central idea of *Thus Spoke Zarathustra*. This self-teaching is for the most part enacted, not narrated. That is, we are not explicitly told what is involved, but rather we see it taking place in act. So we must interpret this enactment. To do so, we need to have certain questions in view in advance, directive questions, ones we can pose to the enactment. To formulate them, let us begin by recalling the passage already cited from *The Gay Science* where the idea of the eternal recurrence makes its first appearance. The title of the section is "The Heaviest Burden," and in it Nietzsche asks how we would respond to a daimon telling us that everything in life will recur: Would we curse that daimon or say we had never heard anything more divine?

To base our questions on that passage, let us first examine the context. The immediately preceding section is called "The Dying Socrates." Here Nietzsche considers the last words of Socrates, the ones in which Socrates betrayed that he had finally attained a glimpse of the failure of Socratism and its optimism. In Nietzsche's eyes, Socrates, by saying he owed a sacrifice to Asclepios for being healed, was in effect acknowledging that he suffered from life and that he sensed the impotence of the optimistic promise of banishing all suffering. Socrates' last words betray his glimpse into that inevitable shortcoming of Socratism which would eventually lead to its collapse and to a renewed need for tragedy. The last words of Socrates serve to highlight that most radical failure on the part of the Greeks, their failure in the task of overcoming the opposition between the Socratic and the tragic, their failure to preserve tragedy in the face of Socratism.

The section ends with Nietzsche's own assumption of that task: "We must overcome even the Greeks!" How is this overcoming to be accomplished? The next section ("The Heaviest Burden") provides the answer. It is by taking on the burden of the idea of the eternal recurrence that even the Greeks are to be overcome. In other words, that is how the opposition of the Socratic and tragic and the resulting destruction of tragedy are to be overcome. It is how there is to be born a kind of tragedy capable of withstanding the power of Socratism (rather than being destroyed by it—as happened to tragedy with the Greeks).

This way of overcoming is confirmed by the section immediately following "The Heaviest Burden" in *The Gay Science*. It is the section ("Tragedy Begins") that is nearly identical with the first words of *Thus Spoke Zarathustra*. Accordingly, the introduction of the idea of the eternal recurrence leads to the beginning of the tragedy, the one by which even the Greeks are to be overcome, the tragedy of *Thus Spoke Zarathustra*.

So our first question is: How does the idea of the eternal recurrence bring about a rebirth of tragedy, a tragedy of such a kind as to overcome even the Greeks? Otherwise expressed, what is the connection between the idea of the eternal recurrence and the tragic? How is the eternal recurrence a tragic idea?

In "The Heaviest Burden," we are told something about the communication of the idea of the eternal recurrence, namely, that it is communicated to one's solitude. Recall what Nietzsche says about solitude in *The Gay Science*: "For a pious man, there is no solitude; we, the godless, have been the first to invent it." Thus solitude is the condition of the godless man, the man who has experienced the death of God; hence, it is to the man in the condition of nihilism that the idea is addressed. This suggests more generally that there are certain existential preconditions necessary in order for one to be genuinely addressed by this idea, that is, in order for one to begin teaching this idea to oneself.

The precondition is confirmed in several other passages. In *The Will to Power*, §1058, Nietzsche speaks of the "ripeness of man for this idea." Another section of that work is more explicit: "Every doctrine for which all accumulated energies and explosives are not yet ready at hand is superfluous. A revaluation of values is achieved only when there is a tension of new needs, of men with new needs, who suffer from the old values without attaining this consciousness" (WP, §1008). Furthermore, Nietzsche tells us that on one who lacks this precondition, the idea is not able to exercise its power: "Our highest insights must—and should—sound like follies and sometimes like crimes when they are heard without permission by those who are not predisposed and predestined for them" (BGE, p. 232).

Thus our second question is: What are the preconditions necessary in order to be able to teach oneself the idea of the eternal recurrence?

"The Heaviest Burden" characterizes the idea of the eternal recurrence as something communicated, handed over. That is elaborated in the passage from *Ecce Homo* in which Nietzsche explicitly identifies the idea of the eternal recurrence as the central idea of *Thus Spoke Zarathustra*: "Now I shall relate the history of *Zarathustra*. The fundamental conception of this work, the idea of the eternal recurrence, this highest formula of affirmation that is at all attainable, traces back to the August of 1881: it was penned on a sheet with the notation, '6,000 feet beyond man and time.' That day I was walking through the woods along the lake of Silvaplana; at a powerful pyramidal rock not far from Surlei I stopped. It was then that this idea came to me" (EH, p. 751).

Nietzsche does *not* say that he discovered the idea, nor that he deduced it from some further ideas or principles, nor even that he invented it; rather, he says it *came to him*. It is a "revelation." That is the term Nietzsche uses to characterize the state of inspiration in which he composed *Thus Spoke Zarathustra*: "The concept of revelation—in the sense that suddenly, with indescribable certainty and subtlety, something becomes visible, audible, something that shakes one to the last depths and throws one down—that merely describes the facts. One hears, one does not seek; one accepts, one does not ask who gives; like lightning, a thought flashes up, with necessity, without hesitation regarding its form—I never had any choice" (EH, p. 756).

In "The Heaviest Burden," Nietzsche identifies the one who communicates this idea: it is a daimon. But that simply means, according to Nietzsche's discussion of Socrates' daimon in *The Birth of Tragedy*, that what communicates the idea remains outside the scope of Socratic uncovering. It is something intrinsically veiled, concealed. So our third question arises: How is the idea communicated? In what form, as what kind of idea, does it come to us? What is the *form* of the idea of the eternal recurrence?

The idea has not only a form but also a *content*. The content is expressed in "The Heaviest Burden" as follows: "This life, as you live it now and have lived it, you must live once more and even innumerable times." The content is expressed more fully by Zarathustra's animals:

> Behold, we know what you teach: that all things recur eternally, and we ourselves too, and that we have already existed an eternal number of times, and all things with us. You teach that there is a Great Year [one complete wobble of the earth on its axis, equivalent to approximately 24,000 calendar years] of becoming, a monster of a Great Year, which must, like an hourglass, turn over again and again so that it may run down and run out again; and all these years are alike in what is grandest as in what is smallest; and we ourselves are alike in every Great Year, in what is grandest as in what is smallest. (TSZ, p. 332)

So the content of the idea can be expressed as follows: it is a *representation* of all things as eternally recurring in identically the same way and form. That raises two further questions. First, what else does this representation entail regarding things and regarding man? That is, what other features must things be implicitly represented as possessing when we represent them as eternally recurring? In other words, what is the *full* content of the idea? Second, what kind of representation is this idea? What (if anything) is the relation between this representation and what is represented? We might at first suppose that this relation is one of correspondence, that the content of the representation corresponds to things as they are, that it is to be a *true* idea. We have seen, however, that nihilism involves the collapse of any such concept of truth and the realization that "truth" is a kind of error. Indeed, in "The Heaviest Burden," the question of whether this is a true idea is not even raised. So what kind of representation is this? Is it perhaps true in a sense that resides outside the traditional, metaphysical, understanding of truth?

If we combine these two questions regarding content, then our fourth question can be simply formulated: What is the *content* of the idea?

The idea of the eternal recurrence is called the "heaviest burden." That means its effect is *not* to relieve man of all burdens. In fact, that relief was already accomplished by the self-destruction of the tradition, by the advent of nihilism in which nothing remains binding upon man. Instead, the effect of the idea of the eternal recurrence is to place a new burden on man, indeed the heaviest burden, one even heavier than that originally placed on him at the stage of the camel.

As a heavier burden, it will more radically reshape man; it will bind man and in doing so will be transformative. For the most part, the passage speaks of nothing else but the binding power of the idea and the transformation of man it can evoke. Specifically, the passage considers what could happen "if that thought acquired power over you." We are told it would be a heavy burden on all man's activities and that it would call for a response on man's part ("how well disposed would you have to become to yourself and to life"). We are told the burden would be a great danger—it would perhaps crush man. On the other hand, however, it might lead man to become so well disposed toward life as to make him long for its eternal recurrence: in this way it holds out the possibility of evoking in man the highest affirmation of life.

A general indication of the transformation of man achievable by this idea is provided in the passage from *Ecce Homo* just cited: it is an idea by which we are placed "6,000 feet beyond man and time." "Beyond man" means the idea can transform man into the overman. "Beyond time" means this transformation involves a radical new relation to time, an overcoming of the relation to time by which man is dragged down, burdened by the weight of time. So our fifth question concerns that transformative relation: What is the transformation of man evoked by his coming to be bound by the idea of the eternal recurrence?

* * *

Let us begin with the second question: What are the preconditions necessary for teaching oneself the idea of the eternal recurrence? In a note from the literary remains, Nietzsche offers an important indication: "Are you now prepared? You must have experienced every grade of skepticism and have bathed with voluptuousness in ice-cold streams—otherwise you have no right to this thought" (IB, vol. 2, §1351). Thus a necessary precondition is the movement through the most radical skepticism, that is, through the recoil of knowledge upon itself, exemplified historically in the self-destruction of Socratism (death of God) and enacted in Nietzsche's own "critique of knowledge" within the framework of the theory of the will to power. The character of this precondition is indicated more fully in "On the Vision and the Riddle": "To you, the bold searchers, researchers, and whoever embarks with cunning sails on terrible seas—to you, drunk with riddles, glad of the twilight, whose soul flutes lure astray to every whirlpool, because you do not want to grope along a thread with cowardly hand; and where you can guess, you hate to deduce—to you alone I tell the riddle that I saw, the vision of the most solitary" (TSZ, pp. 267–68).

Here Nietzsche is describing the condition of those to whom the "vision of the most solitary" can be told. This vision is, of course, that of the eternal recurrence. What follows this introduction is perhaps Zarathustra's most important "account" of the eternal recurrence.

One must be "drunk with riddles." Which riddles? —Precisely the ones encountered in the movement through skepticism, the riddles involved in the self-destruction of the Socratic uncovering, in its being driven to uncover that whose concealment is required by the very possibility of the Socratic project. One must have become *drunk* on these riddles—that is, driven by them back to the god of wine, Dionysus, driven to retrieval of the Dionysian insight, the gaze into the Dionysian abyss.

Zarathustra says that flutes must lure one's soul astray to every whirlpool—because one no longer wants to grope along a thread with cowardly hands. That is, one no longer wants to move along blindly, slowly uncovering things, as the Socratic man does. Instead, flutes now lead one's soul astray. The flute is the instrument of Dionysus; one hears the music of Dionysus and is lured to the whirlpool, to a gaze into the Dionysian abyss.

Therefore, one is "glad of the twilight," namely, the twilight of the idols, the destruction of Socratism, of metaphysics, and of all that was akin to and supported by metaphysics.

The preconditions are further elaborated in terms of the idea of solitude. We know from the passage in *The Gay Science* that the idea of the eternal recurrence is communicated to someone who is in the condition of solitude. Nietzsche identifies this condition with that of man without God, man who has experienced the death of God, man in the condition of nihilism. In "The Return Home," Zarathustra's home is identified as his solitude. He describes this solitude as follows: "Here the words and word-shrines of all being open up before me: here all being wishes to become word, all becoming wishes to learn from me how to speak" (TSZ, p. 296).

In solitude, the "word-shrines of being open up." That is, being is revealed as enshrined in words, as instituted by man in his words and concepts. This is the collapse of being into subjectivity.

Zarathustra says being wishes to become word; all becoming wishes to learn from him. That expresses the same collapse, but in positive terms. It is the experience of oneself as *creator*, as instituting that being by which becoming can be spoken. It is this most intimate presence to self ("feeling of self") that constitutes genuine solitude. Accordingly, Nietzsche says: "In the end, one experiences only oneself" (TSZ, p. 264). So it is to this condition, the recovery of the creative, Dionysian self, that the idea of the eternal recurrence is communicated.

A further issue involved in the preconditions is expressed in "The Wanderer": "Before my highest mountain I stand and before my longest wandering; to that end I must first go down deeper than ever I descended—deeper into pain than ever I descended, down into the blackest flood. . . . It is out of the deepest depth that the highest must come to its height" (TSZ, p. 266). Required is a descent into pain, into suffering. Nietzsche later says: "Divine suffering is the substance of the third part of *Zarathustra*" (Section 77 of "Explanatory notes to *Thus Spoke Zarathustra*," p. 280). That means suffering is fundamentally at issue in the appropriation of the idea of the eternal recurrence.

We have seen that the idea of the eternal recurrence is the formula of the highest affirmation. Nietzsche is now saying that appropriation of the idea, embodiment of such affirmation in oneself, requires the most profound insight into suffering. Indeed, this is the highest affirmation precisely because it takes upon itself and affirms what is most negative—destruction, suffering. Thus Nietzsche says: "Whoever has really . . . looked into, down into the most world-denying of all possible ways of thinking—beyond good and evil and no longer, like the Buddha and Schopenhauer, under the spell and delusion of morality—may just thereby, without really meaning to do so, have opened his eyes to the opposite ideal: the ideal of the most high-spirited, alive, and world-affirming human being who has not only come to terms and learned to get along with whatever was and is, but who wants to have *what was and is* repeated into all eternity" (BGE, p. 258).

Thus the most extreme denial and the highest affirmation lie in closest proximity, and the highest affirmation requires descent into that which provokes the most extreme denial. We can thereby summarize the preconditions: fulfillment of nihilism, solitude, recovery of the Dionysian, descent into suffering.

The delineation of these preconditions and the correlative coming of the idea of the eternal recurrence constitute the principal theme of latter sections of the Second Part of *Thus Spoke Zarathustra*. Thereby we receive several important clues regarding our third question, the one concerning the form of the idea.

After the songs and after the speech on the will to power ("On Self-Overcoming"), the sublime man is portrayed. He is the one who returns gloomy from the hunt for knowledge. By comparing this description with the others given in the Fourth Part, we have seen that the sublime man is the one who has brought Socratism (metaphysics) to the point of radical self-destruction. The sublime man exists in a state of utter nihilism, which is the first precondition for the coming of the idea of the eternal recurrence.

The sublime man still needs to learn laughter and beauty. To learn beauty means, among other things, to become receptive—to let something (the beautiful) come to him: "He must still discard his heroic will. He shall be elevated, not merely sublime: the ether itself should elevate him, the will-less one. . . . But just for the hero the *beautiful* is the most difficult thing. No violent will can attain the beautiful by exertion. A little more, a little less: precisely this counts for much here, this matters most here. To stand with relaxed muscles and unharnessed will: that is the most difficult for all of you who are sublime" (TSZ, p. 230).

What is the beautiful by which the hero (sublime man) must be addressed? Zarathustra says: "When power becomes gracious and descends into the visible—such descent I call beauty" (TSZ, p. 230). Then what is this descent of power into the visible? In "On Immaculate Perception" (primarily an attack on Schopenhauer's concept of beauty as object of disinterested contemplation), Zarathustra provides an indication: "Where is beauty? —Where I must will with all my will; where I want to love and perish that an image may not remain a mere image" (TSZ, p. 235).

So beauty is that which comes to one (for which one must be receptive, will-less) but which in turn provokes the highest degree of willing. In other words, beauty is an image of such a character as to provoke the greatest enhancement of will. Thus, truth (in Nietzsche's sense, as having its criterion in enhancement) is for Nietzsche, as for the Platonic tradition, identical with beauty. What is the image that most enhances the will? To enhance means to be a formula of the highest affirmation, to be an image capable of provoking the highest affirmation. The beautiful (the true) that must come to the hero is the image of the eternal recurrence.

Yet how is this beauty to come to him? The section "On Those Who Are Sublime" concludes with an answer: "For this is the soul's secret: only when the hero has abandoned her is she approached in a dream by the overhero" (TSZ, p. 231). The same point is made negatively in the next section ("On the Hand of Education") where Zarathustra speaks of those who are incapable of achieving what is needed by the sublime man: "You are sterile; that is why you lack faith. But whoever needed to create also had his prophetic dreams and astral signs—and had faith in faith" (TSZ, p. 232). So the beautiful, the image of the eternal recurrence, comes in a dream—it is a dream image.

Yet this dream image is radically different from those of previous poets. Zarathustra says of poets: "I have grown weary of the poets, the old and the new. Superficial they all seem to me and like shallow seas. Their thoughts have not penetrated deeply enough; therefore, their feelings did not touch bottom.... All their harp jingling is to me the breathing and flitting of ghosts. What have they ever known of the fervor of tones?" (TSZ, p. 240).

The poets have not been deep enough and do not know the fervor of tones. In other words, the poets have not descended into the Dionysian, into the depths of suffering, into that which, according to *The Birth of Tragedy*, is the spirit of music. By contrast, Zarathustra's dream image is to be one that in some way does grow out of such a descent.

Zarathustra sums up his critique of the poets by saying: "Ah, how weary I am of all the imperfection which must at all costs become event!" (TSZ, p. 240). There follows a different kind of event, as indicated by the title of the next section, "On Great Events." What is the great event? It is Zarathustra's descent into hell, his descent into the heart of the earth, from which he returns with the teaching that "the heart of the earth is of gold" (TSZ, p. 244).

Zarathustra's task becomes that of preserving this teaching against the great sadness spoken of by the soothsayer, thus the task of teaching this teaching to himself, appropriating it. Therefore, Zarathustra must return to his solitude. Just before he withdraws, he sums up the entire issue: "Do you know the fright of him who falls asleep? He is frightened down to his very toes because the ground gives way under him and the dream begins. This I say to you as a parable" (TSZ, p. 257).

The idea of the eternal recurrence comes in dreams; it comes as an Apollinian image. And the dream begins once "the ground gives way under him"—thus after the collapse of metaphysics and after the renewal of a gaze into the Dionysian abyss. The beginning of such a dream is a rebirth of tragedy.

* * *

Three of our questions remain. A statement in "On the Convalescent" is decisive for all of them. It is Zarathustra's declaration of who he is, and it occurs as he summons the idea of the eternal recurrence: "I, Zarathustra, the advocate of life, the advocate of suffering, the advocate of the circle; I summon you, my most abysmal thought" (TSZ, p. 328). Our answer to the remaining three questions will need to show how the following belong together: advocate of the circle, advocate of life, advocate of suffering.

The fifth and last question we formulated was as follows: How does the idea of the eternal recurrence bind man? This question concerns the transformation brought about when man comes to be bound by the idea of the eternal recurrence. A clue is found in a statement we already quoted, attributable to Zarathustra's animals: "For your animals know well, O Zarathustra, who you are and must become: behold, you are the teacher of the eternal recurrence—that is your destiny." So Zarathustra *is*, and must *become*, the teacher of the eternal recurrence, the advocate of the circle; Zarathustra must become who he is. How? —By teaching the eternal recurrence, by teaching it first of all to himself. To appropriate this idea, to let it be binding on himself, is to become who he is. And that is how the eternal recurrence binds man: in such a way that man can become who he is. What is the character of this transformation by which one becomes who one is? What does it mean to become who one is?

Clearly this is not a transformation in which man actualizes some pregiven ideal. With the advent of nihilism, all such ideals are lacking. Instead, to become who one is means to be related in a new way to who one is. It means no longer to negate and conceal who one is for the sake of some afterworld. It means to affirm the truth of who one is, to love this truth, to love one's fate.

What is this truth? It is not the truth of the Socratic uncovering, not the truth of metaphysics, not the truth merely projected by the subject as a means of fulfilling its preservation-needs. Instead, it is the truth into which man gazes only after the utter collapse of the Socratic project. It is the truth of which we heard Nietzsche speak as follows: "'How much truth can a spirit *endure*, how much truth does a spirit dare?'—This became for me the real standard of value" (WP, §1041). In other words, it is the Dionysian truth.

The idea of the eternal recurrence binds man by binding him to the truth. It binds in such a way as to evoke an affirmation, a love, of the Dionysian truth. What it thus evokes is an enhancement of life over against negation or mere preservation. Zarathustra, the advocate of the circle, is thereby the advocate of life. Moreover, since the criterion of truth resides in enhancement (WP, §534), the idea of the eternal recurrence is itself true. It is so, not in the sense of correspondence with the way things are, not in the Socratic sense, but in the sense of being in accord with life as self-overcoming. It is true in the sense of being able to bind man to that Dionysian truth which intrinsically involves concealment and so can never be represented in a Socratic theory. It binds man to that primordial truth which is not to be viewed as, and transposed into, a theoretical construction but which is to be endured and enacted. Thus the idea of the eternal recurrence is true not by representing things as they are in themselves but by binding man to that primordial truth which escapes every attempt at representation.

To say that the primordial truth escapes representation means that the idea of the eternal recurrence is not a scientific truth, not a cosmology. The eternal recurrence cannot be proved by an appeal to scientific findings. Yet there is a passage in the literary remains that seems in fact to constitute such an appeal. It is a passage that tells how the doctrine of the eternal recurrence is "substantiated":

> The sum total of energy in the universe is a determinate quantity; energy is not "infinite" (let us guard ourselves from such conceptual excesses). Accordingly, the states, changes, combinations, and vicissitudes of this energy, although they may be enormously great and practically speaking "incalculable," are limited in number and are not infinite. Quite to the contrary, however, the time in which the universe exerts its energy is indeed infinite. That is to say, energy remains eternally the same and eternally active. Up to this moment an infinity of time has already elapsed, which means all possible vicissitudes of the available energy must have already occurred. Therefore the present state must be a repetition, as was also the one that gave birth to it, and as will also be the one it gives birth to. And so on and on forwards and backwards! (IB, vol. 2, §1309)

From this and similar passages, commentators have understood the idea of the eternal recurrence as Nietzsche's cosmology, his doctrine of things as they are, a doctrine based on a scientific foundation. We know by now that such an interpretation is totally impossible. The idea of the eternal recurrence is not a scientific truth, not a cosmology, not an objective truth of things as they are in themselves. For Nietzsche, there are no things in themselves, and Nietzsche is not likely to base any philosophical ideas on scientific findings. What is Nietzsche's view of science?

In the "Attempt at a Self-Criticism," Nietzsche claims that even in his first book he was concerned with the problem of science. From his later perspective, as we quoted at the beginning of our study of Nietzsche on truth, he says that the problem really confronting him in *The Birth of Tragedy* was *"the problem of science itself,* science considered for the first time as problematic, as questionable." In *Beyond Good and Evil*, Nietzsche again points to the questionableness of science: "It is perhaps just dawning on five or six minds that physics, too, is only an interpretation and exegesis of the world (to suit us, if I may say so!) and not an explanation" (BGE, p. 211). In *On the Genealogy of Morals*, Nietzsche considers science in relation to the ascetic ideal. It might at first seem that science, with its reliance on the evidence of the senses, offers a genuine alternative to asceticism. But for Nietzsche it is not so; the scientist is rather the most subtle *exponent* of the ascetic ideal. In the first place, the scientist still believes in the truth, truth in the sense of the Socratic uncovering of things as they are in themselves. Secondly, the scientist desires to stop at the brute facts and avoid all interpretation. Therefore, the scientist practices in the theoretical sphere a kind of self-denial comparable to the ascetic's repudiation of the sensual in favor of the spiritual. The scientist is not far removed from the religious ascetic. The scientific ideal is not at all an alternative to the traditional ascetic ideal:

> Don't come to me with science when I ask for the natural antagonist to the ascetic ideal. . . . Science requires in every respect an ideal of value, a value-creating power, in the service of which it could believe in itself—it never creates values. Its relation to the ascetic ideal is by no means essentially antagonistic; science might even be said to represent the driving force in the inner development of that ideal. . . . This pair, science and the ascetic ideal, both rest on the same foundation, on the same overestimation of truth. . . . A depreciation of the ascetic ideal unavoidably involves a depreciation of science. (GM, p. 589)

We know that Nietzsche does depreciate the ascetic ideal, and so he must unavoidably depreciate scientific research. He could not then appeal to science as substantiation for the idea of the eternal recurrence. Therefore, in the quotation above from the literary remains, Nietzsche cannot be propounding a cosmology, especially not one rooted in science. Yet, on the other hand, *The Will to Power* says that the idea of the eternal recurrence is "the most *scientific* of all possible hypotheses" (WP, §55).

When Nietzsche speaks of science in a positive way, he is thinking of its denial of final ends, final goals. For example, Nietzsche says that, ever since

Copernicus, man has been "rolling from the center" but has not been heading toward any definite end, has been heading "toward x" (WP, §1). The crucial point is that in denying final goals, science must deny itself its own final goal, namely, truth as the goal of its uncovering activity. So the idea of the eternal recurrence is scientific not as a cosmology erected on the basis of empirical data but only in the sense of representing the point at which science comes to its fulfillment in the denial of final goals, that is, the point at which science fulfills itself by negating itself, biting its own tail. In *The Will to Power*, Nietzsche says: "Let us think this thought [of the lack of final goals] in its most terrible form: the eternal recurrence. This is the most extreme form of nihilism: nothingness (meaninglessness) eternally!" (WP, §55).

The idea of the eternal recurrence stands at the point of the most extreme nihilism, the point able to generate the need whence can arise a rebirth of tragedy and tragic art. According to *The Birth of Tragedy*, science, when driven to its limit, changes into art (BT, pp. 95–96). Thus the idea of the eternal recurrence is the most scientific in the sense that it expresses the result of science being driven to its limit, the point at which science is transformed into art. The idea of the eternal recurrence is "proved" as art, not as science.

How is art "proved?" —Not by corresponding to things as they are, but by enhancing life. So now we can see what is at issue in the seemingly empirical proof of the eternal recurrence. The theory of the will to power portrays the collapse of science. Thus it is the theory of the will to power, not science as such, that is to be the basis of a "proof" of the idea of the eternal recurrence. The states of energy spoken of in the proof are not states as understood by science but are rather centers of energy in the sense of wills to power. The will to power expresses the basic nature of everything that is. "The world viewed from inside, the world defined according to its intelligible character—this world would be will to power" (BGE, §36).

All things as will to power, and the theory of the will to power as "proof" of the eternal recurrence—are these then the truth? Do the theory of the will to power and the idea of the eternal recurrence correspond to what things are in themselves? No; the theory and the idea are true only in Nietzsche's sense of truths: images projected as all great art is projected, namely, to serve for the enhancement of life. So Nietzsche is not propounding anything that could be called a cosmology. He is not doing science or basing himself on science. He is doing what issues from science when brought to its limit. He is offering artistic images.

Let us now take up our fourth question, the question of content. What is the content of the idea of the eternal recurrence, and how does this content serve to evoke the highest affirmation? In other words, how does the content serve to bind man, in a relation of love, to the truth of Dionysian wisdom? How does the content evoke an *amor fati*?

The content of the idea of the eternal recurrence embodies the collapse of the metaphysical distinction between time and eternity, becoming and being. It does so by representing becoming *as* eternal. The idea represents eternity, not as something over against time, something metaphysical, but rather as belonging to becoming itself. Eternity is the eternity *of* becoming, the eternal recurrence of the moments of becoming. Nietzsche expresses this eternity of becoming in a famous statement from *The Will to Power*: "To impose upon becoming the character of being—that is the supreme will to power.... That everything recurs is the closest approximation of a world of becoming to a world of being: high point of the meditation" (WP, §617).

This content means that the idea presents to man an image of the world as involving no possible escape from time and becoming into an afterworld. It presents to man an image of his indissoluble bond to life, becoming, and time. It is an image according to which there is no escape from life: if one seeks to escape—even by the most extreme denial, suicide—one only escapes to another recurrence of the same life. Thus Zarathustra's animals say to him:

> And if you wanted to die now, O Zarathustra, behold, we also know how you would then speak to yourself.... "Now I die and vanish," you would say, "and all at once I am nothing. The soul is as mortal as the body. But the knot of causes in which I am entangled recurs and will create me again. I myself belong to the causes of the eternal recurrence. I come again, with this sun, with this earth, with this eagle, with this serpent—not to a new life or a better life or a similar life: I come back eternally to this same, selfsame life, in what is greatest as in what is smallest, to teach again the eternal recurrence of all things, to speak again the word of the great noon of earth and man, to proclaim the overman again to men." (TSZ, p. 333)

So the image of the world as one of eternal recurrence is a radical denial of all escape from life and a radical affirmation of man's bond to life. "Everything becomes and recurs eternally—escape is impossible" (WP, §1058).

The idea presents the eternity of becoming as the eternal recurrence of the *same*, of the *same becoming*. The animals speak of coming back not to a new life or better life or worse life but to the selfsame life. Accordingly, for man the eternity of becoming does not consist in a never-ending passage through different lives; the eternal recurrence is not a doctrine of transmigration. The idea of the eternal recurrence says that there is no possibility of escape to an afterlife or to another, different, earthly life. Man returns eternally to live again identically the same life.

Thus the idea portrays man's bond not just to earthly life as such but to a particular earthly life, namely, this one. To say "Yes" to life does not mean simply to affirm one's bond to life and to becoming in general; it means to say "Yes" to one's current life.

Nietzsche speaks of the eternal recurrence of a "Great Year," and, as the animals say, "all these years are alike." This absolute sameness is elaborated in another conception Nietzsche repeatedly presents as belonging to the content of the idea. It could be called a conception of the intertwining of all things.

The intertwining is asserted cryptically in "On the Vision and the Riddle": "And are not all things knotted together so firmly that this moment draws after it *all* that is to come?" (TSZ, p. 270). Thus the idea of the eternal recurrence is an image of things as so thoroughly intertwined that the recurrence of anything must be the recurrence of everything, that is, the recurrence of identically the same Great Year.

What is the import of this intertwining for the way the idea binds man? "In the actual world, everything is so absolutely linked and related to everything else that to condemn or think away anything means to condemn and think away the whole" (WP, §584). Nietzsche expresses the positive side of same issue as follows: "The first question is by no means whether we are content with ourselves but is whether we are content with anything at all. If we affirm one single moment, we thus affirm not only ourselves but all existence" (WP, §1032). The same positive side is elaborated in "The Drunken Song":

> Have you ever said "Yes" to a single joy? O my friends, then you also said "Yes" to all woe. All things are entangled, ensnared, enamored; if ever you wanted one thing twice, if ever you said, "You please me, happiness! Abide, moment!" then you wanted everything back. Everything anew, everything eternally, eternal recurrence entangled, ensnared, enamored. O, you then loved the world. Eternal ones, love it eternally and evermore; and to woe also you say: "Go, but return!" For every joy wants—eternity! (TSZ, p. 435)

The point is that the idea of the eternal recurrence presents man with an image eliminating all "middle ground," that is, excluding the possibility of partial affirmation and partial negation. To affirm a single moment is to affirm life totally, and to deny a single moment is to deny life totally. There are only two alternatives: either a person says "Yes" to life as a whole or he says "No" to it as a whole.

How does the idea of the eternal recurrence evoke a "Yes" rather than a "No"? To see that, we must examine more closely what lies in the way of affirming life. What is it that most drastically serves to prevent man's "Yes" to life in its entirety? What is it about life that provokes man to negation and to an attempted flight into an afterlife? We have seen already that such flight concerns man's relation to suffering. Regarding the conclusions of metaphysics, Nietzsche writes: "It is suffering that inspires these conclusions. Fundamentally they are *desires* that such a world should exist; in the same way, to imagine another, more valuable world is an expression of hatred for that world which makes one suffer. The resentment of metaphysicians against actuality is here creative" (WP, §579).

Nietzsche makes the same point in "On the Afterworldly": "It was suffering and incapacity that created all afterworlds" (TSZ, p. 143). So what stands in the way of man's affirmation is his incapacity to affirm suffering; man can be an advocate of life only by being an advocate of suffering. What stands in the way is man's resentment against suffering, that is, the spirit of revenge. Accordingly, Zarathustra says: "For man to be delivered from revenge, that is for me the bridge to the highest hope and is a rainbow after long storms" (TSZ, p. 211). The question is then: How does this idea of the eternal recurrence evoke from man a transformation by which he is delivered from the spirit of revenge? How is it that the advocate of the circle and of life is also an advocate of suffering?

In order to answer, we must see how Nietzsche understands the spirit of revenge in its most primordial form. His understanding is expressed in "On Redemption":

> Willing liberates; but what is it that puts even the liberator himself in fetters? "It was"—that is the name of the will's gnashing of teeth and most secret melancholy. Powerless against what has been done, the will is an angry spectator of all that is past. The will cannot will backwards; it cannot break time and time's covetousness—that is the will's loneliest melancholy.... Time does not run backwards—that is the will's wrath. "That which was" is the name of the stone the will cannot move. And so the will moves stones out of wrath.... Thus the will, the liberator, took to hurting; and on all who can suffer the will wreaks revenge for the inability to go backwards. This, indeed this alone, is what revenge is: the will's ill will against time and its "It was." (TSZ, p. 251)

So revenge is ill will against time in the character of time as passing, as solidifying into an irretrievable "It was" over which the will to power has absolutely no power. Thus the spirit of revenge (and hence the whole dreadful spectacle that results in nihilism) is rooted in the conflict between the character of subjectivity as will to power (as overpowering) and the subjection of the subject to time (by which everything is withdrawn from the subject's sphere of power into an irretrievable "It was"). Accordingly, what is required in order to deliver man from the spirit of revenge is deliverance from the ceaseless passing, the eternal flux: "I teach you deliverance from eternal flux: the flux flows again and again back into itself and again and again raises you into the same flux, as the same" (IB, vol. 2, §1300).

How then does the idea of the eternal recurrence deliver man from revenge, from resentment against the passing of time? Zarathustra says: "To redeem those who lived in the past and to re-create all 'It was' into a 'Thus I willed it'—that alone would I call redemption" (TSZ, p. 251). Yet how is the "It was" re-created into a "Thus I willed it"? How is the past rendered subject to man's willing in the same way that the future is subject to it? How can the will will backwards? Do not the two paths, past and future, meeting at the gateway called the "moment," in fact "offend each other face to face" (TSZ, p. 270)? Is it not the case that "these paths contradict each other eternally" (TSZ, p. 270)?

Zarathustra says: "The now and the past on earth—alas, my friends, that is what I find most unendurable; and I should not know how to live if I were not also a seer of that which must come" (TSZ, p. 250). The point is that the idea of the eternal recurrence proclaims the abolition of the distinction between past and future. It abolishes the irretrievableness of the "It was" by proclaiming that the "It was" will recur—that it stands as much in the future as in the past. The eternal recurrence holds before man an image capable of evoking a new relation of man to time, capable of so transforming man's relation to time as to exclude the possibility of that relation of resentment lying at the root of the traditional ideal.

W. Conclusion. Song.

Let us conclude with our first question: the connection to tragedy.

The idea of the eternal recurrence presents man with an image capable of evoking an affirmation, a "Yes-saying" to life. This "Yes-saying" is, most fundamentally, a new relation of man to his temporality—a "Yes-saying" to temporality versus resentment against time, the resentment lying at the root of metaphysics. The eternal recurrence binds man by binding him to life, to its Dionysian truth. It binds man by letting him be bound to the creative-destructive play, the very form of which is given in temporality with its existential ambiguity. That which is capable of letting man be bound to this play is what, from early on, Nietzsche calls tragedy.

The idea of the eternal recurrence is a tragic idea. It is an Apollinian image born out of the spirit of Dionysian music. Thus, in the last two sections of the Third Part of *Thus Spoke Zarathustra*, when Zarathustra comes finally to teach this idea to himself and to let it exercise its binding power, he again breaks into song (TSZ, pp. 339–40 and p. 343).

This is what he sings in "The Other Dancing Song":

> O man, take care!
> What does the deep midnight declare?
> "I was asleep—
> From a dream I woke and swear:
> The world is deep
> Deeper than day had been aware.
> Deep is its woe;
> Joy—deeper yet than agony:

Woe implores: Go!
But every joy wants eternity—
Wants deep, wants deep eternity."

And, finally, in "The seven seals, or, The yes and amen song," Zarathustra sings as follows:

> Sing! Speak no more! Are not all words made for the grave and heavy? Are not all words lies to those who are light? Speak no more! Sing!

Editor's Afterword

THIS VOLUME OF John Sallis' Collected Writings presents his two-semester lecture course on Nietzsche offered in the Philosophy Department of Duquesne University during the school year 1971–72.

Only minor editorial intervention was required in preparing the text from Sallis' lecture notes. These are written in a clear longhand and are almost always formulated in full sentences. Sallis did at times depart from his notes as he lectured, and I was able to incorporate that impromptu material thanks to a transcription by John Vielkind. The latter was a graduate student enrolled in the class, and a copy of his careful transcription has been a prized possession of mine for many years. Now it served me well in the task of reconstituting the full content of the lectures. Needless to say, Sallis himself has approved the final text. As editor, I articulated the course into outline form, devised the headings, provided a key to the citations of Nietzsche's works, and verified all the references. Finally, although Sallis' notes display few colloquialisms, I needed to make some changes in phraseology and diction, as might be expected in the transition from oral delivery to printed page.

I thank John Sallis for entrusting this volume of his Collected Writings to me and am grateful to John Vielkind for the transcription. For very helpful comments on the penultimate version of the entire text, I am indebted to one of Sallis' current students, now writing her dissertation under his direction at Boston College, my daughter Christine Rojcewicz.

Richard Rojcewicz

Index

absurdity, inherent in life, 24, 26, 31, 35, 51
abyss, Dionysian, 43, 46, 83, 132, 154, 160, 163
advocate of the circle, Zarathustra as, 163–64, 169
Aeschylus, 40–41
aesthetic, distance and involvement, 24; as phenomenon justifying existence, 25, 33; correspondence as an aesthetic relation, 51
aesthetics, *Birth of Tragedy* as, 24–25
affect, the will as, 142
afternoon, as image, 122, 127
afterworld, 102, 121, 125, 138, 163, 167
agony, 111–12
altruism, 64, 67
amor fati, 19, 27, 102, 166. *See also* love of one's fate
Anaximander, 24
animals, Zarathustra's, 91, 98–99, 115, 122, 158, 163, 167–68
antiquarian history, 56–57
anti-Semite, 8–9, 13
Apollo, versus Dionysus, 29–30; as art-energy, 29, 36; as put to the test by Socrates, 40; and the sun, 99–100, 114; and dreams, 101, 113, 122
apparent world, as also abolished when the true world becomes a fable, 136, 143
appearances, versus things-in-themselves, 5, 40; needed to veil the eternal strife, 32–33; as projected by the primal will, 36; constructed and destroyed in play, 37–38; knowledge restricted to, 46; as world of becoming, 79; as ordered according to value, 143, 146, 148
aristocrat, 40, 65
Aristotle, 1, 24, 35, 134, 138
art, philology as handmaid of, 6; Wagner's conception of as non-Christian, 7; *Birth of Tragedy* as treatise about art as such, 24–25; essence of known only in artistic creation, 28; art states of nature as preconditions of, 29–30; as redeeming existence, 32–33; and Socratism, 44–45; must be viewed from the perspective of life, 61–62; and philosophy, 97; will to power as, 136; priority of over truth, 150–152; as redemption from nihilism, 154; how "proved," 166
asceticism, and Schopenhauer, 6; as way of gaining power, 64; science not an alternative to, 165
Asclepios, 43, 156
ashes, 47, 85, 102, 117, 155
atheism, of Schopenhauer, 5; as not equivalent to asserting the death of God, 69–70; versus mere No-saying, 107
autobiography, 2, 13–14

Bach, Johann Sebastian, 28
barbarism, 31, 58
Basel, 6–8, 13
basic question, versus guiding question, 136
Bayreuth, 8–9
beauty, and the Greeks, 24; and culture, 26; of speech, 125; and truth, 125–26; not learned by the sublime man, 153–54; as provoking enhancement of will, 162
becoming, as self-becoming, 17–20, 27; eternal joy of, 35–36; denied by Socratism, 73; versus being, 77, 79–80, 167–68; chaos of, 81, 146; permanence within, 83, 95; flux of, 110, 144, 162–63; eternity of, 167
being, concept of, 7; mothers of, 30; primal being, 34; abysses of, 42; versus becoming, 77, 79–80, 167–68; an empty fiction, 79, 134–35; as projected by thought, 79, 85; a fallacy and a vapor, 130; being qua being (τὸ ὂν ᾗ ὄν), 134; What is being? (τί τὸ ὄν;), 134; question of versus question of beings, 136; and objectivity, 138; and subjectivity,

175

139–40; a derived concept versus activity, 142; word-shrines of, 160
birth, of tragedy out of the spirit of music, 23–37; death of tragedy and birth of Socratism, 39–41; of a dancing star, 88, 100; of the child as final metamorphosis, 111–12, 115; of the child as equivalent to the eternal recurrence, 120; of the overman, 121; of the child as central event of *Thus Spoke Zarathustra*, 149–50, 156
biting its own tail, by Socratism, 45; by morality, 67; by logic, 46, 59, 149–51; of the question of truth, 145–46; by science, 166
blindness, 8, 70
Bonn, University of, 4
Brahms, Johannes, 8
Brandes, Georg, 13
Buddha, 76, 154, 161
buffoon, 20
Burckhardt, Jacob, 8, 13

camel, as image of first stage of homecoming, 100–6, 112–15
Camus, Albert, 44–45
Cartesian *cogito*, 86, 138–40
causa sui, 89
cave, Zarathustra's versus Plato's, 116
chaos, of instincts, 20; of history, 58; of becoming, 81, 146; in oneself, 88, 95, 100; ordering of by the will, 142; of sensations, 147, 152
child, compared by Heraclitus to the world-building force, 27; as image of final stage of homecoming, 111–12; as innocence and forgetting, 111, 117; as play, 111; as self-propelled wheel, 111, 117; as a sacred "Yes," 117, 149; as overman, 120; with a mirror, 113, 122; as new ideal, 118, 134; birth of as central event of *Thus Spoke Zarathustra*, 149–50, 156
chorus, as satyrs, 29, 36; as living wall, 33–34; as engagement in the destructiveness of the primal will, 83
Christianity, as Platonism for the people, 17, 73; and slave revolt in morals, 65; as

negation of life, 71; as mankind's greatest misfortune, 72; and truthfulness, 76
circle, time as, 79; sun's movement as, 81; as image of the eternal recurrence, 112; as relation of creator to created, 118; Zarathustra as advocate of, 163–64, 169
cleanliness, 20, 23, 104
comedy, 14, 26, 33, 118; *Thus Spoke Zarathustra* as, 97–98, 113
communication, 141
concepts, as involving falsification, 50–53
constructive force, the Apollinian as, 37–38
contempt, 98, 103
Copernicus, 166; Copernican Revolution (Kantian spirit), 48
correspondence, truth as, 50–51, 80, 146, 158, 164; as an aesthetic relation, 51
cosmology, what the doctrine of the eternal recurrence is not, 164–66
creativity, and religion, 4; Wagner's, 7; myth needed for, 26–27; joy of, 38; and values, 119; as lying at the basis of knowledge, 153–54
critical history, 57
the Crucified (Nietzsche), 12–13; versus Dionysus, 21
crucifixion, 72
culture, Greek, 8, 23–28; as stimulus to life, 26; epochs of Greek culture, 30–32; decadent scientific culture, 55; defined as unity of artistic style, 39, 108
Cupid, 131–32

dance, 34, 81, 92, 105, 132, Nietzsche's style as, 92; dancing girls, 131; dancing star, 82, 88, 100; "The dancing song," 121, 126, 131–33, 150; "The other dancing song," 170–71
daimon, of Socrates, 42, 179; as communicating the idea of the eternal recurrence, 90, 156, 158
dawn, as image of revaluation, 99; understandable only in terms of night, 150; birth of the child as, 156
death of God, 68–82, 88, 90, 103–4, 107, 109–11, 132, 143, 157, 159–60
decadence, 40, 154; logic of, 70–71, 80; instincts of, 72

depth dimension, 142
Descartes, 136, 138. *See also* Cartesian *cogito*
descent, Zarathustra's, 116–17, 123, 161–63
desert, 11, 109, 112
despisers of the body, 103
destructive force, the Dionysian as, 37–38
dialectic, 40–41
Dionysus, versus Apollo, 29; as art-energy, 29, 35; as master of the chorus, 34; versus Socrates, 39, 43, 145; Nietzsche a disciple of, 83; Nietzsche's dithyramb to, 84, 104; as image of the earth, 100. *See also* abyss
dissonance, musical, 38–39
distinction, personal, 63–64
dithyramb, 84, 104
divine suffering, 161
Doric culture, 31
dragon, 106
dream, Zarathustra's, 122, 126–27, 162–63
drinking, as image, 129–30
dualism, Schopenhauer's of intellect and will, 5–6; of truth and appearance, 110
duel, 4
dynamite, 1

eagle, circling and as image of pride, 91, 99, 115, 167
earth, and Dionysus, 29; unchained from the sun, 68, 74–75, 81, 100; remaining true to, 81, 93, 105, 112, 116; overman as meaning of, 99–100, 102; friend as celebration of, 109; death as a return to, 111, 126–27; art and faithfulness to, 154; heart of as gold, 163
ecstasy, Dionysian, 29–30, 34–38
ego, as measure and value of things, 139–40
Elisabeth (Nietzsche's sister), 3, 8, 12, 93
Empedocles, 24
empty fiction, being as, 79, 134–35
enemy, suffering as, 123; time as, 134
energy, artistic, 29, 36; states of as wills to power, 164–66
enhancement-needs, 152
epistemological subject, 152
equalizing, of the unequal, 147–48
Eros, 95, 131

eternal recurrence, central idea of *Thus Spoke Zarathustra*, 79, 91, 155–170; and homecoming, 90; Zarathustra as teacher of, 98–99, 105, 116, 122; friend as image of, 110; as Apollinian image, 155; and the rebirth of tragedy, 156; not a cosmology, 164–66; as heaviest burden, 90, 156–59; as deliverance from revenge by transforming man's relation to time, 94, 169–70
eternity, 79, 114, 121, 161, 167–68, 171
Euripides, 39, 41
evening, as image, 100, 114–15, 122, 131, 133
existential ambiguity of time, 94, 170
existential demand, 16
existential meaning, 95
existential need, 151–53

fable, true world as, 79, 99–100, 120, 132, 136, 143
falsification, as equalization of the unequal, 50–52, 148, 152
festivals, Dionysian, 30; of atonement, 68, 74, 82
Fichte, Johann Gottlieb, 138, 142
Fink, Eugen, 15, 41, 137–38
fire, 85, 129
first philosophy, 134
flames, Zarathustra consuming himself in his own, 117, 129–30, 150
flute, 29, 159–60
flux, of becoming, 81, 110, 144, 169
forest, Zarathustra as, 131
forgetfulness, of one's own falsifying, 50–53
forgiveness, 66
fountain, as image, opposed to well, 127, 129, 132
Franco-Prussian War, 7
freedom, 4, 30, 40; and morality, 60–61; freedom *for*, 110
friend, to be created out of oneself, namely, as image of the eternal recurrence, 109–10, 123
friendship, versus love of neighbor, 109

games, sacred, 68, 74, 82
Gast, Peter, 8, 12–13

genealogy of morals, 61, 65–66; from the perspective of life, 63
genius, 7, 26. *See also* nostrils
German Idealism, 138–39, 141
Germans, 9, 93
German spirit, Dionysian root of, 47
girls, 131
gloom, 153–54, 161
God, corrupt Christian conception of, 3; as crime against life, 69; our role in the killing of, 69–73; as God of the sick, 72; as counter-concept to life, 105; as representative of being-in-itself, 139. *See also* atheism; death of God; shadows of God
Goethe, Johann Wolfgang von, 24
going-under, 89, 112
gold, as heart of the earth, 163
golden fishing rod, 132–33
golden laughter, 91
good and bad, versus good and evil, 65
gravediggers, 68, 75, 82, 115
gravity, spirit of, 131–33
great reason, as body, versus little reason as soul, 103, 140
Great Year, 158, 168
Greeks, the fundamental role they play for Nietzsche, 22–47; their failure to put Socrates and Dionysus together, 145, 156; their superficiality—out of profundity, 155
guiding question, versus basic question, 136
guilt, 117; and punishment, 65

hammer, 1, 112, 116
hatred, of reality, 71; of life, 132–33; of the world of suffering, 169
health, 2, 7; requires a certain horizon, 26–27, 56, 62
heaviest burden, idea of eternal recurrence as, 90, 156–59
Hegel, G. W. F., 9, 55, 72, 138, 141
Heidegger, Martin, 1, 63, 92, 125, 127; his claim that Nietzsche is the last metaphysician, 135–37, 149
Heraclitus, 7, 22, 24, 27, 37, 80, 134
herd, 4, 88
hermit, 123

hero, 34, 54, 97, 110, 125–26, 161–62. *See also* overhero
history, need for, 23, 57–58, 95; birth of Socratism as turning point of, 39; and life, 55–56; excess of, 56, 58; as threat to life, 56–59; history turned against itself, 59; of culture, 64, 66; beginning of a higher history, 68, 75, 78, 82; of metaphysics, ending with the consummation of nihilism, 143; kinds of (*see* antiquarian history; critical history; monumental history)
Hölderlin, Friedrich, 4, 28; "Der Freigeist," 94; "Lebenslauf," 96
home, and freedom, 4; mythical home, 27; Zarathustra's, as image, 98, 160
homecoming, Nietzsche's demand for, 26, 75; Zarathustra's task of, 81; equivalent to becoming what one is, 84; as proceeding from homelessness, 84; through solitude, 84–85; as becoming will to power, 85; as a revaluation of all values, 86; and truth, 86; as beyond good and evil, 87; as becoming overman, 87–88; as self-creation, self-overcoming, and going-under, 88–90; as affirming the eternal recurrence, 90–91; *Thus Spoke Zarathustra* as drama of, 98; stages of (*see* camel; child; lion)
homelessness, as destruction of horizons in Socratism, 57–58; Zarathustra's, 84–85, 98, 100
Homer, 6, 31
honey-gatherers, of the spirit, 16
horizon, of permanence, 56–58, 62, 71, 81, 83–85; defined by myths, as horizon of justification, 26–27
horror, 25–26, 31, 35, 45
hubris, 14
human temporality, 55, 94. *See also* "It was"

ice, 11, 16; as image, versus warmth, 127, 130
idealism, as mendacity, 19. *See also* German Idealism
ideals. *See* idols; workshop
ideas, as invented and not discovered, 53, 62, 148

idols, touched lightly by Nietzsche's hammer, 1; no new ones erected by Nietzsche, 17, 87; as moral ideals, 18; the state as, 108
image-language, 91–92
immoderation, 29
imperium Romanum, 108
illnesses, Nietzsche's, 2, 10, 19
illusion, veil of, 25–26; of the dream world, 30; Olympian gods as, 31; Socratic, metaphysical illusion as stimulus to life, 40, 42, 44–45; truth as, 51; art as good will to illusion, 154
imitator, every artist as, 29
innocence, 17; of Zarathustra's animals, 99; of the senses, 108; child as, 111, 117, 120; of all things, 125
inspiration, 29, 33, 93, 157
instinct, replaced by reason in Socratism, 42, 73
institutions, 40, 42, 75, 108
intellect, versus will, 5–6; as means of preserving the individual, 49, 52–53, 145
intertwining, of all things, 168
intoxication, 30, 36, 41
intuitive (artistic) man versus rational (Socratic) man, 53, 145
invention, 75, 148
"It was," as the irretrievable "it was" of time, 134, 150, 169–70

Jena, 13
jester, 89
joy, of becoming, 35–36; of creating, 38–39; inseparable from suffering, 43; life as a well of joy and suffering, 125, 133; "every joy wants eternity," 168, 171
joyful wisdom, 83
justice, 57, 63, 125
justification, aesthetic, 25, 27

Kant, Immanuel, 5, 46–49, 52, 74, 77, 138, 141, 149, 151
knowledge as equalizing and schematizing, 147–48, 149

language, its return to the nature of imagery in *Thus Spoke Zarathustra*, 28, 81, 92, 98; built-in falsification of, 51–52; creative speech as throwing the existing language out of joint, 53, 127; the language of love, 128; and consciousness of self, 141. *See also* image-language
lantern, 68, 73, 76, 81
last man, 88, 111, 120
last metaphysician, Nietzsche as, 135–37, 145, 149
laughter, 68, 74, 91, 96–97, 122, 153–54, 161
laws, of nature, as a regularity we ourselves have introduced, 52–53
Leibniz, Gottfried Wilhelm, 77, 138
Leipzig, University of, 4, 6
life, of a philosopher in relation to his thought, 2–21; eternal life, 26, 36, 38, 121; and history, 55–56; history as threat to, 58–59; as will to power, 62–63; and morality, 63–65; God as crime against, 69; Zarathustra's affirmation of, 91; "Course of life," 96; spirit as life cutting into life, 111–12; as the woman loved by Zarathustra, 121; as a well, 125, 132; art as stimulant to, 154; as creative-destructive play, 155; eternal occurrence as binding humans to life, 170
lightning, 68, 82, 89, 157; not separate from its flash, 141
lion, as image of second stage of homecoming, 100, 104–112, 117, 120, 122–126, 137
little reason, as soul, versus great reason as body, 103, 140
logic, as destructive of tragedy, 41; biting its own tail, 46, 59, 149–51; of decadence, 70–71
love of one's fate, 19–20, 39, 163. *See also amor fati*
lover, as image, opposed to revenger, 127; Zarathustra as, 128, 132
lyric poetry, 30–34, 36

madman, with a lantern, seeking God, 68–76; the madman of *The Gay Science* compared to the Prologue of *Thus Spoke Zarathustra*, 81–85
madness, and the prisoner in Plato's cave allegory, 76

Maenads, 29
magician, 153
marriage, Nietzsche's proposals of, 9; women and marriage, 120–21
masks, 15, 34, 104
meaning, artistic, 37; of suffering, 96; of the earth, 99–100, 102, 119
Merleau-Ponty, Maurice, 126
metamorphosis. *See* camel; child; lion
metaphor, 28, 51, 53, 92–93, 127
metaphysical comfort, 26, 35–36, 38, 46, 74, 83, 97. *See also* this-worldly comfort
metaphysics, of art, 25; Schopenhauer's, 32, 62, 74, 132; morality as, 97; as the lie about an afterworld, 125; relation of will to power to, 134–38; Nietzsche's history of, 143
Midas, 27
midwife, 121
mirror, Olympian gods as, 31; chorus as, 34; face of the friend as, 109; and the child, 113, 122
monumental history, 56–57
morality, 60–67; homecoming as beyond morality, 87; self-overcoming of, 97–98, 106
morning, as image, 73, 99–100, 115, 122
mountains, 16, 84–85, 97–98, 100, 102, 123
mouth, Zarathustra as, before learning silence, 123, 127
murder, 111, 134; we as murderers of God, 68–70
music, its gulf from cognition, 24–25; tragedy and the spirit of, 39, 46, 83, 113, 162; dissonant, 38; music-practicing Socrates, as artist-philosopher, 44, 46, 53–54, 92, 97, 137, 145
myth, and culture, 26–27; and science, 45

Naumburg, 3, 13
nausea, 35, 70, 125
nerve-stimulus, 51
night, Zarathustra's, as preceding the dawn and the birth of the child, 149–151
nihilism, as the point at which the old values destroy themselves, 59; as transitional stage, 75, 79; for Zarathustra, a new beginning, 82, 85; as the death of God, 84; as setting the earth free, 100; danger of, 120; consummation of, 130, 133, 143; as invoked by Nietzsche, 151; art as countermovement to, 154; the eternal recurrence as the most extreme form of, 166
nobility and profound suffering, 95
noble person, as object of resentment, 71
noble taste, 40
noon, as image, 91, 100, 113–115, 122, 167
No-saying, 6, 76, 107, 126
nostrils, genius of Nietzsche in, 86

Olympian gods, all Apollinian, 31
optimism, versus Schopenhauer's pessimism, 5; of Socratism, 42, 45–46, 156; shipwreck of, 45
Overbeck, Franz, 8, 13, 93, 95
overhero, 126, 162
overman, transformation into, 74–75; as the task taught by Zarathustra, 77–81; becoming overman as homecoming, 87–88; as the meaning of the earth, 99–100; as called forth by the friend, 109; as the child from marriage, 120–21

patience, 66
Paul, 69
perspectivism, 144
Pforta, 3
philistinism, 4
philology, classical, 4, 6; as art of slow reading, 15–16
Phoebus, 29, 99
physicians, 123
physics, 165
pity, 64, 97, 124; and terror, 35
Plato, 14, 17, 24, 69, 73, 77, 81, 94, 99, 116, 129
Platonism, Christianity as Platonism for the people, 17, 73; metaphysical world of, 92, 132; question of Nietzsche's overcoming Platonism or merely reversing it, 136–38
play, as only way of associating with great tasks, 20, 74, 94–95; as creating-destroying, 37–41, 45, 83; child as play of creation, 111–12, 117–19; real man wants danger and play, 121

plebeian resentment, 40
poetry, "Der Freigeist" by Nietzsche, 10; lyric poetry, 30, 34–36; science becoming poetry, 45; *Thus Spoke Zarathustra* as, 92–93; tragedy as poetry plus music, 96. *See also* Hölderlin
poverty, Zarathustra's, 128–29
practice, as not opposed to theory for Nietzsche, 2
pregnancy, 121
preservation-needs, 49–50, 152, 164
pre-Socratics, 6, 22
pride, 91, 102, 111, 124; eagle as image of, 99
priests, 105, 124, 126
primal will, of Schopenhauer's metaphysics, 30–38, 74, 83, 102, 132
Procrustes' bed, 147
promises, 55
punishment, 124–25; and guilt, 65
purification, 104, 110

rabble, 125
rancor, 63
rational (Socratic) man, versus intuitive (artistic) man, 53–54, 145
redemption, in annihilation, 9; in appearances, 32–34; from suffering, 117–118, 124; art as, 154; from the past, 169
Rée, Paul, 8–9
religion, 3, 8, 100, 107
Renaissance, 70
Requiem aeternam Deo ("Eternal rest [grant] to God"), 69
resentment, against the past, 58; of the weak, 63, 71; Christian God as vindication of, 72; of the despisers of the body, 103; against suffering, 117, 124, 130, 169; as most fundamentally against time, 150, 169–70. *See also* plebeian resentment
revaluation of all values, 17, 59–60, 75, 77–79, 86–87, 93, 100, 157
revelation, as Nietzsche's state of inspiration, 157
revenge, 66, 117, 120, 125, 130, 169; versus love, 127
rights, as derivative form of justice, 63

"Ring" cycle, 8
rite, of purification, 104, 110
Ritschl, Friedrich, 4
Röcken, 3
Rohde, Erwin, 6, 92

saint, old saint encountered by Zarathustra, 82, 85, 103, 112, 116
Salomé, Lou, 9
sanctified lie, truth as, 50
satyr, chorus as, 29, 34–36
schemata, their role in knowledge, 147–48, 149, 152
Schiller, Friedrich, 24, 32, 34
Schopenhauer, Arthur, 5–7, 9, 30, 32, 36–37, 46–48, 62, 74, 83, 93, 132, 161–62
science, Nietzsche's view of in general, 165–66
scorpion, 106
sculpture, Greek, 24
self-oblivion, 29–30
self-overcoming, 6, 60, 77, 83; homecoming as, 89; of morality, 98, 106; circle of, 118; as willing beyond oneself, 142, 152; life as, 164
self-propelled wheel, 111, 117–20
Semele, 29
seriousness, 74, 92, 97, 118, 153
serpent, wound in a circle and as image of wisdom, 91, 99, 115, 167
shadows of God, 75–76, 79, 89, 107–10
Shakespeare, William, 20
silence, 16, 40, 69, 123, 127
Silenus, pessimistic wisdom of, 27–28, 31, 35–38, 40, 43, 62, 83, 95, 105, 118, 132, 150, 154
Sils-Maria, 10
Silvaplana, 157
sin, 72; against the earth more dreadful than against God, 100; the state as, 108
skepticism, 85, 111, 140, 153–54, 159–60
slave revolt, 65–66, 72
sleep, 101, 105, 116
solitude, and homecoming, 84–85; of Zarathustra, not simply a ten-year prolongation of homelessness, 99, 104–5, 109–114,

116–17, 122–23; pious person has none, 157; as most intimate presence to self, 160

Socrates, most problematic phenomenon of antiquity, 39; Nietzsche's ambivalence toward, 39–40. *See also* Socratism

Socratism, as demand for intelligibility, and tragedy, 39–40; power of, 41–43; relation to Socrates, 43–44; self-destruction of, 44–47, 50–53, 155, 159, 161; versus a rebirth of tragedy, 137, 150–51

songs, Zarathustra's, "The night song," 126–30; "The dancing song," 131–33; "The tomb song," 133–34; "The drunken song," 168; "The other dancing song," 170–71; "The seven seals, or, The yes and amen song," 171. *See also* voice

soul, new soul that should have sung, v, 26; strife as perpetual food of, 4; merely something about the body, 103; of Zarathustra, a fountain, 127–29; as led astray by flutes, 159. *See also* little reason

Sparta, 31

star, dancing, 82, 88, 100

state, versus a people, 108; everything about it false, 108

stone, sleeping image within, 116

Strauss, David, 9, 14, 55

strife, 4, 32

style, of writing involves relation to truth, 14–15, 25; culture as unity of artistic style, 39, 108; giving style to one's character, 90; Nietzsche's style as a dance, 92

subjectivity, in modern philosophy, as ground of objectivity, 137–38; Nietzsche's conception of, 140–42; as will to power, 169

sublime man, 150, 153–54, 161–62

substance, 79, 141; as subject, 138, 142; as something posited, 148

suffering, and primal will, 32; Socratism abolishes and tragedy transforms, 43; senseless suffering leads man to hate reality and create an afterworld, 71, 95, 102; as object of resentment, 117; saying "Yes" to suffering, 120

suicide, 25, 167; of Greek tragedy, 39

sun-nature, Zarathustra's, 129

Surlei, 157

syllogism, 41

tarantula-heart, 125

teacher, Nietzsche as teacher of slow reading, 15; and pupil, 20; Zarathustra as teacher of the overman, 77, 99; Zarathustra as teacher of the eternal recurrence, 98–99, 116, 122, 163

technocrats, 108

technology, 43

temporality. *See* human temporality

terror, 31, 74, 124, 132; and pity, 35

theodicy, 31, 73

theory, as not opposed to life for Nietzsche, 2

things-in-themselves, 5, 51, 146

thirst, as image, 130

this-worldly comfort, 74, 97. *See also* metaphysical comfort

"Thus I willed it," versus the "it was," 169–70

tightrope walker, 82, 89, 113, 115

Titans, 29, 31

tragedy, as poetry plus and music, 96; birth of, 23–26; death of, 39–44; rebirth of, 7, 21–22, 46–48, 93, 137–38, 155–56, 166; *Thus Spoke Zarathustra* as, 83, 92, 96–98, 112–13, 138, 146

Trampedach, Mathilde, 9

transcendence, 111

transiency of time, 151

transmigration, eternal recurrence not a doctrine of, 167

treatise, as style appropriate to metaphysics, 14–15, 25

Tribschen, 7–8

true world, of metaphysics. *See* fable

truth, defined as a kind of error, 25, 50, 81, 146, 152, 158

truthfulness, 18, 69–70, 97–98, 125–26; the truth of truthfulness, 145

Turin, 12–13

twilight, of the idols, as destruction of ideals, 18, 160

unfathomable, life as, 132–33, 150
untimely, Nietzsche as, 22–23, 55; the task of becoming untimely, 107

values, moral, as rooted in the will to power, 63–65, 71, 144; Nietzsche not proposing a new set of, 77, 87, 119; as schemata, 148, 152. *See also* revaluation of all values
voice, strange voice that should have sung, v, 26
von Gersdorff, Carl, 91–92
von Senger, Hugo, 9

Wagner, Richard, 2, 4–9, 20, 47, 93
war, saying "Yes" to, 7; Franco-Prussian, 7; God as war against life, 71–72; among the virtues, 106
warmth, as image, versus ice, 127, 130
warrior, 106–7
wasteland, 84, 109
whip, and women, 121
whirlpool, 159–60
Wilamowitz, Ulrich, 23
will, Schopenhauer's metaphysics of. *See* primal will
will to power, versus Schopenhauer's dualism, 6; its basic structure of preservation and enhancement, 54, 143; life as, 62–63, 81; as will to will, 63; values rooted in, 63–65, 71, 144; and homecoming, 85; not simply a new idol, 87; as creative play, 119; as ordering and thereby gaining mastery, 142; and knowledge, 145–47; will to truth subordinate to, 152; in what sense true, 166. *See also* metaphysics
Winckelmann, Johann, 24
wine, 29–30, 130, 160
women, as riddle the solution to which is pregnancy, 121; the woman loved by Zarathustra is life, 121; woman as the most dangerous plaything, 121. *See also* marriage; whip
words, as involving falsification, 51–52
work, so-called blessings of, 108
workshop, for manufacturing ideals, 65–66, 71
writing, style of not independent of what is at issue in the writing, 14–15, 25; as signaling a victory, 60

Yes-saying, 5, 19, 72, 125, 138, 149, 155, 170
yoke, 18, 110

Zarathustra, why Nietzsche uses the name, as precise opposite of the Persian Zoroaster, the creator of morality, 97
Zeus, 29

JOHN SALLIS is Frederick J. Adelmann Professor of Philosophy at Boston College. He is author of more than twenty books, including *Light Traces*, *The Return of Nature*, *The Figure of Nature*, and *Songs of Nature*.

RICHARD ROJCEWICZ is editor of two previous volumes of the Collected Writings of John Sallis, translator of several works in Continental Philosophy, and author of *The Gods and Technology* and *Heidegger, Plato, Philosophy, Death*.

www.ingramcontent.com/pod-product-compliance
Lightning Source LLC
Chambersburg PA
CBHW030624230426
43661CB00053B/2132